M a d h o u s e

Urmilla Deshpande lived in Bombay in the 1980s, when most of this book took place, and has close connections with IITans herself. This is her first book as editor. Urmilla now lives in Tallahassee, Florida. Her published work includes *A Pack of Lies* (2009, Westland/Tranquebar) and *Kashmir Blues* (2010, Westland/Tranquebar). She is now working on *Slither: Carnal Prose by Urmilla Deshpande* (Westland/Tranquebar). It is a collection of short fiction, and will be available in 2011.

*

Bakul Desai is a Hyderabad-based businessman who graduated from IIT Bombay in 1982. He is currently on the Board of Directors of IIT Bombay Alumni Association. He lives in Hyderabad with his wife, daughter and colourful memories of his days in IIT where he lived for five years in a black-and-white era.

M a d h o u s e:

True Stories of the Inmates of Hostel 4 IITB

Urmilla Deshpande (Editor)
Bakul Desai (Contributing Editor)

westland

westland ltd
Venkat Towers, 165, P.H. Road, Maduravoyal, Chennai 600 095
No.38/10 (New No.5), Raghava Nagar, New Timber Yard Layout, Bangalore 560 026
Survey No. A-9, II Floor, Moula Ali Industrial Area, Moula Ali, Hyderabad 500 040
23/181, Anand Nagar, Nehru Road, Santacruz East, Mumbai 400 055
47, Brij Mohan Road, Daryaganj, New Delhi 110 002

First published by westland ltd 2010

10 9 8 7 6 5 4 3 2 1

ISBN: 978-93-80658-64-3

Typeset in ITC Officina Sans Book by SÜRYA, New Delhi
Printed at Thomson Press

To Blacky

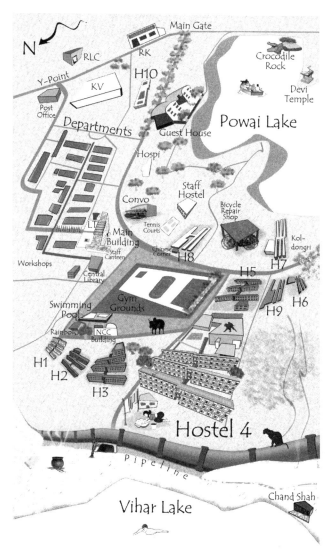

H4 and other places and things of importance including The Dhoban and The Pipeline.

I know it's a cliché, but I'm going to say it, because it's true: My five years at IIT were the best five of my life. We were between fifteen and seventeen when we started at IIT, and when we left, still raw, we were barely over twenty. These were our formative years. We were incubated in the furnace of IIT and shaped in the crucible of H4. Away from the protected and sheltered homes of our parents, thrown into a company of formidable peers and left to fend for ourselves in a high pressure environment, we grew up within our new family. With them we learnt to smoke without coughing on the same day we learnt about induction motors. With them we shared rooms, meals, bidis, beers, Playboys, lecture notes, and even girlfriends.

Ours was a quiet and self-contained world without internet or mobile phones. TV was a single black and white channel, grey in its minimal fare. We had no personal music players, either walkman or iPod, we trudged instead to the lounge where we played LPs on our communal turn table. We listened to whatever was available, and not necessarily of our choosing. We collaborated on projects, hand drew and hand painted everything, those of us lacking artistic talent were the organizational part of the team. We went on group hikes and treks, produced plays, played sports, invented entertainment from gaali spats to anti-chess.

Ironically, we were all learning technologies, the lack of which resulted in this bonhomie in the first place. For many of us, our nearest and closest friends are from those privileged times where we co-existed in a happy equilibrium despite our different cultural and linguistic backgrounds. Time and professional commitments have flung us far across the globe, yet we remain united and bonded by virtue of our growing up together in a mutually beneficial cocoon.

From thirty years ago I knew Jiten Apte, three years my junior and famous for his demonic laughter which could awaken the sleepiest residents in neighbouring H5. Jiten and I re-connected at IIT's formation day on 10th March, 2009. He told me he was in touch with Deepak Patil aka Boss. Anyone in H4 between 1972 and 1985 knew Boss. He is an H4 legend. Tall, bearded and with straight long hair that hung on his shoulders, Boss dominated all the fun proceedings at H4. Except for veteran mess worker Ramchandra More and hostel dog Blacky, no one else was as well known to ten batches of students as Boss. Jiten put me back in touch with him. I wrote him an email, and cc-ed five mutual friends. Boss replied, and added five more to the list. Everyone wrote back adding more of us H4ites to this list. Within a week, almost a hundred emails were exchanged with more than a hundred recipients added to our list. This led me to comment, 'This has become a Madhouse. Let's set up a yahoo group.'

Hilarious anecdotes from the past were exchanged. We all felt that these priceless memories should become a book. The nature of the book was not spelled out. It was still notional. It could as well have been a yearbook for our private circulation. Sandeep Shah, aka Sandhya, was in India on business, and he and various Madhouse members visited H4 to take some photographs for this book. Among the photos were mess workers from our times. Most of us have risen to positions of excellence and achievement in our professions in these last thirty years. But the mess workers, now old and frail were still doing what they were doing all those years ago.

Waiting tables for batch after batch of students who left to pursue their careers. It was a heart-rending moment for all of us, and led to the formation of HATS—Hostel Alumni Team Stewardship, started originally by H7 alumni. Nostalgic and tearful alumni set up an endowment to look after mess workers' interests and address infrastructure needs of the hostel. HATS was launched with great fanfare in December 2009. The book idea was put on the backburner temporarily, but revived during this same December reunion.

1983 graduates Ashish Khosla, Sanjiv Sood, and Arun Jethmalani met in Delhi and they talked about, among other things, Urmilla Deshpande, Ashish's wife. Her first book, A Pack of Lies *(Westland/Tranquebar)* had just been published. Her second, Kashmir Blues *(Westland/Tranquebar)* was in the works, and a collection of short fiction. We asked, and Ashish assured us that Umi would be glad to help with our book.

I spoke to Umi in late March 2010. As Ashish's wife, Umi was both an insider as well as not. She read some of our stories when she found Ashish chortling away at them. After reading a few more anecdotes I sent her, Umi was clear about one thing. Fictionalizing the anecdotes would take away from their charm. All our anecdotes were special and priceless because they were true stories. The audacity of Arun Kaul riding horseback to lectures and tethering the beast in a cycle shed would be construed as a fictional account in the novel form. Umi strongly advocated that we leave the stories in precisely the form they occurred—a collection of anecdotes narrated by different people in different voices.

This idea found favour with most Madhouse members. Umi also reported to us that to her amazement and delight, her *publishers were not only interested, but had agreed to deliver on our impossible deadline—December 2010—to coincide with IIT's annual alumni day. If, that is, we submitted our manuscript by the end of June. This sounded like a daunting task at first, but the looming deadline induced all Madhouse members, even the silent ones, to write their memories in earnest, which finally led us to a new problem. We now had two hundred thousand words—twice what we needed for the book. Many folks worked hard at different tasks—compiling stories, arranging them by topic, providing Umi with background information wherever required. Many stories were authenticated, and in the event of any minor conflicting versions, the least common denominator has been used. Where possible, we sought permission from people named in the stories. Many of them whom today are successful politicians, entrepreneurs, heads of companies, scientists, professors, spiritual gurus, ace mountaineers, even yoga instructors, laughed about unflattering or damning references from thirty years ago and even supplemented our stories with their own outlandish accounts. In just a few cases, we have substituted real names with fictitious ones though the stories are very real and true.*

These stories cover a timeline of less than ten years out of IIT Bombay's chequered history which is more than fifty years old. Accounts cover just a few hundred individuals out of more than thirty-five thousand people believed to have graduated from IITB. The incidents narrated formed a small part of an IITan's life—the time spent in the hostel and time devoted to having fun as a release from the high-pressure academic sessions. References to indulgence in smoking, drinking, reading pornography or about experimenting with birds and bees should in no way take away the reality that an average student pursued his academics diligently and achieved all he is today.

Lastly, there was a debate about how much of our profanity to allow into the book. The verdict was unanimous. This is a collection of true stories, and like all true stories, the truth about this facet should also be left un-tampered with.

The proceeds from this effort go to the HATS fund.

—Bakul Desai

In the Madhouse

When my husband Ashish Khosla, once an inmate of Hostel 4 himself, told me a tale about one of his hostelmates going to lectures on a horse, I was not impressed. Though he is not given to flights of fancy, I thought he was perhaps making a lot of a single incident. Then he showed me the photograph. It had that unmistakable stamp of the early '80s in style and substance, and there was the white horse, and its rider, on their way to a lecture on organic chemistry. I realised that it was not a one-time event. I also commented then that the photo would make a wonderful book cover.

One thing led to another, and in March of 2010 I was given the privilege and frustrations of editing this book.

I have known IITans intimately through my life—father, step-father, husband, boyfriends and many good friends. I made several more friends during the creation of this book. None of what I read and heard explains these guys, though. I still cannot tell whether they chose this gruelling and most prestigious of educational institutions because of the way they were, or they became that way because of those five years they spent at IIT.

In spite of censorship (some language, and some entire incidents were left out due to sheer indecency) it is quite clear that these boys—and they were boys then—indulged in very questionable behaviour. There was substance abuse, and it wasn't the substances that were abused. There was people abuse—in fact abusing each other in picturesque and imaginative ways was a normal pastime. There was delinquency and there were criminal acts. Instincts of various nether levels were indulged endlessly and continuously. This book has chronicled many instances. It is my feeling that these memories are stronger than mundane ones of lectures attended or disciplines learned or even engineering degrees earned. In any case, these were more interesting to both listeners and narrators, and now, will no doubt entertain readers.

There is something that I must make clear to the readers of this book. In spite of all the unsavoury behaviour, I must point out that these same rowdy and rude young men are now captains of industry, science and technology, some are prominent in the political and social arenas, and most are productive members of society. I say this as a reminder, because while reading about their early lives in their own words, a reader might, understandably too, forget this fact.

It is my feeling that in safe and tranquil IIT Bombay, these young men felt free to experiment physically and intellectually. They had all made it into IIT—not an easy task. All they had to do now was make it through the next five years, and life after that could only be, if not easy, then certainly secure. They were far from the rules and conditioning of their homes, thrown together with some like and some utterly unlike themselves. They had unbound and yet protected freedom that allowed them to find themselves. And they looked hard, and pushed themselves and their mates over and under and any which way they could beyond familiar and familial boundaries.

I think such investigations, which might be thought of as foolhardy at best and immoral at worst, informed their morality. These men left IIT with a degree, and also with a self-made morality. Like the degree, that morality, though not conferred, resulted from a process. It involved hypothesis, argument, experimentation, and conclusion. It is perhaps more personal, and more solid than the societal rules and regulations that pass as moral code.

As a project this one was interesting to me in another way. Here was a large number of stories coming to me as they were remembered. One or two or three of the guys are good writers, and I had no trouble with their pieces (other than chopping down some unnecessarily verbose bits, or changing the sequence of the narration to make it more appealing to a reader, moving the twist to the end, emphasizing foreshadowing, deepening suspense). But some of these guys are not writers. They simply put down in words their memory and feeling about an incident with a few relevant and irrelevant details, and sent it off. These are the ones who taught me something about writing. On the first read-through I would think, this story has meat. I then retold the story, in my own 'better' words. And every time I did that, I found that the whole feeling and content changed. I learned firsthand something I had struggled to understand for a long time—something I knew to be true in theory, but didn't understand until this project: that style and content are inseparable. That by adjusting Raj Laad's piece to make it 'better', I was in fact losing the voice of Raj Laad, of course, but also his perspective. And it was his perspective, in his words, which was the content of the piece—not the sequence of events. I promised myself then that I would not change all these pieces to fit an acceptable grammatical or linguistic correctness, especially not a correctness that exists only in texts and classrooms. This was storytelling at its best—the kind of campfire tales that are myth and legend, spoken to the listener from the heart. I knew I must not be overzealous in my editing, or I would make the stories nothing more than a homogenous list of rude and crude incidents in the lives of teenage boys from a certain hostel. I wanted to retain the patina of nostalgia and affectionate remembrance of amazing times. I hope I achieved this.

Without the hard work and dedication of a few people, this project would not have succeeded, let alone got off the ground:

Bakul Desai. Calling him 'contributing editor' just does not cover all he has done. His memory is sharper than most, and though there might be gaps in his memory just the same as anyone else's, we saw no evidence of this. Not too many disagreed with Bakul's elephantine recall, and I suspect that those who did simply preferred the offending anecdote forgotten. The sheer volume of what he wrote makes up a large part of this book, but without his acerbic yet affectionate way of looking at the world and his dear friends and hostelmates, his writing would not have been worth reading. He egged us all on, held the team together, suffered my daily abuse and his team's frustrations, and took on writing, editing, and even marketing to bring his beloved project to life.

Deepak Patil—Boss—whom I came to love for his sweet encouragement, gentle reassurances, and for those amazing word documents which he compiled from thousands of emails between the inmates of H4.

Rohan Menezes, who was put in charge of artwork and photos, who tramped around Mumbai and contrived to get us the photographs and art in the book.

My beloved book committee, who read several drafts, made heartfelt suggestions that I ignored, who encouraged and goaded as the need arose, and above all, did not allow revisionism: Jiten Apte, Hemendra Godbole, Arun Gupta, Ashvin Iyengar, Satish Joshi, Raj Laad, Vikram Modak, Ashvin Sanghvi, Sanjiv Sood.

And most of all, all the inmates of Hostel4, some of whom begged and pleaded with me to not call them 'inmates' because of the connotations associated with other institutions of indoctrination and discipline. Their wonderful memories and writing, but more, those five years of their lives which they have opened up to us readers, have made this book what it is. Thank you to you all for sharing them with us.

—Urmilla Deshpande

<u>M a d h o u s e:</u>

True Stories of the Inmates of Hostel 4 IITB

Sometime between 1962 and 1967: Nestled between the two picturesque lakes Powai and Vihar, tucked behind rolling hills amid abundant greenery, the newly built IIT Bombay campus was taking shape. This was during the early years of its formation and buildings were still coming up.

There were over two hundred species of birds that inhabited this paradise. As a bird flew from east to west, as did the initial crop of the engineers who graduated from IIT, it would see Hostel 1—H1—in the north east corner. This was the first hostel and the most majestic. Further west almost adjoining H1 was the next hostel—H2, north of the gymkhana grounds. Though built later, H2 was definitely a poor cousin of the imposing H1 and yet, larger, roomier and better than all the later built hostels, except H3. H3 was in the north-west corner of the gymkhana and virtually identical to H2. From H3, the road turned southward, and sitting on this corner was H4, a steep comedown from the other three hostels in terms of room size. These rooms were also sans balconies.

A small narrow road between H3 and H4 led to the forbidden zone of a massive water supply line called The Pipeline and beyond it lay the fantastic Vihar lake.

During this time we speak of, hostels 1 to 7 are known to have existed. Accounts from graduates of the class of 1967 suggest that they were among the first inhabitants of these hostels. They lived in a privileged time—BEST buses plied inside the campus right up to the hostels, a good two kilometres away from the main gate. This privilege was withdrawn in the late Sixties. After that era students

1

commuted, and lugged heavy suitcases to and from the hostels on foot. Back then, the buses went straight from the main gate, continued beyond the gymkhana office skirting its southern flank, turned right at H5, continued to H4, and stopped there at a bus stop. The bus stop was a mighty pole with a metal sign plate. All passengers disgorged here. The students of H3, H2 and H1 continued on foot in the same direction that the bus took to turn and exit from the loop. The students of H5 and H6 walked back and walked long to get to their respective hostels.

This is where the ingenuity and the audacity of the elite engineer in the making comes in. Unfettered by parental control, basking in the glory of new-found freedom, endowed with teenage rebelliousness and an alarming willingness to take risks, the long-suffering, long-walking, bus stop-less non-H4 students decided to take the law and the bus stop into their own hands. In an overnight commando operation, they borrowed shovels and spades from the gardening kit of their hostel stores and uprooted the entire bus stop with its pole and its sign and installed it in front of H5. This guerrilla tactic did yield its dividends, much to the delight of students from H5, 6 and 7. A bus driver tended to stop at a bus stop, instantly forgetting where he had stopped countless times before. The end result of the operation is still being debated but there are reasons to believe that the H4 guys, under cover of another dark night, did restore the bus stop to its rightful place where it belonged. In front of Hostel 4.

～

Advancing years have dimmed my memories. While every moment of my seven years (for the record it was seven years and not five because I did my M.Tech back to back with my B.Tech and not because I loved to spend summers in the hostel) was a new adventure, I can't recall all of it now. These seven years were perhaps the best, most alive and most productive of my life, but all of it wasn't fun and frolic and games. It was a period of growing up, of discovering myself in the big bad world outside the sheltered and protected one I had before entering H4. It was a period of cultural shocks, wounded pride, of coming to terms with the fact that I wasn't really quite as special as I had believed in my eighteen years at home. It was a period of coming to terms with myself.

Finding out what's under the skirts of Patty McGuire or Debra Jo Fondren through that educational rag called *Playboy* was as much a part of that growing up as was listening to Prof Patil and discovering the secret of Minkowski forces. Creating a state of entropy in Khupchoo's room by throwing his mattress out and pouring hair oil on it was as much a part of that discovery as finding out what entropy really meant in Prof Sakore's chemistry class—even though he called chaos 'Cha-oo-s' and not 'kay-o-s.' Maxing a brutal test from Prof Kamat made me as triumphant as was watching my first blue film. Finding ways to elude that hawk-eyed Memon so he wouldn't catch and rag me, entering the hostel for a full month by leaping over the wall near the North Wing to avoid Kicks who had vowed to take my pants down in the first year, was as educational in honing my wits as was making sure I didn't flunk KC Mukherjee's surprise quizzes. Catching a few glimpses of naked bathing women through Birjoo's telescope was as much a pleasure as creating a new algorithm for program optimization while working on my M.Tech project. Helping create a boat club for IIT and going hunting for crocodiles in Powai lake was as exciting as the pursuit of an A in App-Mech (Applied Mechanics) in the second year.

Those seven years were years of truly unfettered freedom of a kind I had never experienced before in my life. The exhilaration of that freedom I am sure all of us in IIT experienced at some time or other, because no matter what socio-economic and cultural backgrounds we came from, being in H4 cracked the cocoons families had built around us. While on one level I went red in the face and felt my ears burning when I was forced to describe my technique of shagging by a senior during my first ragging session, on another level, the fact that I could talk freely and without fear of censure about what, until then, was one of the most

4

pleasurable activities I knew, was almost as divine. That freedom, however, came with a cost sometimes. There were those who were bent on destroying themselves, some of whom were close friends.

There was this hike to Prabalgad, I don't now remember who all were in the group, certainly there was Sandeep Bhise, Scratch from H3, Phiroze Madan, perhaps Saheb Patil and Chhukka. It was late, we had just finished dinner and were enjoying a fag under a resplendent full moon when suddenly a slice was eaten out of the full white disk. It was a total lunar eclipse. The only sound was a faint crackle of the forest, the only light a feeble glow from the embers of our dying fire. I have never forgotten the shimmering white dust of the Milky Way and the sparkle of the stars. A sky like that I have never seen since.

And then there was that hike to Nakhind—Sandeep Bhise again, Subs, Selva, Saheb Patil, Tommy Mathews who probably was on his very first hike. We got to Nakhind in daylight, all out of our boiled eggs and bread. All that was left was six ends of the three loaves. Good citizen that Sandeep Bhise was, he didn't want us to litter the sacred caves of Nakhind, so we had packed them in our rucksacks. On the way back down, of course Bhise had to leave the beaten path. We had climbed up from Wangani. He thought he could find a short cut to Karjat if we followed a stream. Flowing water had to go down, and if we just followed the water it should lead us down the mountain, was his logic. Sure it would lead us down if we could have flowed with it down the sheer twenty-foot cliff over which it plunged. It was getting dark, there was no way we were going to find our way in that untamed jungle with not even the stars visible through the thick foliage. So we hunkered down next to the stream. The six end slices was all the food we had. So for dinner, we cut those six slices into twelve pieces and ate them with salt and pepper. And then the sky opened up and the rain beat down on us relentlessly for the next eight hours. Until then I hadn't known that raindrops could hit your bare skin with as much force as if someone was hitting you with a hammer. And neither before that nor ever after have I felt so cold in my life—not even when I was at 18,600 feet up in the Himalayas in Ladakh. Tommy of course never forgave Sandeep Bhise and probably put a curse on his head that Bhise would burn in hell for seven lifetimes.

It was during H4 freshies night that I discovered I could sing. I actually got a certificate to prove it. We sang a chorus (*Ae Malik Tere Bunde Hum*) with lead singer Bokil and won the second prize. When I proudly presented it to my old school friends they were sure I had forged it, and my parents wondered what kind of place they had sent me to and whether its engineering degrees might be as dubious as the singing certificate. But that was as much as part of my self-discovery.

All of this and more through those seven years in H4 made me—and for that I am eternally grateful.

—*Satish (Satkya) Joshi, '73-'80*

~

I met Ashvin (Ghoda) on the registration day. He was just ahead of me paying his registration fee. He had selected

Electrical Engineering, and he had come alone to register, so we had two things in common. The rest of the guys around us were accompanied by their parents. They were either sullen that their parents were with them for something as trivial as deciding which branch of engineering they would do badly in, or were overawed by being received into the most prestigious engineering institute in the country.

It was simple for me to choose my stream. I signed up for the one most in demand. In case I got excited about another, I could always ease myself downstream rather than work myself upstream in the second year. I suspect that Ashvin chose electrical because of a slim fair girl ahead of him choosing electrical.

During registration we were assigned hostels. We both got H4. We had the whole day ahead of us, we thought, what the heck, let's go and see the place which would be our home for the next five years.

We walked from the Main Building toward the hostels. We were vaguely aware that the summer semester had ended, and there would be hardly anyone around to guide us to the hostel. Near the gymkhana, we came across a plump light-eyed fellow and asked him directions. He looked us up and down. He saw before him a dark lanky guy who swayed his arms far behind him when he walked, and another thin tall guy with a baby face. Freshy meat for slaughter.

He nonchalantly said 'follow me.' It hit us that he was a 'seeniorr' and we had unwittingly put ourselves in the position of being ragged even before we were formally into IIT. Our plump light-eyed fellow introduced himself as Vasant Joshi, G Sec (General Secretary) of the hostel. We learnt later that he was Faatu. Ashvin and I had almost lost our nerve and our desire to see the hostel, and prepared for the worst.

Soon we were joined by another guy from H4, Ponga, who we learnt later was the mess sec. Now there were two guys sharing the kill.

There were lots of cows and bulls wandering around IIT, and we managed not to add our contribution to their generous gifts to the roads. With our mouths dry, we got to the hostel. To me, the creepers adorning the south wing reflected our emotional state. We were shown around the mess and the lounge. Whether the seniors felt there was no meat in us or were too busy winding up to leave, they just let us go.

We walked out of the hostel triumphantly. Brave Trekkies out to explore new worlds . Our first brush with the seniors, who were as bored as lions after a good meal, was so uneventful that it made us cocky. We boasted to the other freshies that yeah, we went to see our hostels, we even met the seniors, it was no big deal.

This adventure that wasn't was a start of a great friendship.

The first day of the orientation program I walked with Ashvin to the Main Building. Before the lecture, I went to the bathroom. I walked into the lecture hall to find him chatting up the slim fair girl from registration day. In that one minute he had her agree to be his steady, and from that minute on, she had no eyes for anyone else.

The first lecture left no impression at all. I have no recollection of anything. I do recall Ashvin swearing undying

8

love to the slim fair girl who responded with similar vehemence. I ribbed him on 'ghoda' being hitched to a 'gaadi'. We were walking down the stairs still horsing around when he lunged for me, and my retaliating mock kick hit the glass panel of the main building. It broke with a crash.

For the security guys, this was the most exciting event since they started their career with IIT. With alacrity seldom seen in any security person, two rushed up and held the two of us, shouting to the other guards, 'trouble!' We explained it was an accident but they were heroes who had controlled a riot. They would not let it go.

These were the days of the Emergency. Our friends in IIT security were probably the only Central Government force that had not the smallest chance to commit atrocities others of their ilk were blessed with. They hauled us up to their chief's office. He informed us he has seen many troublemakers in his time, and one look at us told him we were up to no good.

We pleaded with him that it was an accident and we meant no harm, we were innocent. He said he knew that students across universities were involved in anti-national and treasonable acts against the government, and were protesting against the Emergency. He would allow no such thing on his beat. He had so much power that even the police could not enter IIT without his permission. He could put us in jail without trial.

We promised we would reform. We sought his mercy. Sufficiently admonished, we finally made our way back to the hostel. This was my first brush with the IIT security.

In our fifth year, the security and the Diro (Director, the head honcho of IIT) took an equally heavy-handed approach in closing down IIT as the students had restricted his personal movements when he was gheraoed. But that is another story . . .

—*Birjoo (Bacha) Mehta, '76-'81*

~

'Hey Freshy!'

Among the many myths that prevailed about IIT, the biggest were about the intensity of ragging a fresher was subjected to. This induced a lot of anxiety in parents, and it took a lot of convincing to tell them that far from being fierce, ragging in IIT was actually fun. To start with, there was no physical ragging. Every freshy was told in no uncertain terms that he did not have to submit to physical ragging, and that if it ever got out of hand, he should report it to the hostel council immediately. It helped that there were some anti-ragging crusaders like Gautam Barua (currently Director, IIT Guwahati) and Abhiram Ranade (currently Head of Dept, CSE, IIT Bombay) who kept an eye on things and did not allow anything to get out of hand.

The way I see it, ragging was actually an aid to acclimation and assimilation. It helped build bonds among hostel inmates in the fastest possible manner. It also served to detoxify a fresher of ideas of his own greatness. Understandably, a new entrant into IIT came with the preconceived notion that he was God's gift to mankind. After all, he had surely excelled in school, he was one of just two thousand chosen from among 150,000 applicants, and during the party his proud father would have thrown to celebrate his son's entry into IIT, many guests would have convinced Mr. Fresh that he was the answer to India's technological problems, if not the entire world's. Someone had to tell him that he was at best mediocre in this pool of the most brilliant minds from all over the country. Cutting down an arrogant proud being by a few notches and instilling confidence and survival instincts into a shy introverted one were the purported objectives of ragging exercises. Barring a few deviations, ragging usually did meet with its self-declared objectives. This form of ragging was, in a way, legitimized by events like freshies night and Pagal Gymkhana.

It would be no exaggeration to say that ragging changed many lives forever for better or worse, mainly better. The most visible change was that names were altered forever. Many nicknames, originally designed to last the length of an IIT sojourn, have stuck permanently. Kenneth Stuart Robertson's name was found to be too pseudo and was changed first to Pandurang Dagduram Gaitondeson and it went through some natural transformations from Gaitonde to settle finally at G. Any email G signs as Kenneth today is instantly met with a puzzled response of 'who is Kenneth?'

Then there's a totally unknown Jayant Sheth, which is the real name of a very well known Ghatkopar. On his arrival at IIT his heavily Gujju accented English induced the question 'Hey freshy! Are you from vernacular?' His reply, 'No Sir! I am from Ghatkopar' explains his name.

Ragging was of both a personal and of a general nature, and was usually conducted in our small dingy rooms measuring a pathetic six feet by eight feet. There was a two foot deep niche on one side that held a writing table and another two foot deep niche near the door in which was a cupboard. The cupboard hung on the wall with a two foot space at the top with the ostensible purpose of storing suitcases but was the home of pigeons who roosted there. A two foot space at the bottom of the cupboard was designed to store footwear but was home to some educational reading and viewing material. The upstairs pigeon home was called Kashmir and the downstairs shoe space was called Kanyakumari. An erring freshy was often made to travel to Kashmir from where he derived a bird's eye view of the proceedings and when the punishment was stronger, he got a rat's eye view from Kanyakumari.

~

When the seniors saw the new crop of freshies every year, they asked each other, 'So this is the cream of the crop? These are the best minds of the country? We can beat them with half our brains tied behind our backs—can't we?' It was a subtext of ragging, seniors proving to themselves that they were smarter.

Some nuggets encountered by all and remembered by some were as follows:

~ This was generally used on anyone who came from an elite school, fancied himself as witty and was a potential member of the 'pseud' gang.

'Hey freshy! Are you good with riddles?'

'Yes Sir! I am.'

'So tell us, what is black and white and red all over?'

'Sir! That is very easy. It is a newspaper,' he replies with a triumphant smile.

'You ^&$@#! You think we'd ask you kindergarten riddles? Anyway, how is a newspaper red all over?'

Slow-on-the-uptake freshy smiles triumphantly again. 'Sir! Newspaper is read all over. Read as in R-E-A-D'.

'You %^&$@#ing son of a ^&%$@#, I said red, R-E-D. Why do you assume I said R-E-A-D?'

'Come on Sir! How can anything be black and white and also red?'

'If I tell you, will you stop speaking in English for a whole day and if anyone asks you your name, you will say your name is Dick?'

Freshy reluctantly agrees. So he is told, 'It's a blushing zebra, you idiot.'

~ This one was reserved for those who claimed good all-India ranks and fancied themselves good at science.

'Hey freshy! Do you know what 'g' is?'

'Yes Sir! It is acceleration due to gravity and is 9.8 meters per second squared.'

'No one asked you the value of g. In fact, I am asking you how you would measure g with an electron microscope.'

'It is not possible Sir. How can a microscope measure gravity?'

'Bastard! How did a &^%@#$# like you get admitted to IIT? Want to know how it is done?'

'Yes Sir! I still think it can't be done.'

'I'll tell you. You take an electron microscope to the terrace of a building and throw it down while measuring the time of fall with a stop watch.'

'Oh OK. That is funny Sir. But we will need to know the height of the building in order to calculate g.'

'Oboy. What a smartass. Just get a U tube manometer and measure the height of the building.'

'Sir. How can you measure the height with a U-tube manometer?'

'Freshy, you are dumb and I don't know how you cracked the JEE (Joint Entrance Exam). Just tie a string to the manometer, lower it from the terrace and when it lands on the ground, cut the string and measure its length.'

Understandably, these exchanges did deflate a few oversized egos.

~

There was another standard ragging routine which never failed to arouse mirth, no matter how many times one indulged in it. A freshy was given a book or a newspaper and asked to read a passage aloud and add the words 'up my ass' every three or four words. During my freshy days, a victim told me that if you added the words at the right place—that is, used your discretion and added the words where they would be most appropriate—you would be let off easy. The intensity of the ragging would be transferred from you to the one who bungled this up.

When it came to my turn, my reading went something like this:

Waters of the Tungabhadra river will be used to generate 100 MW of hydel power up my ass, announced Secretary, Power, Mr. KK Goyal up my ass at a press conference yesterday held in his chambers at the Secretariat up my ass. A team of experts was appointed up my ass to identify a suitable site up my ass and it was hoped to commence work on the project in six months' time up my ass, added Goyal. The Government was contemplating the import and commissioning of special submersible turbines up my ass which may do away with the necessity of constructing a dam up my ass. In addition to power generation up my ass, Government was also contemplating the construction of special canals up my ass which would help irrigate over one lakh hectares of arid land up my ass in the surrounding under-developed regions up my ass. This would boost cultivation of cash crops up my ass and generate revenue for the landless labour up my ass, said Goyal. The Government is likely to make a formal announcement soon up my ass after the elections to the local bodies are completed up my ass.

When we graduated to senior-dom, the raggers in my wing invented a variation to this UMA routine—MGM. I had a book of Urdu shayaris written in Hindi, and we asked the freshies to read out shayaris with the addition of—*Meri Gaand Mein*—the Hindi equivalent of Up My Ass. What followed was truly hilarious.

Sood: *Dard ke gulistan sajaane hain, meri gaand mein, saikdo zakhm dil pe khane hain, meri gaand mein*
Khosla: *Wah wah meri gaand mein*
Jetu: *Kya baat hai meri gaand mein*
Chitnis: *Koi jawab nahin meri gaand mein .*
Gazdar: *Dubara meri gaand mein*

Back to Sood who acknowledges these words of praise with an 'Adaab meri gaand mein.' And then says, 'Arz kiya hai meri gaand mein. Dard ke gulistan sajaane hain, meri gaand mein, saikdo zakhm dil pe khane hain, meri gaand mein, gham se ghabrake ke kyun mare koi meri gaand mein, maut ke aur bhi bahane hain meri gaand mein.'

There was a lot of laughter all round, and this was one

session in which the raggees enjoyed themselves as much as the raggers.

—*Bakul Desai, '77-'82*

~

Birjoo aka Bacha revelled in those riddles which seemed to have a dirty answer but the actual answer was as clean as Bacha himself. An example: 'Where does a woman's hair grow the densest and curliest?' Freshy's answer: 'Giggle giggle'. Bacha's mock-horrified correction: 'in Africa'. And then, 'what four-letter word ends with U, N, T and is essentially feminine?' Almost all freshies gave an embarrassed giggle except one Ashish Khosla who knew the answer and said with a triumphant smile, 'A is the missing letter. Aunt is the answer.' Bacha was quick to recover and admonished Ashish, 'Are you a kid or what? Living in your aunty's panties? Grow up man. The answer is C.' Bacha, who must have used this word for the first and maybe the last time in his life received resounding applause.

~

For a reason that became clear later, most ragging sessions cantered around sex. Freshies were first asked if they had 'done that' yet. Those few who said 'yes' were instantly elevated to a position of exaltation and given the status of 'consultant'. Most said 'no' and they were asked to imagine and pretend and play-act steamy scenes upon objects such as pillows. And if one resisted, he was asked to do his act on another guy who resisted. This was enough to make them fall in line. They either acted out on pillows or narrated imaginary encounters with a real person. The real person was generally the hottest girl freshy. With as few as

17

four and as many as nine girls joining IIT, everyone knew every girl's name. They rated the best and used her as an example of who the ragged freshy should fantasize about.

While these sessions went on and guys ooh-ed and aah-ed at the tales of imaginary encounters, there was bored Vinay Shah who thought that these juvenile thrills were sick and disgusting and he often walked out.

Pinky was 'the' girl from my batch. She was pretty, smart, wore her hair short, wore Wranglers, and, above all, she was rich. She had just returned from USA. This last led people to hope that this 'phoren maal' was bindaas and lax with her morals. But the most distinctive feature of Pinky was that she stood out for two very good reasons. Yes, God was kind to her in the upstairs department. Thus, during ragging sessions, fantasizing about Pinky was not difficult at all and words flowed freely from the freshies' mouths about what they would do to her and how they would do it if they could do it. Pinky herself was not unaware of the attention she was getting. But if she knew about the way guys doted on her and the ravages they were subjecting her to in the recesses of their own minds, she would have quit IIT much sooner than she did.

It was my second week at IIT when I was talking to Pinky just outside the classroom. To my horror, three seniors from H4 passed by and gave me the knowing look. 'Come back to the hostel, freshy, and we'll rag you to death' was what Parag Mehta said with his eyes, while Ajit Sheth smiled. Vinay Shah was bored, as always, his was a more 'I couldn't care less' look. It was bad enough that my classmates who were trying to hit on her and hadn't even got to say 'hello' to her saw Gourang and me talking to her. Being seen talking to her by my seniors was a new nightmare that I would have to endure.

When I got to H4 at tiffin time, expectedly, I heard a loud 'Hey freshy' beckoning me to the table of the Parag-Ajit-Vinay trio.

And to my amazement, it was Vinay Shah who took the lead in doing the hatchet job on me.

'Ok. That dame wearing Wranglers that you were talking to. Do you know what to do with her?' he asked me.

'No Sir'.

'What! Are you impotent? Are you a homo?'

'No Sir'.

'Anyway, listen to me carefully. Do whatever I tell you. Take her to a deserted spot behind H8'.

'Yes Sir'.

'Find a bush and go behind it'.

'Yes Sir'.

'Then, slowly start unzipping her Wranglers'.

'Yes Sir'.

'You know how to unzip? Will you show me how?'

'I know how to. I will do it. Please don't ask me to demo'.

'OK, after you unzip, remove her Wranglers and fold them neatly'.

'OK Sir'.

'What will you do next?'

'Whatever you ask me to, Sir'.

'Good. Take those Wranglers off her and bring them to me. I don't care what you do with her. I like her Wranglers'.

The whole table erupted in laughter. Vinay was clearly different and I was relieved that I was let off easily enough. But I did have a tough time later with Pinky. I couldn't take my eyes off her Wranglers every time I met her. She must have wondered why I didn't look where everyone else did.

—*Gokul Bhatt*

~

It was 1982 when I met a very scared freshy, Dhananjay Patankar. I was surprised by his terror, because he had arrived at IITB from the Bhosala Military School. The worst ragging in IITB should have been like Montessori lessons for him. But the fact was, this Dhananjay, who, by the way, had a military school-defying cherubic face, was really very very scared.

Within a few days, however, this cherubic Dhananjay was walking around looking way too cheerful for a UG (Undergraduate) freshy. As I had expected, he was now relishing the ragging. As a senior PG (Postgraduate) who seemed to have some rapport with the UGs, I soon gained Dhananjay's confidence. I asked him about his initial reaction to ragging. He laughed happily and told me, 'I thought that all this talk about taking my ass was for real—just like at my earlier school!'

—*Abhay Patil, '81-'83*

~

Two guys from IIT Delhi had come to IITB for practical training, and were put up in H4 SWGF (South Wing Ground Floor). They were both big, brutish, hard-core Northies. They caught hold of two of us. They played all sorts of psychological games to convince us that they were gay. Both brutes expressed more interest in my friend, to my shortlived, selfish relief. The bigger of the two then displayed a huge jar of Vaseline. I eyed it nervously. He asked me sweetly to make a decision as to where the Vaseline should be applied—on his 'source', or my friend's 'destination'. I'm not sure if this is a Hobson's Choice, or a Morton's Fork, or a Buridan's Ass, but one thing I was sure: I didn't want to make any choices regarding forks and asses. Any which way, I was screwed. Had I told him to use it on himself (which I did) he would say (which he did) 'Why, so that I can do you, after I'm done with him?' Had I selected option two, he'd say, 'So, you want to have a go at your friend, after I'm done?' Us two freshies were in that room for more than an hour, but apart from the horrible impending feeling that we were soon to be in deep shit, nothing really happened. Both of us were very unnerved, and then extremely relieved when they sent us away after having their fun. I told some seniors about the incident, and they were outraged that some IITD guys had the gall to rag their H4 boys, and went looking for them, but that must have been their last act in H4—the duo had checked out and vanished.

—*Rohan Menezes, '81-'85*

∿

It is just as well that some H4 residents were temporary, and not really H4ites at all.

Slippery Surd

In the summer of 82, all the laggards in IIT were doing a summer course. They would tell their parents at home that they were doing an extra course during the summer vacation instead of holidaying like their less serious friends. Parents would be impressed and boast to other parents about the prodigy that their son was. Technically, these folks were right. They were doing an extra course. It was only a technicality that it was a repeat course. There were guys in all hostels but were few in number and everyone there knew their fellow summer-ians. Some hostels also played host to students from other IITs who came to Mumbai to do practical training courses. There was a Surd from IIT Kharagpur who came to IIT B to do such a course and stayed at H4. He was a Surd only in technicality because he had cut his hair short and was known as a cut-surd like others of his ilk. The fact that he stayed in H4 was also a technicality since he spent more time absconding from H4 than not. He had to abscond because he was a glib talker who effortlessly took small loans of ten rupees from various guys and defaulted majorly in paying back. For instance, he would come knocking on your door and ask if you had ten rupees to spare for a few minutes. His cab was waiting outside and he had to pay up ten quickly and he would later go to his room in far off NWSF (North Wing Second Floor) and get the money and pay back. At least that's what he told his unsuspecting prey. Those who believed him paid and waited endlessly for the Surd to travel to and from NWSF, only to find later that the Surd was nowhere in H4. That was because he would shift to H5 and do his number there and disappear to some other hostel. Eventually, when circumstances forced him to return to H4, he would pay back a part of the money to a few of the guys and create a false impression that the huge consignment of money that his dad had sent him and which was lying locked in the bank was now clearing up since the error in transfer code was resolved.

One day, Surd, with a woman, came to H4 in a cab. He went to his room with the woman while the cab waited. Within five minutes, Surd and woman came back and drove away. Late at night, Surd returned in the same cab and went to his room. After waiting for more than twenty minutes, the cabbie raised a ruckus and finally, the security guard took him to G Sec Shenoy's room and woke him up. The cabbie said the Surd had hired the cab at Colaba, driven to H4 with the woman, driven back to Colaba where he dropped her off, and then returned to IIT. The total fare was Rs. 180 and the Surd had bolted. He was nowhere to be found.

The next day, one of the taxi unions called IIT and told the authorities that they would stop plying cabs within IIT unless someone paid up. After two days, the Surd turned up, unfazed by whatever he had precipitated earlier. Warden Ram Mohan Rao and Shenoy had a meeting with him in the warden's office. Surd was very cool. According to him, he picked up a girl in Colaba and brought her to H4 but the girl didn't like the room without an air-conditioner. So he agreed to drop her back in Colaba and when he returned to IIT, he realized he had no money. So he decided to give the cabbie the slip. He reached this point when Shenoy exploded. 'Look here, Mr Singh! I talked to the cab driver at length. You have not given him a slip of any sort. If you had, we would have paid him and taken the money from you later.' Anyway, Surd told the warden that he could take whatever action he wanted. He said that the Police Commissioner Rajadhyaksha's son was his friend and that he would get out of trouble even if the warden put him into it. Warden spent a harrowing week trying to locate someone with a connection to the Commissioner so that he could pre-empt Surd's manoeuvres. Finally, warden realized that the Commissioner was Ribeiro and not Rajadhyaksha. By this time, the Surd had fled Mumbai.

And, more importantly, had left H4 for good.

~

As a part of ragging, a freshy was handed a metal U-pin. Then he was asked to insert it into a live electrical socket. This freshy, who must have been one of the extra smart ones, promptly said, 'No way, I will get a shock.' As punishment for disobeying his seniors he was given a two-pin plug and asked to keep it in his underwear at all times. One week later, while he was in the mess eating his dinner, a senior asked him about the plug. Freshy promptly took it out of his underwear and showed it to the senior.

—*Vasudev (Chopper) Gharpure '72-'82, as told to Mukund (Mandy) Karwe, '76-'81*

~

Freshies were very young, and so freshy facial hair was sparse at best. This was a good area for adding insult to injury. Senior asks freshy, 'Do you like Hitler?' And the freshy does some quick thinking and answers 'Yes', trying some reverse logic. The senior then gives freshy a scathing lecture on the most despicable man in the history of the world and further informs him, 'You are going to pay for this for a long time.' Freshy is taken to the bathroom to shave off the sides of his moustache to leave behind the famous Nazi look. He is told, 'you will go to classes and labs looking like this for the whole month'. Now the senior turns to the second freshy who has been lurking, attempting to remain unseen. 'And you, do you like Hitler?' The shaken freshy blurts out 'no' with a sinking feeling that this answer is not going to help either.

Sure enough—he is asked to shave off the middle of the moustache leaving the sides intact.

So for the next few weeks, these two could not decide whether it was less humiliating going to classes together or separately.

Walking into a classroom of over a hundred freshies generally offered this hilarious sight. Some guys with half their moustache shaved off, say the left half. Some with their right half shaved off. And of course, there was a set of Hitler and anti-Hitler moustaches too. Sometimes there were attempts at shaving in an S shape, but given that freshies had just started sprouting facial hair and were not yet adept at shaving, this look was mostly unsuccessful.

From this crazy mix of funny faces, it was easy to identify which hostel a freshy belonged to. Each hostel's seniors sent freshies to classrooms with their hostel's particular shave pattern, which was decided by the seniors' popular vote. In 1977, H6 guys had their left sides shaved off while H4 guys were Hitlers or anti-Hitlers. And to their horror, two bearded freshies, Christopher Fernandes and Edgar Dias were made to shave off half of each other's beards.

—Ashvin (Ghoda) Sanghvi, '76-'81

~

Among these freshy victims falling left and right, there was one Chopra. Someone thought the most appropriate assignment for that smartie was to send him to the Ladies' Hostel to beg, borrow or steal an undergarment from them. Chopra laid on considerable drama, but, he did turn up with an item.

Days and weeks went by, everyone moved on to other freshies and other pranks. One day, one of the girls said to me, 'You should stop it now, and let the poor guy be.' I looked at her quizzically. 'What do you mean?' I asked.

'Every day this poor kid is at our hostel, with a new story on how you are making his life hell.'

'What poor kid?' I asked her.

And she said, 'Chopra, who else? Did you guys not send him for an undergarment?'

'Yes,' I said sheepishly, 'but we have not ragged him since then, in fact we were wondering what became of him.'

So, while we thought our little prank was so clever, our Chopra had been milking the situation for weeks on end, bringing out motherly instincts in the girls by making up tales of tremendous atrocities by seniors.

We realized we had met much more than our match. He was out of our league—he was in a higher one.

—*Ghoda*

~

It was a week or two after our Freshies night. The freshies were now part of us and we were glad we had some fun recruits. Our thoughts had moved on to other things. Panda and I went to get a sandwich at the canteen to find that they had closed for the day. We decided to go to the neighbouring hostel to see if we could find something there.

Hostel 5 was famous for its rock star musicians. Our friend Mogre in H5 was quite a drummer. So it was not a surprise that the place was rocking and reverberating as we walked down the path towards the lounge. But as we get closer, we saw that it was a special occasion. There was a crowd of guys around the tables, clapping with the beat and having a great time. It was dark, with a few coloured spotlights pointing to the table tops.

And this is where Panda and I took a step back. There was actually a good-looking chick, made up pretty well, doing a very sexy dance on the tables. The high heels were kicking up, showing a flash of thigh and she seemed happy with the cat calls and hoots as she suggestively pulled the blouse over her bare shoulder.

We were disoriented. Can this be true? Could this hostel be more fun than ours? How did they even pull this off?

27

Now the girl dancer on the table turned toward us. My jaw dropped. The girl doing this sexy jig was no other than Shona. Same curly hair, same smile, same flashing teeth, same eyes. Shona was in my class and over time I had got to know her pretty well. She was no starched pants—but this? How could this be happening? As I collected my jaw from the floor, I saw that Panda was as perplexed as I was.

The girl was waving a scarf. And as the boys egged her on, she straddled the scarf with its corners in her hands, moving her body and the scarf with the beat. The crowd was wild. This is where I got my final confirmation. This was the same scarf Shona wore to the previous Mood Indigo, the cultural festival. I was definitely rattled.

And then I noticed a whole similarly dressed line-up waiting their turn to be humiliated. And I realized—this was their freshy night and the 'girl' was Shona's kid brother in her borrowed clothes.

—*Ghoda*

~

For those who have forgotten Rupen Anklekar, he was a poor unfortunate soul who was ragged right through his stay at IIT, at least up until when I saw him last in '82. Like a few others, there was something about him that made him vulnerable to ragging. He always spoke in the present continuous tense—'I am not knowing' instead of 'I don't know'.

Pinakin Patel had got hold of a hideous, scary monster mask. One night, he went from room to room and momentarily

28

freaked people out. The initially scared victim then joined him to go to the next door and scare someone else, and there was a lot of laughter after the initial scare. By the time Pinakin got to Anklekar's room, there was a sizeable crowd of ex-victims accompanying him, wanting to see how Anklekar would react. When Anklekar opened his door to Pinakin's knock and saw the monster, he jumped a few feet in the air and shouted 'hoo-hoo-hoo' loud enough to be heard in H5, and then he ran out of his room and started howling in the footer (football) field between south and central wings. For a while, it appeared that Anklekar had lost it and turned insane.

All this happened around 10pm, but there were enough hostelites enraged by Anklekar's insane howling who woke up Warden Lakkad and insisted he come to the hostel and pull up the miscreants. Warden Lakkad wanted to see the offensive mask in order to understand why this was such a big deal. The mask was declared as missing.

I said to Warden Lakkad, 'Sir, the mask is missing, but if you call Ashwin Hattangadi (Hats), you'll understand what the mask looks like.' Hats was sore with me for an entire week after that. He even stopped bumming fags from me. Almost 30 years later, I am making it up to Hats by referring to our grand project as H4 HATS.

—*Bakul*

~

My first day on-campus, I bought a bicycle. The handle swerved around, as did the seat, and as I found out going faster and faster past the Convo (Convocation Hall, which was used more to screen movies and host events and less for annual graduation ceremonies) toward H8, the bike did not have any brakes either. Finally, my front wheel scissored between a guy's legs, and I stopped. Various parts of the guy's body absorbed the shock, and he landed on his feet after defying gravity for a few seconds. On landing, and with a hand firmly massaging his injured parts, he let out a torrent of abuse. I cursed him back. Before we got to a fist-fight, passersby pulled us apart. He stormed away fuming. I picked up my bicycle, a bit shaken up with all the adrenalin coursing through me. I cycled back to H4 keenly aware of my newfound pride in not having backed down at IIT.

Dinner. Across from me at the table was the same angry senior. He recognized me as I tried to shrink and growled at me to sit down.

After a few moments of enduring nothing more than his glare, I thought he was going to be the worst senior I would ever face. After all, as per the conservation of momentum principle, my front-wheel had transferred a huge amount of energy to whatever objects it came into contact with.

But what he asked me next was a revelation unto itself.

One question.

'Asshole. Are you a PG (Postgraduate)?'

We had freshies-orientation that morning, and our senior Jetu had told us that only H4-seniors were allowed to rag us. I knew I was fair game.

'No,' I said. Then I had to play nose football on my knees, pushing a coin (the ball) against the slope, and my nose pretty much peeled off.

Had I been a PG, I would not have been worth ragging, nor therefore considered a part of the H4 culture. I would simply remain a nameless, faceless PG.

—*Hemendra (Gol Dabba) Godbole, '81-85*

⁓

This social engineering had a profound effect on shaping my personality. I was nineteen, I considered myself elite, but, as a PG, I experienced what it means to be a dalit and how it feels to be ostracized the moment I entered the portals of the hostel. In fact I used to feel sad when a UG (Undergraduate) would stop ragging me the moment he realized that I was a PG.

—*Abhay*

⁓

One exception with PG ragging was Pinakin and team with the hideous mask. They in fact primarily targeted PGs who were already fast asleep. These PGs were far more disciplined with their sleep habits—they were in bed by 9:30pm. The attacking team even put a white bed sheet around themselves along with the mask and made some howling sounds for added effect.

After being rudely awoken by a team of ghosts in the midst of their REM sleep phase, the PGs all had different reactions. In some cases it was pure flight and in other cases it was fight. I remember one of the PG victims being so terrified that he took it upon himself to attack the ghost by punching the masked individual wherever he could find an opening all the while yelling 'Go away ghost, go away ghost'. It was hilarious to see how quickly the roles were reversed and the team of attackers now ran helter-skelter to avoid the hysterical kicking and punching. Perhaps, though, this was a smart PG who outwitted all of us and took advantage of the opportunity to legally beat the crap out of us UGs for once.

—*Sanjay Pol, '77-'82*

~

There was one raggee who was allegedly ragged badly enough to drop out of IIT altogether, and squeal to the corporator in his area that IIT ragging was fierce. Mr. Corporator ran his story in a local paper. The story said there were two ragging gangs, and each had its own ringleader. He said one of the rooms was a dreaded chamber of ragging. The room he named, unfortunately for him, belonged to a staunch anti-ragging crusader.

The education minister of the Maharashtra Government called Diro (Director) who passed the call on to DOSA (Dean of Student Affairs) Isaac, who made clear that there were no such ferocious raggers in IIT, let alone gangs and chambers. Still, the education minister sent the education secretary to IIT on a fact-finding mission. DOSA Isaac sent the secretary away without going through the task of rounding up criminals, as there were none, and he knew it. The newspaper article had listed some thirteen organised events during which ragging took place, including Pagal Gymkhana and the freshies night. Isaac said he had been the chief guest of every Pagal Gym, and it was a fun-and-games event and not a ragging routine at all.

It turned out that this raggee was reluctant to join IIT in the first place. His father had coerced him to join, and he used this story of bullying to get out, sullying names in the process.

~

Ragging freshies was something all of us sometimes did—just as we sometimes took baths, had breakfast, went for lectures and spent hours faating (talking about nothing important, aka cacking) in the corridors. After a number of years of this regular ritual, the urge to do it waned considerably. One evening I came across a bunch of 2nd-year guys whose enthusiasm for their new-found power was still alive. They had themselves a freshy victim, I think his name was Poddar. I watched as they tried out the routines played on them the previous year—describe your girlfriend's assets, be a cuckoo clock, compare the measurement of your penis, praying to God vs. Zeenat Aman, and so on. This guy—Poddar perhaps—stood there stony-faced, hands folded across chest, eyes firmly directed at ground. He did not respond to anything. He didn't utter a word or move a muscle, no expression altered his face—not embarrassment, rage, disgust, nothing. Classical detachment, the personification of Leibniz's Monad. Almost a half hour of persistent effort yielded naught. It was interesting to watch the faces of his tormentors change from excited to outraged to puzzled to outraged to dejected to outraged to bored to

33

outraged and finally to defeated and reconciled to their failure. If the freshy had even smiled his raggers would have thought their job done. This was a truly Gandhian counter to ragging, more effective than any subterfuge I had seen generations of freshies use over the years.

And then there was Chitnis. I remember this non-incident because it ended my enthusiasm for ragging freshies once and for all. One evening, Blondie Mittal and I were sitting in the corridor by the stairs in NWSF (North Wing Second Floor). There was a gloomy, listless rain falling. This meant no volleyball, no boating, no cricket and nothing exciting to do. Mittal spotted Chitnis, then freshy, and thought, here is one way of making our time interesting. Chitnis looked like a fawn in the headlights. The usual ragging routine followed. Chitnis answered everything, responded to every probing question, every ribald joke about him, each lewd comment about his girlfriends. But his every answer was mundane and monochromatic. About the only thing that livened up the moment was a Beatles song he sang, and that was vaguely interesting not because he sang it well, simply because it was a Beatles song. The event couldn't have been better designed to bore even Mittal to death, not an easy thing to do. If we were gloomy before we ragged Chitnis, we were ready to jump off the ledge from the second floor after.

—*Satkya*

~

An interesting ragging incident involved one Sonawane who would have graduated in'83. I say 'would have' for a reason. Sonawane was a sneaky guy who kept away from the hostel during his entire first year in order to avoid getting ragged. But in his second year, he became a new-born lion who not only stayed in the hostel, he would actually rag folks from the '84 batch.

During a Pagal Gymkhana in the hostel the few C'84 (graduating Class of '84) folks that we had regaled us with some fun and games by playing three-legged and five-legged race and hop-jump-squish in the mud and stuff like that. I also remember that Subodh Mhaisalkar was the star performer on that day. Sonawane was very much present and was enjoying himself seeing his juniors suffer in a way that he was smart enough to avoid.

Toward the end of the event, some signals were exchanged.

Nobody is sure what exactly went down, but I know that Sood was one of the guys who gave a signal to the C84 guys. Quick as a flash, all these freshies suddenly converged upon Sonawane. Sonawane, at first too stunned to react, recovered fast enough and sprinted like his life depended on running away fast enough. He did precisely that. He ran out of the hostel and kept running. The freshies gave up the chase near the gymkhana but Sonawane continued running till he was out of the main gate.

During dinnertime that same evening, Warden Lakkad came to the hostel with the Deputy Diro to inquire about the 'Sonawane episode'. This was already classified as an episode and had a senior level delegation out on a fact finding mission. Deputy Diro asked me, 'Who was responsible?' I tried telling him that the freshies chased Sonawane because they were told to do so by the seniors and were certainly not responsible, and, before I could explain further, junta began to run down Sonawane vociferously. To our pleasant surprise, Lakkad too opined that it was better that people like Sonawane don't come back and spoil the atmosphere. So that was Sonawane, who would have graduated in '83. He did not ever return, that day when he left the gate, he ran away into permanent oblivion.

—*Bakul*

~

The inter-hostel drama competition was a good time to add some extra-curricular drama to the lives of the hostelites. We were staging the play *The Bet*. One of the props required for the play was a door. Memon, Giri, and company thought it would be a bright idea to borrow the Convo door for this purpose. The main door and other doors at the architecturally aesthetic Convocation Hall were heavy-duty doors carved in solid wood and very impressive looking. They also thought it would be a good idea to assign this project to the freshies under their guidance. Sandeep Bhise, Kicks, Duddy, Kripalani, and a few others were the chosen ones for this important mission. These chosen ones expressed their concern about what would happen to them if they were caught. Their guides informed them that they would be kicked out of the institute. But ever the logical minds of IIT, they also pointed out that if unable to perform this simple task, they were not fit to be there anyway.

For the next ten days, the freshies practiced unscrewing and screwing doors. They had a plan. Duties were assigned: Duddy would turn off the Convo lights. The practiced unscrewers would unscrew. Others would stand watch, and raise the alarm in case of danger.

The day arrived. Memon led the would-be borrowers of the Convo door to the hall. He instructed the guards to yell 'Run, You Bastards' in case there was need to do so. He instructed that the bastards, on hearing the alarm, should then run in different directions, and stay away for a couple of hours.

As soon as Duddy turned off the lights, they all heard the call, 'Run, You Bastards!'

Run they did, all the way to Powai Lake.

After their return two hours later, and for the rest of the two years that Memon and Giri had left at IIT, the gang were the objects of derision. They were the useless ones who could not carry out a simple mission.

Two years later when Memon was leaving the institute on his graduation, he explained to the suitably vilified and much insulted group that not only was it not possible to remove the Convo door without getting caught, it was not possible to remove the door at all.

—told by Sandeep Bhise, '72-'77 to Pradeep (Blondie) Mittal, '72-'77

~

The year was 1973, the first month of term was just over. Ragging was fading away, and there was a kind of feeling of being settled. H4 was beginning to feel like home. Seniors were friendlier. Freshies night was approaching. There is an unwritten rule that this night is the end of ragging. This was a well-established tradition, with a party, and a big meal. Freshers are expected to serve seniors that night. Lucky seniors would bring guests from H10 (The Ladies' Hostel), and professors and the warden and their families were also guests.

That year the meal was to be cooked by the mess, but the special dish was Tandoori Chicken from A1 Grill on Linking Road, Juhu. In those days this was a famous joint, and one I could not afford to patronize with my meagre pocket money (It cost Rs. 11/- for a full chicken). I was in the team which would serve the Tandoori Chicken. After its long journey from Juhu to H4 the poor Tandoori Chicken would be cold by the time we served it, and I suggested we set up an open grill to warm the dead bird in its final journey, give it a warm send-off to heaven. The mess committee accepted my bright idea. We set up a grill with bricks and a piece of welded mesh with a coal fire below. Everything was ready when a taxi arrived with the birds, and we got to work.

Dinner was to start around 8pm. The first six chickens were laid out on the grill. As the delicious red juicy meat got warmed up, it sizzled and crackled. Its enticing aroma wafted through the air. The first batch was served. It was greatly appreciated. We became proficient by the fourth batch.

The whole fireside experience was exciting, adding to the gastronomical delight of those at the tables. For us, as the initial excitement waned, it became a torture to see and smell the juicy, tasty inviting meat, and feel the ensuing agony of hunger. Soon enough, my three colleagues and I could hardly bear the pangs. The birds were flying off our grill, and we knew we wouldn't get any dinner until 10pm at the earliest. We became utterly helpless and miserable.

The Great Hunger finally won. I plucked a small piece of a wing. Before I could think, it disappeared into my mouth. My colleagues were aghast. Ethics was not much of an issue, Maslow's hierarchy of needs took over. They thought we would be caught. Even so, by and by, poor chickens went to the tables without a wing or part of a leg. Who can be blamed for natural inadequacies, but God himself?

Nobody noticed their mutant chickens. We got away with it, and were quite full. As luck would have it, the number of chickens turned out to be inadequate—many took extras (maybe those who got lame chickens). Some of the volunteers had to go without Tandoori Chicken for their dinner—us. There was much sympathy and perhaps some guilt, and we were compensated with Tandoori Chicken coupons to A1 Grill.

Fortune does favour the hungry sometimes. And the greedy.

—*Vasant Vasant (Balya / V Square) Limaye, '73-'78)*

~

Sometime in '80, a freshy called Nene walked into H4 with his dad. They were from a small hamlet in Maharashtra. They were both short, mousy and timid-looking, and they both had mouths that looked as if they were always smiling. Even when the Nenes scowled, they scowled with a smile. Nene Sr. was clearly proud of his son who had made it to IIT, but he was also protective towards him and worried that he would get ravaged by the sinister ragging squads that his whole town had heard about. So the father decided to stay with his son in H4 and move around with him until the 'ragging period' was over. He had been told that there was something called Freshers night which heralded the end of ragging.

These Nenes, like Anklekar, always spoke in a present continuous tense. 'I am not knowing', 'I am eating and sleeping with my son' and so on. This look-alike father son duo walked alike and ate alike and beside each other. Or, to put it in Nene terms, they are always walking alike and eating alike and sitting alike. They are not letting seniors come near them. If seniors are troubling son, father is stepping forward and telling seniors to stop trouble. Why unnecessary doing trouble? What the son is spoiling of seniors that they are looking for him to be coming out of room alone? And what nonsense the management is talking? Management people are telling that ragging is doing good for the son.

So like this two weeks are passing and father is smiling more and more and eating boldly in mess, Hasmukh KT is going to him and asking if he is forgetting his villaze address. If he is missing the bus or train that is taking him to his villaze. Father is saying that Hasmukh is saying whatever he is wanting but father is not leaving till it is settling down. Gogate is getting angry and asking father which department he is joining. Why he is doing BTech at such old aze? Father then saying that he is staying in hostel only because seniors are doing ragging. Gogate is telling that when father is going, son is getting ragging. Father is staying five years or what? Father is telling that if it is necessary, he is staying five years. Gogate is then telling father that like this his son's life is getting ruined. If he is wanting his son repaired and moving like proper man, father must be leaving him alone and letting son find his own way in life so that he is standing alone. Nene Sr. is agreeing and going to villaze.

Nene jr. is being ragged and becoming good person on own merit.

~

A freshy was asked by seniors if he was a virgin. Highly embarrassed, he blurted out, 'not yet!'

—*Ashanka Sen, '83-'87*

~

Prickly Times

People who remember Mukesh Parikh from the batch of '84 may also remember why he was called Mukesh Prick before he left H4 in disgrace and moved to H5.

After a gruelling ragging session, he said to the ragging senior, 'You seem to be very popular. Can you sell my shampoo in your wing? I will give you exclusive rights for the whole wing.'

Mukesh, like any other Gujju pronounced his own name 'Mukes'. He came to IIT with ambitious and grandiose plans of making it big as a business tycoon, and started off in right earnest from day one—even while he was being ragged. He started off by trying to sell shampoo (pronounced 'samepoo') at Rs 12 per bottle. He claimed it was manufactured in his father's factory, but, as Rajesh Devi told us later, was actually being made by his Mummy in her kitchen as a 'side' business. The marketing strategist in Mukes compelled him to look for an 'agent' in every wing who could promote his sales with an inducement of a Rs 2 per bottle commission. It didn't take long for him to realize that IITans who bathed once a week didn't exactly use samepoo. In fact, most of them didn't even know what it meant.

But that didn't deter our never-say-die businessman. A quick market survey told Mukesbhai that IITans needed a 'calekey' (Gujju for calcy—calculator) like junkies need their fix. Enter Pappa's side business. The next day saw a stunning array of Casio calekeys doing the rounds in all wings. Calekeys were priced at Rs. 500, and, with a calekey, you got an added bonus: one bottle samepoo free. This was a coup. Mummy's and Pappa's business interests were covered. I suspect that future ad gurus who started this 'Buy One, Get One Free' idea were inspired by our very own entrepreneur. Business began to pick up. Mukesbhai even toyed with the idea of a reversal—sell 1 bottle samepoo with 1 calekey thrown in free. But after working the economics on the same calekey, he realized it was a bad idea.

Alas! This dream run was to end. The 'calekeys' began to malfunction. They would not work. And when they did, a simple 2X2 gave you 3.99999999999 as the answer. Irate purchasers hounded Mukes. Warden JC Chandrashekhar had to step in. Pappa was summoned to the hostel at 8pm. Pappa came in at 7.30 sharp and father/son duo had a wholesome dinner in the mess. When mess worker More took the 'extras' notebook to Mukes to sign for an extra meal, he was rudely told by the senior Parikh, 'Your own warden called me here at dinner time, surely you don't think I'm required to pay for this meal?' More could not handle such strong Gujju logic. It took Fish (G Sec Ashvin Iyengar who was fondly called Fish) to intervene and extract the prized signature. JC could not believe what happened during the meeting. Pappa first said that 'there are no guarantees for 'without-bill' goods' and 'does the Casio company belong to my father or what?' And finally, he alluded to a pay-off, saying, 'let's come to some understanding and settle this matter between us.'

In the end Mukes was asked to take back a few calekeys and refund half the money. Of course, he asked for a samepoo return too as a pre-condition for the money refund. He was also induced to change hostels. On the day of his departure Mukes was seen walking into H4 with a bucket in his hand, and

43

in the bucket was a frothy foamy liquid which turned out to be the same notorious samepoo. Hasmukh KT was accosted first. He was offered a bucket of samepoo for only Rs. 25. Provided the bucket was returned. Suspicious KT asked what the catch was. To start with, he asked why the samepoo was in a bucket. 'Well', boasted the triumphant tycoon, 'I was carrying 6 bottles which fell and broke. I quickly scooped up the contents and poured them in this bucket.' Aghast KT asked him if broken glass pieces were also part of this wholesale deal. Mukes was worried for exactly ten seconds before he broke into a triumphant smile and told KT, 'If you keep silent about this, I will give you Rs 5 from the 25.'

~

Partition

Our hostel was one of those at IIT with the privilege of having partitions between two 'rooms' instead of complete walls. These partitions left about six inches of space at the bottom and about two feet on the top. This space was the source of interesting dynamics between partition mates.

Each year, only a handful rooms came vacant on the upper floors, so most freshies ended up in a room on the ground floor. These were not the most desirable—they hosted snails and other creatures during the monsoon. Everyone aspired to be on the first or second floor. The only way for a freshy to get a room upstairs was to have some talent, or at least convince the seniors at the Pearly Gates that you were a freshy with some talent—at sports, or something cultural, or just that you were a fun person.

Raj Laad, one of the leaders in SWSF (South Wing Second Floor) ordered me to come and make my home in SWSF. As an obedient freshy, I didn't have a choice. My partition mate was Pardikar, about seven or eight years my senior. He had returned to IIT to do his M.Tech.

There were the usual greetings when I moved in. After that we adopted the British policy of 'Don't speak until you are spoken to'. Both of us followed this policy to the dot. As a freshy, I hoped that he would break the ice. He, I'm sure, thought I was a snob. Our only cross-partition conversation took place when we discussed the scroll of honour GBM (General Body Meeting) at the end of a whole year of co-habitation.

As the first year was wrapping up, some of my friends— Nikhil Tikekar (Tikya), Hemen Godbole (Dabba), Makarand Gokhale (Fakrya) and Chris Fernandes moved to NWSF (North Wing Second Floor). I moved with them, by then I had enough courage to resist any pleas from the SWSFers. I got Room 215 and my new partition mate was Prashant Khambekar (Khambu).

At IIT you can categorize people into (a) sloggers—who took studying very seriously, (b) get by-ers—who got by with a 6 or 7 point something GPA and spent lot of time on fun, and (c) given up-ers—who had given up on studies. Fortunately, very few fell into category c. I was a get by-er, Khambu was a slogger. The chemistry did not match. And then there was the matter of the tubelight that Khambu and his former partition mate, Adke, had installed right above the partition. Khambu studied late into every night. So late that it could be thought of as early. While I was not an early-to-bed kind of a guy, post 10pm was reserved for 'cack sessions' which lasted until midnight. After which I wanted my eight hours sleep. Bathed in the glare of the giant tubelight of death, however, it was extremely difficult to sleep.

First there were polite requests, then, strong language was thrown in, including threats of pulling down the tubelight. Khambu did not budge. So, then, the usual gang—Tikya, Dabba, Fakrya and I—hatched a plot that was bound to succeed. We moved our post-10pm cack sessions to my room and extended them way beyond midnight. These sessions were not soft-spoken polite discussions. They were filled with high-pitched impassioned debates and loud laugher. Enough to disturb any slogger's meditation. Sure enough, the tables turned—there were requests at first and then threats of complaints to Wardy (the hostel warden). We offered the middle ground of a tubelight-out policy at the stroke of midnight, but this was not acceptable to the other party. So we kept our strategy going, relentlessly, day after day. Khambu moved out. He went to live on the ground floor in the safe haven of freshies and snails.

We were successful at achieving our objective. The 'room' next door was vacant. We wanted to get the 'right' kind of person there. But it was hi-jacked by a PG. Madhav Kale moved in without even asking our permission. This was not done. Again, there were requests to move out—softer at first, stronger later. But none of it yielded any result. The cack session strategy did not work. We tried others. First, we put glue in the keyhole of his padlock. He cut open the lock. Next, we put our own padlock on, an expensive one not easy to cut. He called in a locksmith. Next, we put decorative wall paper in his room while he was out. He removed it. All of our schemes and plans had failed. We gave up, and slowly but surely welcomed Kale to our fold. After all, someone who could resist us UGs to this degree had to be a special PG.

Our creative conspiracies are more than a quarter century old and we can all only look back on them in amusement now.

—Amol Mahajani, '81-'85

~

Talking about partition mates reminds me that Ram Chopra had quite a few partition mates in his time. He also had—well, let's just call them visitors. He had visitors visiting his side of the partition, and the not-yet-asleep partition mate would later narrate eye-witness accounts—change that to ear-witness accounts. Subir Saha was one such partition mate who did not believe in the 'hear no evil, speak no evil, see no evil' doctrine of the three monkeys. He would excitedly narrate to some of us all that he heard (and smelt when the perfume was strong) the previous night while he was feigning sleep.

We had some amorous adventurers in my own wing too, with the critical difference that the dormant partition mate was asked to leave his room. It helped that my room, 252, doubled as a refugee camp for Soumitra Banerjee when he was chucked out by Shashank Shah and my room also served Shashank Shah when Soumitra Banerjee caused his exit more often than the other way around.

And may I boast that my room was refugee-friendly, and my experience in dealing with refugees could have served as the starting point for a successful career in the hospitality business. Room 252 was always open, there were welcome pin-ups on the walls, and, when finances were good, there was a welcome drink to be had too. All kinds of cigarettes were provided except on days Fish Iyengar raided my room, and my later day partition mate Mad Rao stocked up well on—let's just call them educational books, which could be accessed with a quick jump over the partition. (Note to Mad: No, I swear I did not wack the Debra Jo Fondren playmate pin-up and neither did any of my guests. Please check elsewhere and stop asking me to return it.)

—*Bakul*

~

Vasu and I were roommates (partition mates) in our first year and he had this strange habit of locking his room. He would lock it even when he left to take a shower. That innocent act irritated me, since I was of the firm conviction that hostel rooms should never be locked. How else could I steal cigarettes and pondies (what we called educational material of a certain genre) otherwise? So one day I jumped over the partition and bolted his room from the inside, jumped back into my room, locked my room and left. Poor Vasu was pacing the corridor in his towel when I returned much later, but, as always, he did not pitch a fit about it. I knew that he would return the favour, and he did. But little did he know that I had planned for it by keeping the window ajar. And he did not know about my flexible ways and that my wiry hands could somehow squeeze in through the bars and extend far enough to open the door.

—*Ashvin (Fish) Iyengar, '77-'83*

~

Fishing

This Fish is a character who can inspire many books, leave alone a chapter or a few lines. There exists a video which shows this Fish bringing his clasped hands from his front to his back from over his head, without unclasping them. Fish was tall, wiry, nervous twitches, curly hair (if you blew smoke into his hair, it would remain trapped, and only came out when you patted his head, and then the smoke came out very confused). He bunked lectures but worked like a horse in the mess. And he wrote melancholic poems. He got off on imagining that he was jilted. If a girl was nice to him, he would somehow manoeuvre events forcing the girl to jilt him so he could indulge in his melancholia for the day. Perpetually poverty stricken, he would bum cigarettes from anybody and everybody, and I was his lifeline and assured supplier. During my occasional absence from IIT, Fish would be driven to despair. He once actually chided me for changing my brand from filterless Panama cigs to the more respectable Wills Navy Cut. 'I do not like Wills. So why do you buy them?'

Among his millions of quirks, there was this one where he walked meanderingly alongside a wall and touched it every seven or eight feet. And if he passed a bicycle, that would be his crowning moment. He got a lot of surface area to touch. Carrier, seat and handle. Many wondered if he was aroused by this touching business, so passionately would he indulge in it.

And like many things that happened backwards for him in life, his rendition of his melancholic poems aroused sniggers and giggles, but his delivery of good but deadpan jokes saw more frowns than smiles. There's more, but for now, this is an anecdote which will make you wonder why nobody has killed this poor dear yet.

Ashvin Iyengar woke up unusually early one day. And for a good reason, he was disoriented. Time was around 10am and there was a heavenly body called the sun which was shining in a direction called the East. Now this Iyengar, or Fish, as he was called, had neither seen the sun nor the east in a while and he

49

was quite distraught trying to figure out this new stellar configuration God had delivered him this day.

With a forehead furrowed with lines of worry, this aimless wanderer made his way to an approximate mess. The mess was exact but this Fish had to meander his way to it at a time of day he had never seen until that morning, and therefore this mess is designated as approximate while this Fish tried to find an exact way to this approximate piece of infrastructure.

Fish had reasons to worry. Where would he get his next fag from? Guys were refusing to lend him a matchstick, leave alone a half-smoked Panama. His darling Billee had walked out to God-knows-where before he woke up. His Jotter refill pen had been flicked by a miscreant and he did not know how to close the stanza of his melancholic poem. Was the mess open at this unearthly hour? Would a Gopi-what's-his-name deliver a whatchmacallit-omelette? Would this Vishnu something guy let him at least sniff a cig, if not smoke it?

And while this aimless wanderer trudged his wavy way to the mess performing arm-twisting calisthenics and touching walls and cycles in the corridor, there was another guy on a cycle, and this guy had a mission. For want of identification and for the purpose of telling a story, let us assume that this guy was Subodh Gadgil. Gadgil had come to IIT to become an engineer. He wanted to design a turbine that would rid India of her energy problems. And so here was Subodh Gadgil on his cycle with eight thick text books in his right hand and a delicately positioned T-square under his left armpit, trying to race to the lecture hall before someone else designed the turbine.

And as Gadgil passed Fish in the corridor, Fish called out, 'What's the time?'

Now, if you are an average man, 52,000 questions will run through your mind. Why does Fish want to know the time? Does he know what time is? Does it matter to him whether it is 10 o'clock or 48 thousand o' clock or one crore o'clock? Why doesn't he wear his own frigging wristwatch? How does he expect me to tell the time when I am racing on a cycle with my eight fat textbooks in my right arm and my T-square under my left armpit and I'm about to turn from the corridor onto the main road?

But Subodh Gadgil was nicer than the average man and he actually shuffled his eight textbooks from his right arm to his left, traded the T-square's designated armpit from left to right, stretched his wristwatch arm out to squint at it and announce to Fish that the time was 'Dus-Dus.'

And thus, as a triumphant Gadgil who had performed the acrobatic feat of deciphering his wristwatch while in motion pursed his lips to say 'welcome' to Fish's imminent 'thanks', he had to stop dead in his track at what followed.

A quick recap: Fish said, 'What's the time?' Gadgil said: 'Dus-Dus.'

And Fish replied, 'Why are you telling me twice? I asked you just once.' Coming from a guy who was sleep-deprived, alcohol-deprived, Panama-deprived, cat-deprived, omelette-deprived, end of melancholic poem-deprived, this was too much and Subodh Gadgil's expression told a story that may well take a whole chapter to describe.

Had it been anyone else but this nice man Subodh Gadgil, he would have stopped his bike, thrown the eight fat textbooks to the ground, gone after Fish, and posited the T-square exactly where it belonged. In Fish's hinterland.

—Bakul

~

These memories about partition mates reminded me of a rare distinction I had that you guys never did. I had a 'pole-mate' in Subramanian S. Iyer who later came to be known as the more famous Subrah Iyer—founder and CEO of a $4.5 billion Webex.

This took place sometime in August 1978, early in my second year. The mess workers were giving us a hard time and we had an angry GBM in which we authorized G Sec Manu (future CM of Goa, Manohar Parrikar) to take strong action against them. The GBM stretched late into the night. Soon after that, I had to make a phone call to someone, and as usual, our H4 phone was out of order. By strange coincidence, Subra too had to make a call and we found ourselves walking together to neighbouring H5 to try our luck there. While in H5, I got my mischief itch. To scratch it, I called up H4 on the internal line. (The number was 383, and changed to 583 later.) The phone was answered by councillor Chandu Tambat aka Hechku. (I later learned that Hechku was short for Hugroo Kumar. Hug was a slang for a flop and I was soon to understand why Tambat was a champion Hugroo.) I told Hechku that the mess workers had learned about impending action against them and they were on their way to H4 carrying cans of petrol and planned to set H4 ablaze. I said all this quite casually and without excitement and was amazed that Hechku took me seriously and began to ask me panic-stricken questions. I was beside myself laughing, so I passed the phone to Subra, telling Hechku that the Security Officer wanted to have a word with him. Guys may remember Subra's booming voice that boomed louder than Security Officer Singh's voice. And while 'Security Officer' Subra counselled Hechku to 'be careful and on your guard', he went one step further to hint that this was a prank. Subra said, 'Be careful with your Kreyzigs. Kreyzigs are important. Be sure to save your Kreyzigs.' (Kreyzig was a crazy monster of a Math book for MA courses). And with that, he hung up and we walked back to H4 laughing at what had just transpired and smug and secure in the belief that the Kreyzig googly would prevent Hechku from raising an alarm.

When we got back to H4, it was ablaze with all lights on and guys were running down the corridors in unison. If one could have filmed that scene on that day, it would put the most disciplined military drill to shame. Every H4 guy who was unfortunate enough to be in H4 that night was woken up, and each guy ran in a file formation from the wing to the stairwell and then down the staircase, and converged near the entrance. Some guys were seen brandishing hockey sticks. When Subra and I got to the entrance there were more than two hundred sleepy yet enraged folks looking at us with a questioning look which said, 'Where are the bastards?' Subra first, and I later, committed the mistake of laughing out loud and asked, 'Did you guys take us so seriously or what?'

What followed is something that I remember in slow motion and in a blur. Satish Joshi aka Satkya lunged at me and caught me by the collar while Boss Patil reached out and restrained him. There was a plethora of abuses hurled at us. Many hands materialized from nowhere, and soon, Subra's and my wrists were tied back to back on the pole near the entrance. I always wondered where the ropes materialized from, and later found out that they were supplied by Chopper and the mountaineering gang. For want of anything better, H4 rubber stamps were taken out from the warden's office and we were stamped all over our shirt and trousers and finally on our faces. We were made to say sorry a few thousand times and made to promise 'I will not do it again' in primary school punishment fashion. A photograph was taken (I am unable to find my copy) and all our pleas to be released were not entertained for the next three hours. During this ordeal, Subra kept shouting, 'Tambat, you idiot! I told you to save your Kreyzigs. Could you not see it was a joke?' Tambat denied having heard the Kreyzig word, possibly due to the stress caused by this unexpected alarm. I tried to entreat guys to look at the bright side of things. After all, two hours earlier, they all thought they had a malicious fire on their hands. Now, they didn't. Shouldn't that make them happy and grant us amnesty? I tried praising the guys for the quick, efficient and organized manner in which they rallied around to deal with an emergency. Could they not look at this prank as a test for a successful demonstration of H4 spirit?

Finally, G Sec Manu and ex G Sec Latku issued the release order at around 3am. My pole mate remained un-amused throughout the night. His eyes stabbed me with the 'you and your bright ideas' look.

The next day, while everyone in H4 was laughing at what had transpired the previous night, we were faced with an unexpected twist of events. The mess workers accused Manu of spreading false rumours to discredit them and some 'concerned' students (including later day BJP bigwig Sudheendra Kulkarni) came to H4 to seek our signature on an apology letter. And ironically, many H4 guys rallied behind us in the same manner demonstrated the previous night and got together to tell Sudheen and others to 'take a hike.' That pole still exists, but the mates are ensconced in two different parts of the world.

—*Bakul*

~

54

This one aspect of my H4-life—my partition mates—makes the title 'Madhouse' truly resonate with me.

Take Vinayak Dravid, one partition mate I had. Vinayak, two years my senior in calendar years but several years my senior in terms of spiritual awakening, was lying on his broken bed (two slats missing) one Saturday afternoon. His room—and hence mine—reeked of pigeon droppings. Our joint space was rocking to the sounds of two pigeons singing a mesmerizing tune. I just had to peer over our partition. The scene before me: One of the pigeons was going around in circles on the built-in cupboard. The other pigeon was circling Dravid's half-smoked cigarette, an arm's length away from a very glazed Dravid himself, looking at said pigeon. There was pigeon crap on the desk right before him. I was stunned, and yelled first at Dravid, and when he was unresponsive, I yelled at the pigeon. Neither missed a beat in their divine state of togetherness.

Dravid eventually looked at me quizzically, his brows furrowing. 'They are living things too. They are bound to crap. Why are you so upset?' I was at a complete loss.

I don't recall exactly what made Dravid's pets fly away eventually, but, mercifully, they did.

—*Dabba*

~

Selva in particular, and NWSF occupants of his time, had some of the strangest pets that I know of. One of them was called Gharpure. This Gharpure was a monitor lizard caught by Selva near Vihar lake behind H4. Monitor lizards are dangerous carnivores—too small to eat a human but aggressive enough to hurt one in the process of trying to do so. Only Selva knows how he caught this thing. He then spent one whole afternoon converting his chair into a cage for Gharpure by hammering a grill he stole from the Mech Engg workshop around the legs of the chair. That evening Gharpure was proudly on display as the newest pet of NWSF.

The next morning Gharpure was gone. It had broken through the grill with his claws and teeth. The reason it was called Gharpure? In Marathi the monitor lizard is called a 'ghorpad'.

To Selva's Malaysian ears that sounded too close to poor Gharpure's name to give up the opportunity to call it Gharpure. (According to some other opinions the man and the lizard even looked alike and had similar sharp claws but that is something Gharpure AKA Chopper, the man didn't quite agree with.)

Then there was a time we all went to Naneghat and Selva caught a snake. Actually the snake was peacefully going about its business when Selva stepped on it and tripped. The snake did not have much of a complaint about it but Selva did. For this brazen act of tripping, Selva the snake was imprisoned in a bottle and brought to NWSF. The next morning saw Selva jumping around trying to catch flies, grasshoppers and earthworms to feed the snake. The snake, however, had a Gandhian gene in its DNA and had decided to go on a hunger strike to protest the gross injustice of being imprisoned for no fault of his. For three days our wing became a veritable zoo containing all manner of creatures Selva had caught that he thought the snake would find tempting. But to no avail. Finally Selva decided to let it go and released it in the jungle behind H4 (perhaps half hoping he will bite the Dhobi—more on that later).

And then after Selva's fame (about his pets) had spread far and wide a kingfisher (yes, a real live one) came seeking shelter in Selva's arms. Its wing was injured and it wasn't flying very well. That whole week you would find Selva crooning to the kingfisher, nursing it back to health. He even negotiated a deal with a fisherwoman from YP (Y-Point) to come and deliver a fish (small, just about as long as his index finger) to H4 every morning. Apparently the fisherwoman didn't find the deal particularly lucrative and didn't come on the fifth day. The kingfisher decided he had taken enough advantage of Selva's hospitality and vanished the next morning.

—*Satkya*

~

Animals in H4—I got my H4 mates involved in an animal episode myself. In our final year, H4 was paired with H10 for the EP (Entertainment Program) competition. The theme was 'The Court of the Crimson King.' Points for publicity were 10 out of 100. During tiffin time discussions, there was desultory talk of making posters. I said maybe we should bring an elephant to campus. We could have the Queen (Mukta Ghate) and King (Sameer Vijaykar) sit on the elephant with a retinue of courtiers and maybe some drum beaters leading the procession. I thought we would present this tamasha during Friday evening movie time at the Convo where all of IIT would be headed. Everyone laughed except the Social Secretary Jetu (Arun Jethmalani, '83 batch), who chided me for being too flippant and not serious enough. He ended his lecture with 'who will get this elephant?' My impulsive response to his question turned out to be my biggest nightmare.

I roped in some very reluctant friends. Vasu and Soumitra initially and, when the going got really tough, Fish (Ashvin Iyengar) and our warden Prof. Suresh Dixit as well. I spread the word to all watchmen and all shopkeepers from Y-Point to main gate that I was in the market for an elephant. They would look at me with amusement and smirked openly whenever I rode past them on my mini Rajdoot.

To start with, I borrowed Rs. 20 from Jetu everyday for gas for my mobike. I would make a round of all temples, police stations, beaches, parks and studios. After logging 300 kms without getting within sniffing distance of an elephant, Jetu pulled back from financing this project and left me to devise ingenious ways to conserve on fuel. I did the best I could. On the Western Express Highway, where I did most of my elephant hunting, I would rev up to 80kmph, locate a down slope, and then switch off my ignition and let the bike roll for a km at least. It helped that my tires were bald—I saved massively on frictional losses.

During this self-inflicted elephant finding mission, I found out something I did not know: that India abounds with comedians.

The head trustee at Ramakrishna Mission temple in Powai sent me to Swami Acharya Jignasu at a temple in Juhu with a written request to show me the elephants. He was talking plurals here. Acharya Jignasu made me wait for half an hour. He made me go through the temple's daily aarti, break a coconut, apply a two-inch-wide-deep and dark red tikka on my forehead and deposit Rs 1.25 in the hundi. Then he led me outside and showed me two beautiful elephants. The ones at the entrance. Carved in stone.

One Mr. Kelkar who registered animals and pets at a run-down BMC office in Sakinaka invited me to sit, offered me tea, and told me he could provide me with hundreds of elephants. 'White elephants,' he said. 'Our government is full of white elephants' he was heartily delighted with his own joke, and laughed while I cried.

Sub Inspector Sawant at the Goregaon police station was a burly man. When I told him I was looking for an elephant, he dragged me by my collar to the entrance and I thought he would throw me out, but he pointed at the signboard and said, 'Padh isko. Read this. Kya likha hai?'

'Police thane,' I said in order to prove that I was a man of letters.

'To kya samjha? What do you understand by this?'

In spite of my vulnerable state I did not resist: 'I thought that this was Goregaon,' I said. 'Why does it say Thane?' His expletives convinced me I had been unwise to attempt a wisecrack, particularly when in the grip of a burly policeman with a thick lathi. He told me where he would put it.

At Jogeshwari police station the chief was an affable man. While I waited he said he would draw me a route map to the place I could get an elephant. After 15 minutes, he showed it to me with a smile on his face. It was a route map, complete with traffic signals, to the Byculla zoo. He then informed the handful of constables around, 'This guy is asking me for an elephant's address. I'm sending him to the zoo.' And they laughed and I cried some more.

At the Vikhroli temple I was assured that I would get at least one elephant from the Guruvayoor temple. And to my next question, the man replied nonchalantly that Guruvayoor was in Kerala.

The watchman at Navrang studios gave us the address to Varmaji ka tabelas in Film City. Varmaji personally showed us around his stables, his beautiful black Arab mustangs. He informed us that horses were in and elephants were a no-no. No film featuring an elephant, according to him, ever fared well at the box-office. 'Box-office? Do we look like film-makers?'

He gave Vasu and me, in our slippers, T-shirts and torn jeans, the once-over. Nowadays, he said, people like us (aap ke jaise fatru log) had taken to making films. After Shyam Benegal's success.

Shyamballi the watchman barged into my room and told me excitedly that his friend had just called him (on the decrepit old H4 phone which never worked) to report that he had seen an elephant near Odeon cinema. If I rushed there, I could probably find him within a kilometre radius of Odeon, it could not have travelled much further by then. After a futile chase all over Ghatkopar, I returned to a sheepish Shyamballi who swore that he had said Oscar cinema and not Odeon.

The camel-ride merchants at Juhu beach were incredulous. Did I expect jungle inhabiting elephants to walk on beaches? Considering that their desert camels were at the beach, I did not understand their reaction. In any case, they were no help with finding elephants.

By now, I was totally out of fuel. Prof Dixit stepped in to help me out. Dixit, Soumitra, Vasu and I set out on Dixit's scooter and Soumitra's bike on Wednesday night to a Jain dharamshala in Goregaon. The Jains there had hired a convoy of elephants for a three-day ritual, or anyway, that is what our informants told us. If we did not get an elephant that night, it was curtains for the project because the crucial Friday was just a day and a half away. The Jains were secretive about their elephants, and would not divulge their sources. The paan shop owner outside the dharamshala, however, told us where the elephants were parked at night. There were no elephants there. Soumitra turned on his headlights and Vasu scouted for tell-tale signs of elephant dung. Evidence was that they had indeed been parked there, but had now migrated to another parking lot.

On the way back to the hostel, we picked up a bottle of whiskey from RLC (RLC is the Ratna Country Liquor Bar just outside the Y-Point gate of IIT. The correct acronym would have been RCL but it was corrupted to RLC to match with electrical RLC circuits that all of us were taught about. In elec-ese, RLC refers to resistors/inductors/capacitors). I was wondering how I would pay back Jetu for this failed project, and how we would cope with all the jeering and barbs that awaited us. As I unwrapped the bottle that would help us drown our sorrows, something caught my eye. On the newspaper wrapping was a photograph of an elephant. We were seeing elephants already, and we had not even opened the bottle yet! It was a photo of a procession of someone's birthday bash. The newspaper was in Tamil. It was close to midnight, but we went to the telephone exchange. Vasu, our Tamil speaker, called the Tamil newspaper editor. We discovered that Tamil editors do not take kindly to being woken up at night with 'who was the man on the elephant in your paper two days ago and what is his number and address?' From amid his swearing we got that the man was Vardarajan Mudaliar. The editor, for reasons we did not comprehend at that point, did not believe that we asked for Varda's address. Did we not know Varda of Antop Hill? We did not, and nor did we know what Antop Hill was.

But here was a ray of hope. We chalked out a plan to go to Antop Hill on Thursday and look for Varda and tell him to please get us this pachyderm, and for that we would bless him and pinch his cheek. Vasu refused to bunk his test on Thursday. Varda was definitely a Tamil name, and Soumitra did not understand Tamil even though he was dating a Tamilian (he said he was dating in English). I finally settled on Sukumar who was a JTA (Junior Tech asst.) in the chemical engineering department. Sukumar was a Keralite but understood Tamil and could even speak it in a Malayali accent. Most important, he had a scooter with petrol in it and he would wait to be paid till Jetu paid me.

Antop Hill seemed seedy as hell. The stench of brewing hooch was in the air. The streets were populated by muscled men wearing banyans and rolled up lungis and thick gold chains and thicker belts (on their lungis). A band of menacing looking men escorted us to a tin-roofed shed on a hillock. Varda was in this shed, sitting on a chair watching the game of carom in progress. Sukumar started the conversation in Tamil. I caught the word 'Yaan' (I found out later that the Tamil word for elephant is 'yaanai'). Varda looked up at me. He continued to stare at me for five whole minutes without saying a word.

Then Vardabhai began to laugh. What began as a mellow unthreatening chortle soon became a bellowing uncontrolled guffawing. The henchmen joined in, just like they do in the movies, and so did I. Sukumar tried to shush me, he had some knowledge I did not. Vardabhai was amused enough by us to ask his deputy, Selvan, to call the elephant vendor in Borivali and instruct him to bring down the rental from

63

2,500 to 2,000, and if it was a problem, Vardabhai said, he would pay the 500 difference himself. '2,000 Rs?' I said to myself.' Was this guy loco? Did he not know Jetu who would not part with even 200?'

I went to the vendor's house in Borivali, this time on Deepak Tiwary's scooter. The sixteen-year-old Lankesh Pathak, his twelve-year-old sister, his aged mother and his invalid grandfather received us as VIPs. His father had passed away recently and the boy was making ends meet by renting out elephants and horses. He started our negotiations at 2,000. I started at 200. His grandfather threatened to throw us out. Lankesh reminded him that we were Varda's men. As we were walking out, Lankesh followed us and told us that he would close the deal at 500, provided we coughed up the money on the spot. Between Tiwary and I, we materialized Rs 100. Lankesh was desperate. He wanted to buy medicines for his grandfather. He agreed to take the 100 then and balance on Friday evening. I made a mental note that I would pay him 2,000 whenever I was able to. I must admit, regretfully, that I have not done it, and don't know how.

The elephant arrived, but thirty minutes late. Several people had stopped it on the way and asked the mahout his address, because there was this IIT student who wanted an elephant. Mukta and Sameer took their spots upon the elephant's back. We all sang and danced. It was a sensation and a hit.

Prof Subhash Babu from HSS (Humanities & Social Sciences dept.) saw the commotion and jostled his way through the crowd. He sought out Fish and asked him, 'What is this?' Fish looked over to where the Professor's finger was pointing and answered, 'This is an elephant.'

The elephant was a cow named 'Haathi' and was parked in H10 (a girls' hostel). Later at night, I got senti. I bought a stick of sugarcane and went to visit her. I said to her, 'Thank you Haathi for saving my skin.' I heard giggling. I turned to see four girls who found my tender moment with Haathi funny.

I saw our Vardabhai staring at me again two years later. This time though, he was on the covers of national magazines. Had I known then what I know now, I may have reacted to his stare, and to his subsequent laughter with discomfort at least, but I think I might have wet my pants.

Sukumar had translated his words for me that night when he had stared at me the first time and then dissolved into laughter: People come to me for everything. People say Vardabhai, give me naukri. Some say Vardabhai give me chokri. Some say Vardabhai, give me 5-lakh donation, Some say Vardabhai, kill my enemy. Women say Vardabhai, become the father of my child. But nobody has ever asked Vardabhai for an elephant.

Vardarajan Munniswamy Mudaliar. He, like his contemporaries Haji Mastan, Yusuf Patel and Karim Lala, was into illicit liquor, matka dens, drugs, prostitution rings, extortion, supari killings, and everything else that we knew nothing about. I had gone to him to ask him for an elephant. And had even thought about pinching his cheek. One of the most wanted, most notorious dons in Bombay's formidable underworld.

—*Bakul*

~

Some of the animals in H4 were there by choice, and because they were wanted. Take Blacky—he was as much a hostel inmate as any of us students. He didn't go to classes, like some of his co-inhabitants, but he didn't have to. He had to make do with the same terrible food that we all got—he partook in the good and the bad with the rest of us.

Blacky was a great dog, the real H4 pet. Jack spent a lot of his time fondling Blacky's ears every night and would feed him omelettes at breakfast. Blacky would beg for food by placing his paw gently in your lap. If you raised a glass of water, Blacky understood it as the signal to take the hint and move on.

One Sunday morning the BMC (Bombay Municipal Corporation) dog pound guys took Blacky away. First we scrapped with Dr. Lokeshwar at the hospi (affectionate term for the IIT hospital) for calling those guys in. He thought he was doing us all a favour by ridding the campus of the health hazard of stray dogs. Then we scrapped with Scrooty (affectionate term for all security personnel) officer Singh for allowing those guys in. Then we collected Rs.60 from Junta and sent office asst. Shinde to the dog pound to secure Blacky's release and bring him back home to us in a cab. Blacky was no stray dog, he was one of us.

~

I think Blacky died of old age circa '82. He was survived by Blacky Jr. (of dubious ancestry) who later became B'lock, and spent many an amorous night with Mad Rao.

Though tough, having been raised on H4 grub, unlike Blacky, B'lock was quite a goofball. He once chased a goat on the gym grounds, but after cornering it, didn't quite know what to do, and gazed at us stupidly with the goat entwined in his paws. He survived several seasons of Dina's (un)holi concoctions, and also general abuse from the likes of G and KT.

Poor B'lock finally went a little crazy, chasing and barking at arb (arbitrary) buggers, and finally, and fatally pissing off some NCC dude, who put a bullet through his head.

B'lock was buried behind CWGF (H3 side) on a hot Palm Sunday in '85. B'lock RIP.

—*Rohan*

⁓

One day, the darkest H4-ite, Waghamare, went to see *Kaalia*, bought a ticket in black for the late night show, and Blacky accompanied him to Huma theatre in Kanjurmarg. This came to be known as the height of blackness.

⁓

Blacky had a Pal called Brownie (whoever named these inmates was not terribly imaginative, it seems). Some say they enjoyed a relationship socially acceptable only in California. Be that as it may, he was forever following Blacky in whatever may be going on in H4—whether it was a bunch of guys boozing on the second floor landing, or a bunch of guys going to Vihar lake for a swim (or even getting caught and being taken to the Police Thana—both of these guys Blacky and Brownie were seen following them all the way up to Vikhroli). Or whether it was a Hostel function where movies of a certain tint were being shown—whatever. They were always around.

—*Satkya*

~

Summer of '77, we (Ravi Poovaiah, Peter, Vilas) joined the H1 mess (to see if the food was any better there than at our sorry mess). Blacky would follow us to get his tidbits (and to see if the food was any better there than at his sorry mess). H1 G Sec did not take kindly to dogs in the mess. He told us, 'This dog must get out.' We agreed. We told him, 'Throw him out.'

When he went to hold Blacky's collar, Blacky bared his teeth. G Sec backed away and ordered the watchman to tackle Blacky. The watchman refused to touch him saying that when he went to H4 for his shift there, the dog would attack him.

Blacky came with us to the H1 mess every day after that. I think he was the only dog allowed in H1 mess.

—*Sharookh Dara Lashkari, '75-'80*

~

I have lived with many cats, but Billee, one of the cats I had in H4, was unlike any other. He was a beautiful black and white cat, mine since he was a very small kitten. Billee would not only respond to his name but come running to me like a dog when I called him. He went for walks with me. He did not like to be carried, but if a dog came after him, he would let me carry him for a while on my shoulders, draped around my neck. Billee liked Energee Milk and I fed him by emptying the few drops from empty bottles in the crate.

One day I was in the H2 lounge chatting with a friend and I saw Billee wandering around. He hadn't seen me. In those days, a considerable amount of my creativity was occupied with funding my cigarettes. 'Cats know they are called *billee* in Hindi,' I told my friend. He stared at me incredulously. 'See that cat over there?' I continued, 'he will come running to me if I call him Billee.'

'Balls he is going to come running to you,' said my friend confidently and we bet a buck.

I still remember the look of incomprehension on his face when I called 'Billee!' and Billee, delighted to see me in H2, came running to me and jumped into my lap. Easiest buck I ever made.

One day I noticed a chirping sound in my small loft and I realized that there was a baby sparrow in a nest. Its mother did not come back, so I would get up on my chair and feed the baby sparrow milk and water using an ink dropper. One day I came back to my room to find feathers all over the floor and a small chewed up dead bird. The bird had flown and Billee had probably thought I had brought him a special treat. That's the one and only time in my life when I have hit a cat. Poor bird and poor Billee.

Billee was with me for about two-and-half years. One day, without any warning, when I got back to the hostel from one of the few labs I ever attended, Billee was dead. My friends and I buried him in the hostel grounds and I was so distraught that I wasn't able to cry. I still feel the loss thirty years later. I have had other cats since then, but none like Billee.

—*Fish*

~

Dogs and cats were common enough pets, of course, in H4 as anywhere else. But then there was Arun-organic-chemistry-Kaul who actually had a horse he found somewhere. He would go for lectures to the MB (Main Building) on his horse and would park it in a cycle shed. The horse was his pet as well as his transport.

Equinimity

This Arun Kaul was an aspiring aeronautical engineer who would deliberately duck Organic Chemistry simply because he was happy to hang out on the campus and eat subsidized mess food and not work for a living. He managed to duck this course for at least two years before he was asked to graduate or be thrown out. Kaul was short and diminutive and incredibly talented. He devised humorous skits for many EPs and would sing 'Aye meri zohrazabeen' while playing the harmonium and he used to publish a hand-written magazine called MUDD (The first D is silent) and put it up on the notice board. He was also an exponent of Urdu and was the only guy who knew the meaning of *'goya ke chunache'* in the song from Manoranjan (goya means 'if' and chunache means 'therefore'). When guys discovered that he was from Kashmir and his last name was Kaul, they would inevitably ask him something like 'Do you know SK Kaul from Srinagar?' and his answer to them would be 'Do you know SK Joshi from Bombay?'

For a guy who smoked borrowed Charminars, every hostel function night was a lavish feast he would look forward to while recollecting the feast he had as a kid in the Raj Bhavan, Srinagar at the birthday party of his classmate who was Maharaja Karan Singh's daughter.

Arun had found this sickly horse which had been abandoned by its owner. Arun adopted it and would go to lectures on horseback and audaciously park it in the cycle stand outside the library. There is also a story about how Ayaz Janjua rode this horse to MB accompanied by a gang of fifty H4 punters who beat drums and sounded bugles on the way. Finally, the horse was reclaimed by its owner. All this happened before '77, so this info is hearsay from the horse's mouth—Arun Kaul himself.

Everyone will surely remember a particular weird multi-coloured, multi-patterned pair of bell bottomed trousers he wore for an entire semester without ever washing them. There is a photograph of Arun Kaul in his pristine glory, bell-bottoms and slippers and all, seated upon his white steed.

～

Not all the animals in the hostel were pets, nor were they welcome. There were the monkeys, of course, and that is a whole continuing saga in the history of H4. They were a menace, and sometimes dangerous. And there was the smaller menace of the pigeons. One year a horde of pigeons infested the NWSF bogs (affectionate term for our toilets). Selva took offense at their unruly behaviour. He thought he would teach them a lesson. His lesson technique was to catch one, pour a bucket of water on it that he kept just for that purpose, and then let it go. The poor scared pigeon floundered around, unable to fly with wet feathers. That is the only time I have ever seen a bird trip on its own feet and fall over. After he had caught each and every one Selva

was content that he had taught them the intended lesson. Unfortunately those bird-brains never did learn Selva's lessons. One day one of them used Selva's head for excretory activities. Selva was mighty pissed at this blow to his dignity. He caught the offending pigeon and five more for good measure. He killed them all, lit a bonfire between the two halves of NWSF and fed all of us roast pigeon for dinner that night.

—*Satkya*

~

One time we decided to have kheema in the mess (separate utensils of course). Co-incidentally the day of the kheema, someone noticed that two of our pet dogs had gone missing, and that 'Thapa' had cooked the kheema.

—*Dabba*

~

Mess and Despair

My first meal on my first day in IIT was a glimpse into the culinary ordeals in store for me for the next five years. Like most people, I was adept at eating with my right hand, and particularly adept at breaking off pieces of my chapatti with only three fingers. My first attempt to do so that first dinner time in the mess made me acutely aware that my survival would depend on evolving my technique to a higher level (or lower level depending on how you look at it) of sophistication. I had to bring my teeth into play to tackle the version of chapatti the cook saw fit to serve us. After the first bit of subji went down my gullet I could hear strong protests from within. There was potato in the concoction, which is something I ordinarily liked very much. In my chemistry class I was being taught about inert elements in the periodic table like Argon and Xenon. These substances are odourless, tasteless and don't react with anything. I began to feel that potato, especially after passing through our mess kitchen, belonged on this list. Evidently Mendeleev wasn't as knowledgeable as our cooks were in this regard.

I suppose I should be grateful for the disaster that was our mess. It was there, after all, that I learned the healthy habit of eating a big breakfast, a light lunch and a lighter dinner. The high point of meals in H4 were the breakfasts. It is almost impossible to make an egg taste bad, I think, unless it has actually gone bad and is emitting H_2S.

The other culinary high point came only once a week—dry dinner on Friday nights after the Convo movies. This dry dinner consisted of omelettes, bread, jam and potato chips (which, thankfully, were not made in-house), all of which would have required exceptional skills to convert into inert substances. I was a Mumbai boy and could easily have forsaken the Friday night dinner by going home after the movie. But I felt I had to get something in return for the mess bills I was paying.

Among all this food-related misery were two gourmet experiences. For one Friday evening meal, I don't know who, but I suspect Selva, strong-armed somebody in the mess to make sweet corn soup. After a long wait in hungry anticipation of this soup, steaming cauldrons came out and were placed on the table. As people attempted to dive in and help themselves they realized that what they needed was not serving spoons but knives to cut pieces off this soup before they could eat it. It was certainly corn, it also was certainly sweet, but somebody had taken the concept of a soup—as something that it expected to be thicker than water—to the limit. But, such was the level of desperation where food was concerned, that every one happily chewed the soup and asked for more. Whatever it was, it certainly tasted better than the regular fare we were dished out every day.

On another occasion, someone (again I don't know who) incited some adventurous guy in the mess to make *puran poli*. For those not in the know, making puran poli requires skills handed down through generations. So again we all waited hungrily, and anxiously, and finally the puran polis came out. Each was about half an inch thick, solid and heavy enough that they could have been used to replace the tires on Faatu's scooty and he would have had a sweeter ride. When I managed to break one open, I could count each grain of the daal used to make the puran. But, they were sweet, and nobody was going to quibble about minor details like the thickness and weight.

There was one thing made in the mess that was truly, genuinely, world class. There were a couple of mango trees in H4. Early in the summer somebody would pick the raw mangoes from the trees and make a pickle of freshly cut mangoes. And it was as good as any that my mom ever made.

—*Satkya*

~

The branches of one of those mango trees came within a foot of my window in room 252. Once, when my juvenile wing mates locked me out of my own room, I used the tree to get back in. And this reminds me of the day when Faatu was monkeying around on the tree to get those raw mangoes. Faatu, sometimes known as Vasant Joshi, was fair with green eyes, pleasantly plump, a non-stop talker who could talk his way out of any situation, could debate endlessly with me for socialism, who could debate against socialism with a diehard commie, who was always looking for fun and mischief. Hence, it was not surprising to see Faatu perched on a tree to find his thrill of the day in the branches of the mango tree. When guys asked him to be careful, Faatu said he would be—he had climbed lots of mango trees in his village and found the mango branches very treacherous. They would snap when you least expected them to, but he had experience, and could tell a suddenly snapping branch from a non-snapping one. Just as he finished saying this, there was a snapping sound and Faatu was seen accelerating to earth at 9.8 metres per second squared with branch attached to his feet. He said something like 'Who am I? Where am I?' before passing out.

Nursing a hip bone fracture, he spent three treacherous months at the hospi and another two on a walking stick. The relief was that he was saved from sampling mess food. Punishment was that he had to drink the stale broth which the hospi served and he started hankering for mess food again. And to add insult to injury, among the treats we took him from the mess was that pickle made from the same mangoes from the same tree with the snapping branches.

—*Bakul*

~

Like everyone else, I was looking forward to the fruit salad my very first week at H4. I imagined lots of fruits—chickoo, pineapple, apple, banana, in nicely flavoured milk. I wasn't up to eating the dinner, just wanted to enjoy the fruit salad. I even had a dream about it the night before. But, as was usual in this mess of ours, there were many disappointments in store for me. First I was disappointed when I saw the small bowl (*wati*). Then I had to really search to find any fruits and I discovered two small pieces of banana. That brought *shikaran* (fruit salad containing only banana) to mind, and I became homesick. And my dream of the night before, well that was just a dream, and much better than the real thing.

—*Raj Laad, '77-'82*

~

My Dad (God bless his soul) had come to the hostel one weekday morning to get my signature on some papers. After signing the papers, I insisted dad eat in the hostel with me, saying the food was special on that day (it was a day we got bhindi with the ubiquitous potato). Breaking the chapatti was, like for the rest of us, a struggle for him. After tasting the vegetables, he asked me if there was a restaurant nearby. Dad and I, along with a couple of inmates (Kumar Ramnathan and Uday) went off to RK (affectionate term for our Hotel Radhakrishna) for a proper lunch.

When Dad left us at H4 after lunch, he gave me a C note (Rs.100), and said, 'If you require more money please ask me, and eat well.' I was never broke after that day. Whenever I left home for H4, dad would pass me a C note, which in those days could buy quite a lot.

That I did not spend the money on food was another story.

—*Sharookh*

~

On one of those rare occasions when they ran out of potatoes the mess workers would serve up a *mutter paneer* concoction. I used to find it a matter of strange coincidence that by the time the bowl made it to our end of the table, it would be devoid of all the paneer and most of the mutter as well. I discovered that the culprits were a couple of PGs who would quickly go into action as soon as each bowl of mutter paneer was placed on the table. In fact, I believe they had strategized where to sit so that they could get to it first. While the UGs were busy chatting away about how

77

badly they got screwed in some test du jour, the PG closest to the bowl would pick out every little piece of paneer from the bowl. And I mean every single piece. After he was satisfied that he had done a good job of de-paneering the bowl, he would pass of the bowl to the next PG with a victorious smile. The next PG would repeat the process, this time de-muttering the bowl. I imagined Gabbar saying, *'Kitne mutter hai is bowl mein, Samba? Kitne? Kitne? (Teen Huzoor!) Sirf teen? Izzat mitti mey mila diye. Iska Jawab milega, zaroor milega!'*

After being robbed of all that IIT had to offer in a non-potato dish, I decided to embark on a competitive strategy. If I couldn't move fast enough to grab the bowl as soon as it came, I had to make the bowl come to us first. During one of the breaks, I buttered up the mess workers by chatting with them in Marathi about a variety of sundry stuff. I didn't ask them to do anything different, but the next time and every time from then on, the new bowl of mutter paneer was placed right in front of me. Now it was our turn to beam a victorious smile to the PG end of the table.

Today, the H4 dining experience is more of a buffet style so this unique IIT style competitive learning opportunity is lost on the new junta.

—Pol

~

This is one topic on which there may be total unanimity. Mess food sucked, and sucked bad. When folks at home asked us how our mess food was, we answered in what has now become a cliché. 'We have a lot of variety. We eat potatoes for lunch, aloo for tiffin and *batata* for dinner.' Curries were insipid and tasteless, chapattis were thick and one needed both hands to tear them. Even Blacky, while receiving a freebie chapatti, would chew at it distastefully and make faces at Takat Singh the cook. During one attempt at making gulab jamun, folks asked the serving staff to supply chisels and hammers to deal with them. These gulab jamuns were taken to the wings to use as cricket balls.

Every mess coordinator thought he would change the situation without realizing that the mess in the mess was staff-driven. Manu, Gadgil, Chris, KK, Fish, Idi, Waghamare and many more tried their hand at the impossible and came out badly burned. Gadgil was pilloried after one valedictory function because the chicken procured from outside the mess was so good that some guys polished off two and three pieces and many vegetarians changed their religion in order to savour the delicacy. As a result, many guys went chickenless and Gadgil was hauled up for others' greed. In Manu's time, the food quality was better because the mess workers spent more time fighting him and less time cooking, resulting in a few culinary specialist students to fill in for them.

But without doubt, a special mention has to be reserved for Idi Amin. This Idi was once called SS Sawant in some forgotten chapter in history. Short and portly with curly hair and Afro features, this cute guy resembled his more notorious namesake in Uganda. Idi's stamp, in this line of valiant soldiers who were brave enough to coordinate messy matters, was the memorable and free use of oil. Everything that could be classified as a food item reeked of oil during Idi's tenure. If you ever ran out of hair oil, you would be advised to run one of Idi's chapattis on your head. If the hinge of your door creaked, you could oil it with one of Idi's potatoes. Very soon, Idi came to be known as the oil sheikh of Uganda. In a cartoon contest, the prize-winning entry was by Sandeep Vichare. In this, Idi is shown as an Arab sheikh and is being administered an 'oral remedy' by a belly dancer and she is seen exclaiming, 'Yuck! It's oil!'

Those poor mess coordinators could write a tome about the trials and tribulation they endured while trying to keep us alive.

~

In his new avatar in H5 far away from his tryst with tycoonism, Mukes was back to being a student. One fine day he shocked his batchmates by announcing, 'Tomorrow go-slow.' Students enjoying an uneasy relationship with mess-workers and psyched out by the frequent 'go-slow' strikes were worried. Eventually, the council members in H5 were informed and a worried lot of anxious students made their way to the mess-workers to ask them why there was going to be a 'go-slow', and to persuade them to call it off. Puzzled mess workers swore that they knew of no such plan but took time off to check with union bosses (read our very own Takat Singh Purohit from H4). Takat Singh thought that a go-slow was a great idea but alas, there was absolutely no motivation or cause for one. He regretfully announced that no such go-slow plan was afoot.

Angry councillors turned to hostelites who angrily turned to 84-ites who angrily turned to Mukes and asked him who told him there was to be a go-slow the next day. Mukes's answer was swift, and simple: 'Prof. KD Joshi from Maths dept'.

'Now wait a minute, Mukes you prick. What does KD Joshi have to do with a go-slow?'

'Why not? He's the one who taught us go-slow and he told me that it is there in tomorrow's test.'

'What! You jerk! There is a go-slow in a KD Joshi test? What are you talking about?'

It took time for the realization to set in that Gujju bhai Mukes was referring to Gauss' Law which was a part of the dreaded Math course called MA 202.

~

Considering our messy circumstances, it was an especial treat to be invited to the family function of a hostelite. We would head out from H4, bathed and groomed, sporting long-sleeved shirts tucked into well-pressed trousers, some occasionally wore a tie, and much less occasionally, even shoes.

A bunch of guys was seated for lunch at one such Maharashtrian wedding feast. Pu was enjoying the delicious vegetarian meal immensely. The mother of the bride was making the traditional rounds among the guests, with hospitable chitchat, imploring them to feel at home, making sure they were looked after. When she came to Pu, she smiled politely, and with delicate hand gestures said, *'Saavkaash jeva'* (meaning, 'Take your time and enjoy this food').

81

Pu, who thought she was introducing herself, swiftly swallowed the sumptuous morsel in his mouth, and reciprocated: 'Srinivas Ketavarapu.'

—Rohan

~

Once during a boring faat session in front of room 204 a Malaysian friend of Selva's from H3 arrived with a packet. The friend had just returned from home and had brought Selva's favourite grub. Grub from home. Considering our food situation, grub from home was like manna from heaven. Everybody's eyes lit up. Selva licked his chops loudly and dramatically, and opened his packet with a flourish. The stench went all the way to the other end of NWSF. The packet contained dried squid, and that is the only time that I know of when Selva's famous cry of 'If you want you will come, if you don't want you won't come' went unanswered.

—Satkya

~

Shobhan Mondal, swarthy, dusky footballer with Mithun Chakraborty looks, Rajeev Deodhar aka Child, clean-shaven, well-scrubbed, spectacled, and brooding, and I, were sitting at a table in the cafeteria. Our humble wallets meant Child and I ordered one tea each. Optimistic Mondal ordered a plate of fried rice while he scanned the tables to see who he could order to pay his tab when it came. Anirban (pronounced Onirbon) Sen from H3 joined us. He spearheaded the poet's corner movement in IIT. Guys gathered every Monday in the Convo foyer in soiled kurtas and beards and recited poems into a cloud of bidi smoke. Late into the night they talked about cataclysm and protoplasm and asked the 'who am I' question and answered that they were withered leaves that crumbled in Sen's hand while the more bearded ones with more soiled kurtas opined that they were a bar of soap dipped in bovine excreta.

Our conversation at the cafeteria too soon veered toward poetry. We asked the senile Sen to explain the meaning behind his poems. Mondal, still awaiting his fried rice, remarked that modern poetry was easy and poets faked their nonsense and passed it off as sublime thought processes. Sen challenged Mondal to write one then, if it was so easy. Mondal took the offer. He grabbed a pen from the nearest passerby and turned over an unpaid bill. The first line came instantaneously.

Sometimes

What next? Mondal lit up a cigarette and watched the smoke go up in lazy curves and form abstract patterns in the still air of the cafeteria. He studied the smoke intently and looked for a sign or a hint of a metamorphic suggestion of what the swirl implied. Was it an infinity on trial? Was it a somnambulist's ombudsman? Was it as stale and as cheap as the Charminar it emanated from? The answer eluded Mondal. Time to light up a joint and find ethereal meaning in his existence. The lit joint lit up his eyes. The second line would come soon, he was sure about that. It had to be something as mystical as Mona Lisa's smile.

Just then, his fried rice plate arrived. He touched the plate. It was cold and he was hungry and he still had no one who would pay for it. While he stabbed at the rice with his spoon, his eyes lit up and he wrote his second line. It was a direct reflection of his current status. The line was 'When the food is cold'. So now this masterpiece read:

Sometimes
When the food is cold

He took another spoonful but moved it back to the plate slowly. What should his third line be? A description of the sensory palette that was affected by his gastronomical satiety? Or that this necessity to cater to biological needs was as illusory a phenomenon as his very existence? Was it a cry of an animal? A song for the moribund? A scream of anguish? The magical line still eluded him. The mocking trio of Sen, Child and I did nothing to help matters. He was hungrier than a starving Ethiopian and he had to dive into his plate and finish off the fried rice to its last grain. And in this state where he had reached a state of deglutition consistent with his dietetic integrity, Mondal smiled and wrote his third and last line and proudly passed the prize-winning masterpiece to Sen.

Sometimes
When the food is cold
I eat it that way

That poetry session ended with Child and me penning our own poems. Mine was,

If you love me
The way I love you
Then
Shame on us

And Child responded with a three lettered poem:

Sic

As to who paid for the fried rice, let me settle this suspense over Mondal's bill. The truth is that I do not know. The trend in the cafe was to tell Joe (and later John, Thomas, Big Joe, Duh Joe, Benny) 'Joe! Add that to my tab.' When Joe flashed our tab bill at us and told us 'Your bill', we would tell him that we didn't know any Bill. We only knew Jack.

Sometimes
When the bill comes
I don't pay anyway

—*Bakul*

∽

Given our mess food, our paunch competition was particularly pathetic.

∽

KK (Krishna Kumar Purswani, my predecessor as the Mess Coordinator) and I decided that the only way to improve the mess food quality was to hire a cook from outside. We stole ourselves Thapa from a restaurant in Koliwada. Thapa was indeed a good cook, but predictably, there was a lot of resistance from all the other cooks. They were jealous, and probably sabotaged Thapa's culinary efforts. Every time I tried to inspire Thapa to cook better and ignore the pressures from his colleagues who were dedicated to serving the most God-awful fare, Thapa got emotional and assured

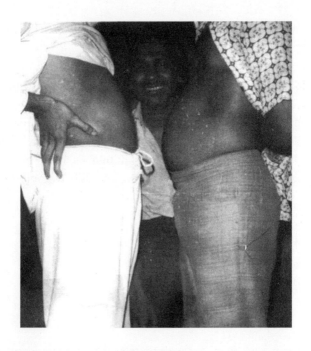

me, 'Yes. Thapa cook'. We did manage to get some decent meals once in a while. But Thapa was emotional and prone to drink not unlike another cook named Bevda Nair who used to smuggle eggs out of the mess to exchange at YP for liquor.

Every time I praised Thapa's cooking, he asked that I join him in his room for a drink. Going into the stinky mess quarters was a daunting prospect and I avoided it. But once, when Thapa had outdone himself at a hostel function, I could turn him down no more. In his room, Thapa pulled out a bottle. 'Oh my God—illicit liquor! Don't people go blind from it?' I was terrified at the prospect. 'If I go blind from this, people will take it as proof that masturbation indeed makes you go blind,' I thought ruefully as I raised the foul smelling brew to my lips. After every sip, I looked at my hands to make sure I could still see.

I survived that night but Thapa did not survive the stress of being treated as an outcast by his colleagues, and he vanished for good one day, leaving us to our mess and its food.

Our survival is proof that 'that which does not kill you, makes you stronger'.

—*Fish*

~

H4 Life

A lot of action took place around the two decrepit old phones near the entrance of H4 just outside the Warden's office. A lot of this action has been captured in history by countless narrations of folklore handed down from generation to generation. One of these phones was a pay phone that generally did not work and gobbled up tons of minted metal before ingenuous IIT minds devised contraptions to make the phone believe that it was swallowing yet another coin. This was called the 'external line' and its purported objective was to allow communion with the outside world. In 1977, this phone had the number 581008. The other phone was a more reliable 'internal line', 383, which changed to 583, and which allowed for an intra-IIT communication with a high domination of H4-H10 conversations. Had a secret webcam been installed then, we would have been sitting on a treasure trove of incredible stories. Isn't it amazing that two majorly non-performing assets were the centre of so much confabulation?

Lines were either incoming or outgoing. On the external line, outgoing was a no-no expensive affair so it was reserved mainly for an incoming call. The internal line was predominantly outgoing because H10 had only one line, and there were nine boys' hostels in all, and the first past the post could get a call through. Hence, people with patience and perseverance and strong abrasion-proof fingers would dial away endlessly before they struck gold. It should be remembered that dialling then was a full clockwise motion of a finger inserted in a numbered slot and not a push-button affair.

Now, the question arises that if an incoming call came in (what else can it do?), and the caller asked to speak to so and so from room number so-other-so, who would call the called and bring him to the caller? This story now brings in a creature called 'scrooty' which was short for security guard who always wore khaki and mostly was a Nepali. If you looked at one and addressed him as Bahadur or Singh or Thapa, you were likely to be accorded a royal salute from a beaming gorkha who would wonder how 'Shaabji' knew his name. A name generally was Shamsher Singh Bahadur Thapa or Govind Singh Bahadur Thapa or just-about-anything Singh Bahadur Thapa.

The arrangement of wings and rooms was well structured but taxing on the feet. The North wing housing room numbers 1 to 28 on GF, 101 to 128 on FF and 201 to 228 on SF was maybe 240 feet away from the phone. Similarly, the central wing with 29 to 56 was maybe 160 feet away and South wing with 57 to 84 numbers was 80 feet away. Answering a phone, putting it on hold and walking over to the desired wing to shout out the room number was not a part of a scrooty's job description, but he obliged. A posting in the hostel was highly coveted because of the perks of free meals, watching a daily circus for free (or maybe you could call it a cartoon network), TV programs like *Chhaya Geet* for free, and getting a trickled-down booty of *daaru*, chocolates, pondies and gaalis, all free. The remuneration far outweighed the additional walks up and down to rooms, no matter how far they were. In this idyllic setting where calls were made to and fro and an informal scrooty calling system was in place, here are some samples of related events:

~ Vikram Modak and friends were outside the Manager's office when the watchman, who had been working at the hostel for well over a year, ambled over. They didn't want the watchman to see what they were up to (something that need not be discussed here). They told the watchman that there was a phone-call for Room 285.

He promptly said 'OK Saboo' and walked down the passage and started yelling 'Tooo ettie phaaaaiu, phooon, tooo ettie phaaaaiu, phooon'. This bellowing went on for well over five minutes, after which he suddenly stopped, and walked back toward them. He had a sheepish look on his face, and said, 'Saboo, Hostel 4 mei Room 285 nahi hai'(In those days, the last room number was 284.)

By this time they had finished what they were doing.

~ Ashvin Sanghvi (Ghoda) had a cheerful disposition and for a good reason. There was always an incoming call for him on the internal line. The identity of the caller was not known for a long time but Ghoda could often be overheard talking about spring and sunsets and a walk by the lake. He lived in the far-off room 222—in scrooty-ese, he lived in tooooo-toooo-toooooo. Everyone knew when he had a call because the scrooty's loud announcement and the unmistakable number of his room gave it away. One afternoon, Ghoda spent a lot of time on the phone and had sealed up plans for the evening for a walk to the lake and had detailed it up to but not after the moonlit part of the date. Ghoda returned to his far out and far up room with his trademark swagger, and he began to get into kurta and pyjamas in order to grab some shut-eye prior to the promising date that awaited him. And while he was in the middle of his changing, came the same familiar loud 'Tooooo-tooooo-tooooo, phooon.' Ghoda was stunned. What happened now? Was the date off? Had she come to know about the Rekha in his building? Or did she want to change the lake venue from Powai to Vihar? Or did he have to pick up roses on the way? Still speculating on the possibilities and also speculating on whether to continue the change to pyjamas or halt and revert to jeans and T-shirt, Ghoda shouted out 'Aata hai' to the scrooty. Finally, after re-changing into his old gear, anxious Ghoda went galloping back to the phone in what must have been ten minutes in all. After another two minutes, we could hear Ghoda shout out like a scrooty ... ...'toooooooo-threeeeeeeeeeeeee-toooooooo, phooon' and then suddenly he says, 'Oye Shelat, the bloody phone is for you' and then there was another shout from Ghoda at the scrooty, 'Theek se number sunta nahin hai kya?'

Nobody dared ask Ghoda how his date went.

~ This one was commonly used. If you wanted to call a guy from his room for anything, say a walk or a game of carom or TT, asking him to join you would not work. Folks were too lazy to slip out from the comfort of their jocks and take a long walk to join you for something strenuous. But the ingenuous IIT mind always found a way out. If you wanted to call out, say Soumitra, pick up a phone, pretend to speak on it for a minute and then send a scrooty to shout 'Tooooooooo phore shevan, phoon' and the job was done.

~ Viren Pathare was dating his childhood sweetheart and needed to speak to her on the external phone everyday for at least an hour. For a few months, I too needed to speak on the same phone everyday and while one hour was not mandatory, I had figured that an investment of 50 paise, if stretched over at least 50 minutes, brought down the cost of lovey-dovey talk to a paisa per minute. It made good commercial sense but with two poachers chasing the same target, life was becoming difficult. So Viren and I settled matters in a gentlemanly fashion. He would speak from 6pm to 7pm and make way for me to be on the phone from 7pm to 8pm This arrangement worked fine by and large, but one particular day, it was already 7pm and Viren was still extolling the virtues of Meera's limpid pools and I was needling him to hang up and make way for me. Clearly, multi-tasking was not Viren's forte—in fact, multi-tasking wasn't even invented then. So what did Viren do? While telling Meera what her eyes were like, he exclaimed a loud 'Just fuck off!' while looking at me. And while all bystanders broke out into a loud laugh, Viren could be heard saying 'sorry, sorry, sorry' umpteen times and Meera apparently hung up on him. While leaving the place in a huff, Viren warned me that if he lost this girlfriend, I would have to give him mine.

~ Apparently, there were many who resented Viren and me jamming the phone for long stretches and complained to G Sec Manu. Manu put up a notice announcing a time limit of five minutes of talk time and that he would fine all defaulters a hefty Rs. 50 fine. This was not so fine for Viren and me. The next time there was a complaint, Viren and I both protested that we spoke for no more than five minutes each. It was the complainant's word against ours. So Manu evolved a new system. Every time Viren or I got on the phone, scrooty would alert Manu who would stand there himself timing the call duration on his wristwatch. One day, I lost it and shouted at Manu, 'How can you be so heartless? Anyway, what will you understand? What do you know about love? You're better off slogging in the mess so please go back there.' Manu did not say anything then but did call me to his room on the next day because 'I want to show you something.' 'Something' turned out to be a photograph of smiling, pleasant faced girl with clean scrubbed looks. Manu held up the photo with great admiration. She was Medha

Kotnis, the girl he loved and doted on and the girl he would marry after graduating. It was clear that Manu was smitten and had great affection for her. He was shy about displaying this side of his very human nature, but he needed to tell me that he was not a heartless brute who fined people for fun. He wanted us to live disciplined lives and show concern for common hostel property.

Manu lost his Medha in 2000 when she went down fighting terminal cancer and this experience has left Manu very shattered and he has stopped visiting his room at the hostel since it brings back memories of Medha for him.

—*Bakul*

~

Back to those old decrepit phones. You dialled a number, when the called party said hello, you dropped a 50p coin in the slot for the phone call to continue. 50p was a princely sum, a luxury for most of us non-princes.

In the early days of H4—the '62 to '67 era—everyone operated the phone with a crooked wire without putting in any coins. For the convenience of all the inmates, the wire contraption was permanently kept next to the phone itself. The inmates from this time report that the telephone department finally removed the phone from such an unprofitable location. They did put it back, thankfully, at some later time. The inventors of the wire contraption had long graduated, and the wire contraption itself disappeared with the phone, but poverty was still the norm when we came along, and so was the ingenuity of the new inmates.

We devised a contraption we called a tickler by drilling a hole in the coin, and tying a string to it. We lowered the tickler into the coin slot for the call, and yanked it out once the call was done. The general average tickler user got his economics to work at 1p per call. Some of the more enterprising amongst us rented out a tickler at 10p per call.

The even more inventive who moreover had the time to read up on the mechanism of a public phone devised a method less cumbersome than drilling a hole through a coin. They used a computer punch card folded in half to make it slightly rigid. They pried the front and side panels of the phone box apart by a millimetre and brought the card down on the wire which would have moved down under the luxurious weight of the 50p coin.

Guys from Kolhapur and Sangli used a method which they swore worked well in their Kolhapur and Sangli. They simply brought the earpiece to their mouth, shouted through it, and quickly moved the earpiece back to their ear to listen to counter shouting. Nobody understood the logic but empirical evidence suggests that it worked quite well, given the number of shouting goons seen with the earpiece of a phone at their mouth.

I still remember the day when an official in a khaki uniform came to the hostel on his cycle carrying a big bag. He was from the telephone department and the big bag was to carry back the millions of 50p coins he hoped would come trickling down from the phone as soon as he opened it with an official key. His confidence at striking gold stemmed from the fact that the phone meter records showed H4 guys as champion callers. Overcome by curiosity, all of us gathered around Mr. Khaki as he pulled a funny looking key from his pocket and deftly opened and slid out the coin tray while using his palm to obstruct the valuable coins from flowing out like lava. Nothing flowed out. He looked down, and looked again, and his jaw dropped. He turned his gaze to the assembled and amused onlookers and then stared in disbelief at the coin tray. Amid all the laughter that ensued, I waded my way through the crowd and got a quick peek at the tray. Right in the centre of the tray lay a solitary 50p coin basking in the glory of its coinly solitude. It was surrounded by matchsticks, broken strings, crumpled computer cards, rubber bands, clips, pins and an assortment of wires made of steel, copper, plastic, and a wad of chewed chewing gum.

—*Bakul*

~

IIT showed us four movies in a month with four Fridays and five in some months. The monthly pass came at a princely Rs. 2, which was sheer highway robbery as far as some scientific minds were concerned. If Necessity is the Mother of Invention, IIT was her maternity ward. The necessity of spreading this Rs. 2 expense over ten people led to an invention called 'coat the pass with wax'. Once the pass was ticked with a pen, or so thought the usher who actually ticked on wax, the successful entrant into the Convo (convocation hall where the movies were screened) rubbed the tick away and slipped the pass out through a grill for the second man to attempt entry. In IIT guys asked each other for the usual match, lighter, cigarette of course. But sometimes they asked if anyone had a candle to spare. If you carried a candle in your pocket, you were respected as an individual with foresight.

~

Some of our inventions were certainly illegitimate children of Mother Necessity, like the wax pass, or the devices produced because of the necessity to make phone calls in spite of dire poverty. But some were the result of our ever-restless brains, and a real desire to create.

Sandeep Bhise had this urge to follow in the footsteps of famous seafarers Columbus and Vasco da Gama, and circumnavigate the globe. But for starters he set a more modest goal: cross Vihar lake on a vessel made by his very own hands.

Many a night and drawing paper was consumed making ever more sophisticated designs of all manners of craft which would float on water. It was soon realized that acquiring the raw materials needed to convert these designs into reality would wipe out Bhise's net worth (at that time) several times over. But the intrepid adventurer in his heart found a way. He befriended the then Mess Secy and collected all the empty kerosene cans that were lying around the kitchen. There were about twenty. The next few days were spent gathering the construction materials—wires to tie the cans, beeswax to plug their openings to make them water proof, and so on.

After a few weeks the raft was ready and was christened SS H4Whore. Bhise, in a cap and undies—he didn't want to risk his clothes getting wet in case the raft sank—and a bunch of guys from H4 took the raft to Vihar lake. A makeshift oar was hastily fashioned out of a piece of wood—everybody had forgotten we would need one to steer the raft.

Bhise mounted the H4Whore and off he went, surrounded by the bunch of guys swimming alongside. Wonder of wonders, the raft did not sink, and Bhise actually made it to the opposite end of the lake. The entourage made it too, in spite of the crocodiles of Vihar.

—*Satkya*

~

Those Who can't Do . . .

I had a lifelong ambition. To learn and master the art of swimming. While in school, my mother never allowed me to try, or learn. Every Sunday, my friends splashed and played in the near-by well. I tried to convince my mother how safe it was, to no avail. Still, I would wake up early every Sunday, go down to the well, and watch.

IIT Bombay. Lakes everywhere. Vihar, Tulsi, Powai. And Vihar lake so close to H4. Away from home. No mother to stop me. What more could you ask for to fulfil the long cherished childhood dream?

Freshies night went by and one felt a bit free and breathed easy in one's own space. One evening, chatting with the guys, I found out that they swam in Vihar Lake on weekends. Being a Mumbaikar, come Friday evening I went home after the movie and dry dinner only to reappear in the hostel late Sunday night. What a luxury it was. Friday evening movie in Convo, Dry Dinner at the hostel, getting the week's dirty clothes washed at home, Sunday evening movie on Doordarshan while eating mutton curry and rice made by my mother. (Could today's kids ever imagine the pleasure we derived out of these simple things, I wonder?)

Coming back to the chatting session that evening. I felt exposed in the sense that everyone got to know that I didn't know how to swim. But, no one laughed at me. This bunch of guys were much more interested in knowing how come I got to that age without learning to swim. I told them how come, and I also told them it was a childhood wish to swim. But who would teach me? And, there was no equipment, and neither was the lake ideal to learn swimming in, with its unpredictable depth and dangerous crocodiles.

It was Sandeep Bhise who said, 'I will teach you to swim. It is so easy.' Sandeep is the guy who is very sincere, committed, methodical, confident and persuasive. I decided to spend the next weekend at H4, even though it meant sacrificing home food and washing my clothes myself.

Saturday, after a late breakfast, was my first lesson in Vihar Lake. I was not afraid, but I was definitely a bit nervous at the prospect of getting in the water for the first time. Sandeep, like a seasoned coach, was with me when we left hostel, encouraging me and calming my nerves. We got to the lake and everyone, Selva, Chhuck, Chandu (he hadn't yet acquired the name H-Ku), Mike buddy, jumped in and started swimming. Sandeep also got in to warm up for 5 minutes. Everyone said, swimming is so easy, our body just floats, even the dogs and buffaloes can swim without coaching when thrown in the water, the natural survival instinct makes one swim. Remember Archimedes Principle, they said. I was convinced. IITans can never be wrong, at least technically. I jumped in the water where I was told the depth was no more than five feet out to a distance of ten feet. I was safe there, no chance of drowning.

The next thing I knew was my body was neither horizontal nor vertical, and I was inhaling water instead of oxygen. Probably ten or fifteen seconds later, though it seemed an eternity to me, someone pulled me up and stood me upright in the waist-level water. I was panting and struggling to breathe. A lot of water had already passed through my nostrils and wind pipe and safely deposited itself in my stomach. It took me some time to get over the first experience of swimming and then came a comforting pat on the back by Guru Sandeep. The wise words followed.

'Don't worry, you have learnt the first lesson. Do not try to breathe while your head is under the water.' I nodded dumbly. 'How do I breathe then?' I ask my Guru.

'It is very simple. Listen to me carefully. Take a deep breath and jump in the water horizontally, keep your head in the water, move your hands sideways, from front to back, under the water, and at the same time move your legs up and down. The hand movement will take you further and the leg movement will keep you horizontal. When the stored oxygen supply is used up, bring your head above the water level, breathe deeply and then continue the way you started till the oxygen is depleted again. Repeat. Simple.'

It looked pretty simple. I could see other guys doing the same. Some of them, in fact didn't even find the need to keep the head under the water. Probably they were a step ahead. Everything looked very easy. I prepared myself mentally, did a rehearsal in my mind a couple of times and collected all my courage. I reminded myself of my ambition. I was ready for the next lesson. I asked couple of guys to stay close by me, just in case.

I took a deep breath and flung myself horizontally in the water, kept my head under the water as I had been told, and moved my hands and legs as instructed. That felt so easy, no anxiety, no fear and I was quite comfortable for the next two minutes or so. I hadn't yet started smoking then and the lungs were quite powerful. After a while, I felt the need to breathe and tried to get my head above the water level. With all the concentration on getting the head above water (not wanting to flood nostrils and windpipe again), along with my head my whole body too became vertically oriented and I was breathing normally. I was standing with my feet touching the bottom in water all of four feet deep.

Sandeep who was watching me carefully, came along and congratulated me on my achievement and was pleased that I had listened and followed his instruction to the tee. It was a different matter that I couldn't get my head above the water while keeping my body floating. I tried that again and again but couldn't. I asked Sandeep for the Guru Mantra on how to do that. He kept saying just try and you will succeed, just the same way you succeeded with the first part.

To this day, after about 38 years after my first lesson in swimming I can swim exactly the same way and only as much as I learned that day. The only difference perhaps is that I could swim for two minutes then, and today for about one minute. I am still confused who is at fault—the Guru or the disciple.

—Deepak (Boss) Patil, '72-'85

~

In those days I was teaching Bhise how to swim and in return he was trying to teach me how to fish. At four in the morning. My lazy bones were refusing to learn because my mind knew that at four in the morning it should be asleep.

101

Swimming or no swimming, Bhise did make that raft. I still remember, as we walked to the hostel and tipped the H4Whore over the boundary wall, hearing Vijay Merchant on the radio saying 'au revoir' at the end of his radio programme about cricket. He would sign off every day with a French word.

The H4Whore had only one more outing on the water, because we were accosted by guards on her next voyage. Those were the days when Black September was threatening to poison Vihar and other lakes around Bombay. We had to dismantle her and return the oil cans to the mess.

—*Ramesh (Chukker) Chauhan, '72-'78*

~

H4 was easily the wackiest. We had Bhise on a raft, Arun Kaul going to lectures on horseback and actually 'parking' the horse in the cycle shed by the library, Coover and Bhingri making hand gliders (one each) crash effortlessly into the hill behind H4. To top it all, we once saw Batty travelling around all day with two bicycles. He cycled on one and wheeled the other one along by holding the handle. After watching him do it five times in one day, an exasperated Fish asked him, 'What is your ambition in life?' Before Batty could react, Birjoo Mehta answered on his behalf, 'His ambition is to own a four-wheeler.'

~

I read a news story in the *Indian Express* (August 2010) of a poor bloke who was literally eaten up by crocs in Powai lake just off Devi Temple. And this reminded me of some dangerous brushes some of us have had with these beasts in that same lake. KV was the first guy to photograph crocs and put them up on the notice board to get all doubting Thomases to shut up. KV had told us that he had sighted the crocs on an island towards the far end from the guest house bank. Soumitra and I tried in vain to sight them. Eventually, KV volunteered to row with us and Shyam Arora was the fourth guy in our boat and sure enough, the first thing we saw as we approached the island was a solitary croc sleeping on a rock with a prominent knife-like tooth sticking out. Our 'Shhhhhhh . . . here's the croc' must have travelled fast on the water because Mr Croc, got up, let out a whistling hiss and rapidly crawled into the water. We panicked momentarily wondering if he was heading towards our boat. KV reasoned that crocs cannot differentiate between us and the boat and is most likely to have slithered away to some safe recess within the lake bed. We saw the same beast on the same rock several times after that. Once Shobhan Mondal and Meenakshi Rao were with Soumitra and me. Mondal shocked us by diving into the water and swimming alongside our boat and boasting, 'This bugger does not have the balls to bite me.'

How do we know it was the same croc? It was the same unmistakable hiss. Soumitra named him Marlex because his hiss sounded like a Marlex pressure cooker whose whistle greeted us during ad-breaks before *Chhaya Geet*. And of course, the island rock was named Crocodile Rock after an Elton John song by the same name. And there are stories about how Coover dived in the lake and swam furiously and fast toward the croc as if he was dying to shake hands with him.

The *Indian Express* story made me think, today's generation of crocs are an aggressive lot who killed one guy and then attacked the rescue team as well. Clearly, they do not have the DNA of good old shy Marlex who whistled at us and then hid himself from us till his next picnic on the rock. Had these present rogues been around during our time, we would have been writing an obituary about good old KV or Coover or any of us.

—*Bakul*

~

Maybe it was just as well that the raft sailed no more. The crocodiles of Vihar Lake, even Marlex, were very real and vicious. The following story is about a singular H4-ite who combined many of the qualities we talk about: inventiveness, stick-to-it-iveness, audacity, eccentricity. And about those crocodiles of Vihar Lake.

Red Badge of Courage

Jetu narrated this story, bringing back vivid images to all present. It features an eccentric bawa from C83 named Cyrus Gazdar aka Coover. I know that 'eccentric bawa' is a tautological statement much like hot sun or cold ice or four-legged dog. But this Coover guy was clearly over the hill, even for a bawa. So think of it as really saying something when we call him an eccentric bawa: he was an eccentric even among bawas. He tried to make a hang glider. We would see him carrying it back to the hostel in a mutilated condition after he had crashed it on some hill or other.

Back to Jetu's story. Coover was fond of swimming, and Vihar lake was his favourite pool. Coover was slim, fair and the most 'chikna' bawa compared to others from his tribe like Sharookh, Irani, Kersi Dotiwala, Khushroo Lakdawala, Chikliwala, Rustom 'quack' Sethna and Rustom Homi Sethna.

This chikna, eccentric bawa Cyrus Gazdar-Coover wore swimming trunks that were a dazzling red and skimpier than a bikini. One day, he heard that the authorities had begun to crack down on all illegal swimmers who treated Vihar lake as their pool. The cops would come, confiscate swimmer's clothes if they lay on the bank, wait for the swimmer to come ashore, bundle him into their jeep, drive down to Andheri police station, and leave him there to find his way home. This was a really strong measure and scary enough to deter even the bravest. But not for nothing was this Coover known as Mr. Eccentric. His passion for swimming in Vihar was greater than the fear of even death penalty, leave alone something as petty as this. He stitched a pocket on the inside of his dazzling red skimpy bikini look-alike jocks. He would put a one rupee coin and his room key in that pocket, walk in these trunks to the lake and dive into the cold crocodile-infested waters.

And did the inevitable happen? Yes, it did. There were no clothes to confiscate, but the cops were glad to sit beside a gora, chikna, skimpy red bikini-ed bawa who would be their companion from Vihar to Andheri, and it was with a heavy heart that they let him off at Andheri. And what did our intrepid friend do? Simple. He stood in a bus queue, boarded the 396 when it came, dug into the pocket of the skimpy, pulled out a coin and said casually to a flabbergasted conductor, *'Ek Powai'.* We can only imagine how the other passengers took this, but there were several who espied him walking the two kilometres from the main gate back to H4, where he dug into the pocket of the skimpy yet again to retrieve his room key and finally disappeared from sight.

~

Inventiveness in IIT, it goes without saying, was widespread. Take Rane. There is a gadget used to extract old nails (or perhaps teeth), bend wires, and so on. Of course it can also be used for some more interesting applications such as pinching female bottoms but that has its attendant risks. I am referring to the humble pliers. So there was Rane (Boss's bosom buddy, I must add). His one passion in life—I'll illustrate with a hypothetical example—give him a pondy and give him a pair of pliers and he would use the former to lovingly wipe and clean the latter. Every waking moment of his life he spent furiously thinking of ways to make the pliers multi-purpose. Perhaps he even did that in his dreams while sleeping, but I wouldn't know about that since I never slept with him. So one day he realized that using pliers can be hazardous (no, not because he tried one of the interesting applications mentioned above). For example, he learned that you could get electrocuted if you used it to bend a wire that was live and carrying a current. Why anyone would be stupid enough to do that was not a question entertained by our intrepid inventor. What if somebody was? So he hit upon the idea of creating a pair of pliers that would have an 'integrated' tester. Of course 'integrated' is a modern management mantra that you cannot learn without paying a million bucks to Wharton or Sloan's School. Fortunately for Rane this mantra wasn't invented then. So he saved the million bucks, simply called it the Rane Tester-plier and started making plans to set up a factory with the million bucks that he had saved. For the rest of the semester and the next one that began after summer, he didn't stop talking about his tester-plier (or plier-tester depending on whether your political inclination was to the left or to the right). So Doody made a jingle about the world famous Rane Pliers—sung to the tune of a famous ad jungle 'Ranipal Ranipal Ranipal'. It goes,

Rane Pliers, Rane Pliers, Rane Pliers
Is it a tester– no, no, no!
Is it a plier—no, no, no!
It's a tester-plier, plier-tester, tester-plier
Rane Pliers, Rane Pliers, Rane Pliers

Every time anybody saw Rane in the corridor or in the mess, they would break out into this jingle. Loudly. Every time someone from H4 bumped into Rane in the library or in the department or in the Ac Office in MB, they would go—'Hey! Rane pliers, Rane Pliers . . .'. Friday evening while watching the movie in Convo, every time the hero smooched the heroine some group of H4 guys would start singing 'Rane Pliers, Rane Pliers . . .'. This was the theme song for that semester all over the campus. I even saw some guys from H5 singing 'Rane Pliers, Rane pliers' when they saw Rane walk past H5 gate towards the Gymkhana. It was a special favourite of Saheb Patil (not to be confused with Boss Patil) who was known to even sing it in his weekly bath.

—Satkya

~

Some of this inventiveness was sometimes visible in other areas as well.

Bingri's (Sanjay Bhingardevi) hang glider, Kaivan's geodesic domes for low cost housing, KT's 'KT-ism', featuring a convoluted arrangement of pipes and ingenious mixing contraptions to get hot water in the bathroom in shower format (as opposed to using a bucket), which was a big hit and enjoyed by all in the wing, the Boat Club dudes figuring out solutions to rid Powai lake of the dreadful water hyacinth (aka 'vile weed'), Milind Sohoni and gang's enviro attempts to re-green the hill by H4, which kept getting set on fire by the territorial hooch lobby, Sharookh / KRD's electrical circuitry (with built-in AI) to operate appliances (and simultaneously shut unneeded ones) in the room from the bed with a single flick of a switch, and the same Sharookh's masterful crafting of an electric guitar using wood from a bed, the list is long.

~

And then, there were some inventions that were, well . . . everyone starts somewhere.

Wasteland

For most IITans, professors, elders and even lab assistants were 'Sirs'. A fellow student, no matter what his seniority was always 'oye hero' if one did not know his name. Watchmen, mess workers, canteen boys, sweepers and so on were also generally 'oye-hero'. If you met someone in the corridor and say, asked him the time, you would generally ask, 'What is the time, Sir?' or 'What is the time, hero?'

Shashank Shah, though a bird of a different feather, abided by this timeless custom initially. In later years, when he found that many 'heroes' did not read TS Eliot and Geoffrey Chaucer, he decided to refer to erstwhile heroes as 'oye-chutiya' and sometimes as 'oye-gaandu'.

Hence, most of Shashank's salutations were Sir and Chutiya/ Gaandu and a hero was a scarce commodity on his radar. But there was also another problem. Most IITans attended classes and labs and generally knew which a Sir was and which a Hero. Shashank was clearly handicapped here. Neither his paltry attendance record nor his atrocious memory helped him distinguish a Sir from a Hero or a Chutiya. This led to several hilarious moments which saw Shashank Shah slapping a Prof with a rare spirit of bonhomie and asking him, 'Abbey oye chutiya! Did you see Professor Lele? I have to join his lab assignment'. The professor shot daggers through his eyes (unnoticed by Shashank) before announcing that he was Professor Lele. Then there was the time when Shashank was approached by a helpful gent while he was stuck in the middle of a bothersome experiment. Before the gent could utter a word, Shashank shot out, 'Fuck off ya chutiya! You are not in my group. I will go over to Yedkar's table and copy down his readings. You go and help chutiyas from your group.' He barely finished saying this when Yedkar walked over to tell Shashank's chutiya, 'Sir! We have finished this experiment. What should we do next?'

These minor misdemeanours did not deter our adventurer, however. He went about his business as usual, confident that he would get it all right one day. So, on the day he went to a lab exclusively allotted for him, he was in an upbeat mood. He wore his patented green trousers with a shocking pink kurta. (Not for nothing was Shashank Shah known as a colourful man.) Accompanying him was his flute (he was a wannabe flautist and didn't abandon his ambition till someone stole his flute and made it disappear), and along with the flute, a copy of TS Eliot's *Wasteland* was very much in tow, as was a scrap of paper on which he penned a verse for Gauri every day. And of course, there was a copy of abstracts that told him that if he could chlorinate atactic polypropylene, he could create a paste which could be used in footwear manufacture. Incidentally, that was the reason he was in the lab which was allotted for his exclusive use that day. He had convinced some 'Sirs' that IPCL Baroda generated a huge waste product in the form of the atactic which was useless to mankind, but he, Shashank Shah, would chlorinate it into a footwear paste and would give some credit to IIT during his acceptance speech at Stockholm when he was conferred with the Nobel prize. Whether the Sirs bought the idea or wanted to get rid of this persistent inventor/scientist is not clear, but the end result was that Shashank walked into the lab with his green trousers, pink kurta, flute, copy of *Wasteland*, a paper of poems scribbled for Gauri and the abstracts which would launch him into inventordom. And, there was a hanky full of atactic polypropylene crystals. And, there was a guy in the lab to whom Shashank said, 'Abbe Gaandu! Thoda chlorine de.' The un-amused guy who was of course a 'Sir' replied in English that chlorine does not flow from taps. Undeterred, Shashank ran his eyes quickly over the labels of all the bottles of reagent and finally stopped at chloroform. He was reasonably sure that chloroform contained chlorine and maybe the chlorine would move out of the chloroform and stick to the atactic fellow if Shashank played a lilting melody on his flute.

Finally, due to circumstances which need not be explained, Shashank was heating atactic with chloroform in a test tube when it happened: A loud deafening explosion that shook the entire building housing the lab. This explosion was preceded by a yellow effervescence that mesmerized Shashank. In his narration of the incident later, he said he was struck by the yellowness of the effervescence and not the explosion per se. The yellow, according to him, was ochre-ish though not quite there. It was ethereal. Surrealistic. Mystical. Magical. Exuberant. And mythical enough to establish Shashank's communion with a supra personal absolute.

When reality struck and the scorching flames reached close enough to scald his skin, Shashank fled. And then he remembered that his prized possessions were left to burn. So he turned back, did a Rajnikanth and dived through the flames to retrieve his flute, poems, Eliot, and extracts, and fled again to finally report that this atactic was a useless by-product that looked better in the stockyards of IPCL and could not be chlorinated.

⌒

The academic inventions, successful or not, were immortalised in BTPs—the mandatory B.Tech projects. Inventiveness abounded in this area.

Shashank Shah, 770239, Room 248 still felt on the verge of a breakthrough discovery, in spite of his recent setback. In order to immortalize his landmark discovery, he decided to ink his findings—type actually—in a BTP style book, before realizing that it was mandatory to do so. It was mandatory, in fact, to report the observations he had made in the lab.

Now normal mortals like us went to the library, cogged (IIT-ese for copied) notes, sat up nights with a department typist, plied him with chai and cigarettes and then carried the typewritten ream to Sudhir's book binding works where we oversaw the glossy black binding with embossed gold letters. And most of us had to buy 'Sunlit' brand bond paper A4 size at Rs. 45 a ream. But Shashank was a do-it-yourself man all the way, and in no way a normal mortal. He borrowed his dad's portable small font typewriter and composed the matter while typing it out himself. Of course, there was a remnant of Gujju genes in him which made him type out just one copy on the bond paper. He used thin tissue paper for the remaining three copies which got typed as carbon copies. Sudhir's brief was to bind just the one set typed on bond paper and the other three tissue copies were wrapped in a dirty pink hard paper and stitched and stapled crudely to vaguely suggest a bookish look.

Shashank was proud of what he got from Sudhir's binding shop. A dazzling, professional-looking black hardcover document with gold letters announcing that it was a 'B Tech project on Finding Use for Atactic Polypropylene by Shashank N Shah'. This was so good compared to the pink hardpaper stapled/stitched rag with the title written in red ink, that Shashank decided to retain the black book for himself and offered the pink book for appraisal to the panel of internal and external examiners. Talking about suicide bombers, you now know where the first one originated from.

There are several hilarious anecdotes about this BTP which actually need to be serialized, but for now, a mention has to be made about Chapter 13. The title was at least seven lines long. Something like 'Chlorinating atactic polypropylene crystals at so and so temperature using so and so catalyst over a period of so many hours etc and so forth to extract a paste to be used in footwear manufacture.' That was the title. Clearly, the compose-as-you-type routine had taken its toll. Shashank, typing himself into dead of night must have worn out his fingers to the last phalanges, because the total content of Chapter 13 after the title was exactly this: 'Do the above to get footwear paste'. History was being created and some of us were around to witness it. A chapter with a seven-line heading had a seven-word text. We managed to talk Shashank out of typing Chapter 14 on the same sheet even if it had to cost 1 sheet of bond paper and 3 sheets of tissue paper extra.

~

I had the distinction of being the partition mate of noted scientist and Advisory Council member of IITB, Prof. Vinayak Dravid (and his pigeons) who at the time was learning his now famous skills with metallurgy and material science in the labs of IIT Bombay. For his research work he enlisted the services of one Jadhav whose sole task was to 'furnace on karo' and 'furnace off karo' depending on whether Dravid was entering the lab or exiting the lab.

For his BTP he was required to submit his project outline to his guide. Normally, a student scripted a long outline for an even longer project, but Dravid was conscious of his time and wanted to maximize his ROI (returns on investment) for the time invested in preparing a project outline. He picked up twelve thick text books, found the pages where his project outline matter appeared, and used computer punch cards as bookmarks. He then told his guide that the outline started from 'this'—being punch card No.1 to 'that'—being punch card No. 2 and then from #3 to #4 and so on.

Despite this short cut, Dravid managed to score a perfect A for his BTP. Not surprising, he had superb presentation skills.

—*Dabba*

~

All of us had to do a mini BTP—a seminar module. Bakul chose the topic Mini Cement Plant. His guide was Professor Mandal. Bakul was informed that he should buy a small notebook, visit the central library frequently (perhaps it was daily), take meticulous notes of his research and references, and report back to the guide every week (for sure it was weekly). This was a routine most of us had left behind with school, but Bakul was the most unlikely among even us to follow it. There was little or no contact between the guide and the follower thereafter. The time to submit the bound treatise of his labour closed in. The follower had to produce one. Then there was one brief (I imagine stormy) contact between guide and follower. The outcome was predictable— follower had to produce a paper any which way he could.

Bakul parked himself outside his room and started writing the paper. Taking into account the negligible information he had on the topic and the nonexistent research he had done, he decided to seek public help. Bakul was in the central wing with full view of corridors and other wings, and everyone gave input on capacities, feed rate, power consumption and what not. With the resulting paper, Bakul managed to meet the deadline, and also clear the module.

Industrialist Bakul, I am quite sure, has avoided mini cement plant business opportunities if they were ever presented to him.

—*Deepak (Tweedy) Tiwary, '77-'82*

~

Trust Tweedy to remember and narrate unsavoury incidents from my past. Yes, my seminar project was 'Manufacture of Portland Cement in mini-cement plants', and senior Prof. G Mandal was my guide. The night before my presentation, I fake-limped to his house and asked him if I could be excused for having met with a leg accident. When he asked me how I injured my foot, I fumbled a wee bit longer than I should have and Mandal told me that I would genuinely suffer a leg-break if I bunked the seminar. My esteemed seniors had told me that after the presentation, your guide was generally sympathetic to you while rest of the panellists would grill you black and blue. Taking this cue, I asked Mandal what kind of questions he would ask me and what the others would ask. He just advised me to read up my notes and prepare well and not be worried about questions. It was then that I confessed that I had no notes and that I had not even started writing the seminar. Prof. G Mandal was incredulous. Shocked. His face changed colours faster than a chameleon ever did. While driving me out of his house, he smelt the tell-tale signs of an RK Beer unsuccessfully concealed by a YP paan and he cursed me enough to announce my doom.

Friends, Romans and countrymen helped me out, as Deepak says. They told me what cement is, told me how to spell chute (it was not what I thought it was), and some even wrote the acetate slides for me. Staying up all night and transforming yourself into a cement tycoon from a drinking-beer-on-credit-student was an experience, as was the experience of making it to the mess for breakfast—a never-before-happened phenomenon.

I was sober during the seminar and tried to act collected and confident. Even while the panellists demolished topper after topper, I kept my plastic smile intact, as if I knew how to conjure cement from my nostrils at three seconds' notice. The panel was headed by Prof Samir Sarkar and consisted of Prof Dwivedi, Prof Patwardhan and, of course, my guide Prof Mandal. Dwivedi and Pattu were doing a hatchet job on guys in a synchronized alternation while Prof Sarkar was trying to regulate them. Prof. Mandal behaved like a quiet, good boy.

It took my entry to transform Mandal from a timid rabbit to an angry, hungry lion. He went hammer and tongs at me from the word go. He was on the warpath and justifiably so. He was teaching me to make cement and I was experimenting with alcohol on the sly.

Prof Samir Sarkar stepped in and asked me to speak about what aspect of cement manufacture interested me. This was a cue and I took it. I talked about the economics of a small investment which yielded a higher profit/investment ratio.

Pattu asked me why a product costing Rs 31.25 per bag should sell at just 33 per bag. Dwivedi answered by saying that the black market rate for cement was 90 per bag and therefore profitable. This began an animated discussion amongst the panellists about the parallel economy and government policies. Mandal tried hard to veer the debate back to shafts and nodulizers. I coerced the panellists to fight on.

I escaped relatively unscathed. As Deepak says, I have bought a lot of cement in my days, and keep buying it, but never did I endeavour its manufacture.

—*Bakul*

~

It was the first day of orientation, and all the freshies were being taken around all the departments. Pretty boring stuff I thought, except that most of the freshies seemed to be absorbing all the inane trivia with wide-eyed enthusiasm. After the first session, I left for the hostel. You've seen one department, you've seen them all, I thought. Bakul must have had the same thought, he was walking with me. We were chatting happily, till we turned to look behind us. A group of forty freshies were on our tail. They thought we were going to the next session in a hurry and decided to follow us. At some point they realized we were going away from and not toward the departments and left. Bakul and I went to the hostel and bunked the rest of the orientation. That was a sign of things to come, I guess, for that behaviour continued for five years in Bakul's case and six in mine.

—*Fish*

∼

Fish and I had started the 'let's see who bunks more labs' contest early enough—in our very first semester. As a result, I was three assignments down in the machine drawing class, had bunked one quiz and scored a neat, perfect duck in the only other quiz I tried to participate in. Ergo, it meant that I would have to max the drawing endsem (end-semester exam which has 50% weightage, the other 50% coming from in-semester evaluation) in order to pass. Some well-meaning seniors, including one Abbasi who had been that route before, offered me a simple solution. According to his nuggets of wisdom, Prof Gadgil who conducted the drawing class was a trustee on the board of the Devi Padmavati temple and his one-point agenda in life outside the drawing class was to raise funds for his temple. 'If you contribute two rupees for the Devi temple, Gadgil is bound to pass you.' Thus spake Abbasi.

So just before the endsem started, I wondered for a fleeting moment whether or not I should walk up to Gadgil and make my 'humble' offering for the divine cause. Unfortunately however, the eternal optimist in me rose to the fore. When you are down and out, things can only improve, right? So in the manner of a tramp who goes to a swank restaurant and believes that he will pay the bill with the valuable pearl that he will uncover from an oyster that he will order, I decided that I would not risk my investment of Rs 2 on Goddess Devi till I had tried my hand at drawing some beautiful shafts and cylinders. And in case my cylinder didn't look like a cylinder, only then would I invest in half a brick for the temple.

Needless to say that my cylinders lacked in cylindricity. They looked more like battered pistons. Prof Gadgil came walking down the aisle collecting everyone's drawing sheets and balancing them delicately in his hand. When he approached my table and asked me to place my sheet on top of the pile he was deftly carrying, I put a two-rupee note on the sheet and said, 'For your temple fund, Sir'. Gadgil was aghast. 'Who told you about my involvement with the temple? Why are you giving the money here? I have to give you a proper receipt and I need your name, address and other details. Can you please wait till I have collected all sheets?' I said that I would be glad to wait. Later, when he came back to the table with a receipt book in hand, I had scribbled down all my information on a scrap of paper. My name, my address, my roll number, my drawing class serial number, my division. Sir Gadgil was aghast again, 'Why are you giving roll numbers and division numbers for a donation receipt?' I knew why I was doing it, but did not tell him.

After a couple of days, Fish and I dropped in to the drawing class to find out the fate of my endsem. Had Devi Padmavati decided to pass me? Gadgil looked at us, dug into his pocket and pulled out the same two rupee note that I had given him and said angrily, 'Please take this back. I do not want any correlation with your exam and this noble cause.' Fish and I acted offended and wondered how Sir could even think anything so slimy about us. To prove his point, Sir asked, 'Have you even seen the temple?'

'Yes!' I shot back, 'We were passing by the temple during our evening walk and Ashvin told me that you are involved with this temple and I decided to offer my own small contribution for this big cause.' This line would have ordinarily impressed, but Gadgil looked aghast again and I could feel Fish kick me under the table. As I was to learn later, the temple was at the edge of one bank of Powai lake and you could not 'pass by' the temple. If you passed it by, you would be swimming in Powai.

Nevertheless, I kept up with my protests and kept insisting how genuinely I believed in the temple cause. 'Sir! I am a God-fearing man ...' I could not complete this sentence because at this point the idiot Fish burst out laughing uncontrollably and ran out of the room. To top it all, his parting words while running out of the room were, 'That's a good one Bakul!' Gadgil took all of two seconds to thrust the vilified note in my hand and turn away. Surprisingly however, I learnt later that I had passed. Maybe Gadgil did not want to see me again begging, grovelling and pleading with another two rupee note. And ironically, almost two years later, I had plenty of opportunities to visit the Devi temple because that was the haunt of Soumitra and Tara. Whenever there was an urgent message from Soumitra's home for him, I would bike to the Devi temple to deliver the message in those non-mobile phone days. And I must add that the temple had come up very well and was set amidst the most beautiful and serene surroundings within IIT and I always made it a point to drop Rs 2 in the temple hundi whenever I was there.

—*Bakul*

~

Love Byte

Good old Radha from batch of '81, NWFF (North wing first floor) fame, is really one Raghunath Iyer. If I remember correctly, (which I generally do) he is Thiru Tharagad Raghunath Shivasubramanian Iyer. Our Radha was madly and passionately in love with EC 1030, the antique Russian computer of IITB. Radha would spend hours and hours at the CC (Computer Centre) punching out big fat decks of computer cards. He would give it to his beloved as his 'input' and collect the 'output' the next day. It was a common sight to see Radha walk into the CC with a 'deck' that must have weighed at least 2 Kg.

All departments had to do one course in CS (Computer Science) and unfortunately, each of us also had to do a project. For my project I helped myself to a thick deck from my senior Ajit Kumar Panda (it was a program simulating a cricket match) and went to CC for the first time to figure out where I give it and where I collect the printout.

Expectedly, Radha was there and he was smirking at me for looking like a Martian navigating through Dharavi. He walked up to help me out and casually enquired what I was doing there. Equally casually, I pointed to my deck and asked where I should deposit it. Radha's jaw dropped when he saw the deck. The deck was at least one inch thicker than the one he was carrying.

Fortunately, for him, he was relieved of the horror of considering the possibility that his darling EC 1030 was walking away from him because Prof Phatak walked in, looked at my deck and remarked, '*Kya re!* Panda *ka* deck *utha ke laaya kya?*'

—*Bakul*

~

In the 6th semester we had a Professor Nandedkar. I have no idea what he taught. Maybe wave guides? Even folks who normally bunked classes would not miss his lectures because of the entertainment value. He taught in all seriousness, completely unaware of his own oddness. So, he kept saying things and doing things while the class was laughing, rolling on the floor-with tears in their eyes. Literally. If you had to make a movie—here is the continuous shot you could have had focusing on him:

Nandedkar arrives at the department on his scooter. He gives hand signals for every little curve he negotiates along the path. He has a raincoat on, and a rain cap—with the ear flaps sticking out on both sides, flapping in the breeze (it isn't raining). Now he parks the scooter and starts walking toward the department—continuing to give hand signals at every turn. As he walks into the class, some clown tells him— 'Sir, we are prepared for the surprise quiz'. And now Nandedkar says, 'Then it is not a surprise?' (He made questions out of sentences where they should not be). And as a result he gives up on giving the quiz.

There is a quick exchange between Subharao Shenoy and him. As the professor is talking, he has already taken off his raincoat but not the rain cap. He forgets, in that exchange that he needs to take off his cap. Instead, he continues to take off the already taken-off raincoat. This time he unbuttons his shirt completely. You can see a funky undershirt (made out of a netlike material). The girls in the front row are completely aghast not just about the undershirt, but perhaps at what might be taken off next. And of course the class is now rolling on the floor.

At the end of the year, the professors gave out eval (evaluation) forms to fill out. This guy was such a hoot that most people gave him top marks on everything. This happened every year. And every year he would show his scores to KCM, Homo Kamat and others, who, I am sure would be gnashing their teeth.

—Ghoda

~

Nandedkar taught Electronics, at least to non EE majors. I remember him believing in theories that things can travel faster than the speed of light. I have actually personally seen him giving the turn signal before walking into the EE department building.

—*Vijay Desai, '76-'81*

~

I don't know how the profs put up with it but they were frequently accosted by students pleading for a change in their grade. For me, it was a matter of survival and therefore totally justified. But for some others I suspect it was some kind of a hobby—an unseemly obsession with a good grade point average.

On one such occasion (and I regret to say there were many such occasions), I had flunked a course I really needed to pass with even a D and I decided to go and fall at the professor's feet, and kiss them if necessary.

So I went to this prof (whose name I have forgotten) and told him how I misunderstood the question and how I meant to answer it differently and so on. This man pulled out my answer paper and asked me, 'OK Mr. Iyengar. Now tell me what would you do differently?'

I had no idea he would be that organized. I thought he would have sent all the papers to some irretrievable mass storage and I could just bluff my way out. Or I hoped he would take pity on me and pass me.

I persisted. I tried bluffing, refusing to let the professor's increasingly amused expression unnerve me. After about ten minutes of frantic and outrageous begging, I thought the prof would throw me out and warn me never to bother him again, but to my surprise, he grimaced, changed my grade to a 'D' and told me about it. I was so ecstatic I almost did cartwheels all the way out of his office. I would have been in dire straits on my probation status if I hadn't cleared that course.

I went back to the hostel and shared my good news. One of the guys I told about this went to the prof in question and requested a grade change from a 'D' to a 'C'.

The prof said, 'Sorry Mr. So-and-so, I don't change grades.'

Mr. So-and-so was outraged at this blatant lie.

'But you changed Ashvin Iyengar's grade, Sir,' he protested.

'Ahhhh. Ashvin Iyengar. Well that was different,' said the professor.

'How was that different, Sir?' the student persisted.

The professor explained kindly, 'when I first failed Ashvin, it was in the hope that he would repeat the course and learn something. But after listening to him for ten whole minutes, I realized that even if he repeated the course, he would learn nothing. So I did not see any point in flunking him.'

When I heard this story I thought it was very unfair. It was very unfair that there weren't more such enlightened profs in IIT.

—*Fish*

~

Prof Burragohain (later Director of IIT Guwahati) from Civil Engg was teaching us App Mech. (Don't ask me what App

Mech means. I know as much about it now as I did then.) In one of his tests, he had devised a problem. When I got my paper back, I realized that I had 3 out of 5 for one particular answer. The answer was correct, except, I had added two numbers instead of subtracting them, and that cost me 2 marks. When I was told that 2 marks would get me out of the D grade into a C grade, I braved it to Burragohain's office and told him, 'Sir, because of a silly mistake, I got 3 marks. If you can pardon my mistake, I can get 5 and therefore, a C grade.' Burragohain snatched the paper from my hand and exclaimed, 'You are right! It is a silly mistake. It is *my* silly mistake. Why did I give you three marks? Let me correct my mistake.' And he scratched out my 3 marks entirely. And ensured that I remained degraded.

—*Bakul*

~

In December '77, we had a lab endsem for physics. This was our first endsem and the lab endsems were always conducted before the main endsems. Shashank walked in twenty minutes late because he had lost his way to the physics lab, having visited that place on only a handful of occasions. By this time, Shashank had already acquired his now famous green trouser, pink kurta and flute, and he came to this lab with all these aforementioned embellishments which came with him equally twenty minutes late. Shashank was quickly ushered in and escorted by anxious lab assistants to his table where he had to perform his experiment. He was given a large beaker filled with water, he was given a block of wood approximately 6′ in length, breadth and height, he was given a spring balance, he was given a hook to attach between the wood and spring balance, and he was also given a question paper which read, 'Using Archimedes' principle, calculate the volume of the block of wood assuming the specific gravity of wood is 0.20.' The question ended but the ruckus started at this point. Shashank was vociferously calling out 'oye hero! Come here.' He barked this instruction in a general direction to all who qualified to be called heroes. This was a general broadcast to fellow students, lab assistants, exam invigilators and Professors, all of whom were equal strangers to Shashank. When it came to giving out bad treatment, Shashank did not discriminate. He was equally scathing towards all. Some five wannabe heroes including Prof Ghattikar rushed to Shashank's table. Shashank's instruction was crisp. 'Bring me a scale quickly. A scale' (Shashank has repeater syndrome). Five heroes looked at each other and nodded. Yes, they all had heard the same thing. This man was asking for a scale. In a very matter-of-fact manner. There was a no-nonsense aura to his instruction. Shashank, with a dazzling pink kurta and a big flute sticking out of his pocket had walked in twenty minutes late and was asking for a scale. One of them had to be brave enough to ask him a stupid question. What exactly entitled Shashank to demand a scale and hope to get it and why did he need it anyway?

Shashank's answer was simple and crisp again like his kurta. He wanted a scale so that he could measure the volume of the block of wood. Now will the kindly gents please move their butts and round up a set of scales so that Shashank could pick one that he fancied and if it was nice, he would order another couple to take home to Mom. Will the gentlemen please move and show some action? Once again,

Prof Ghattikar decided to be the brave one. He stepped forward and requested Shashank to please use the Archimedes principle to measure the volume. Archimedes did not use a scale, did he? Shashank was very forthright again. He did not know Archimedes. In fact, Shashank did not think that Archie-something was even in our batch. Anyway, Shashank always measured volume with a scale and he would be glad to teach Archie how to do it.

In the remaining two hours of the endsem, Ghattikar had not recovered.

~

I had hoped that none would remember my tryst with the matak (MTech) in the physics lab where I calculated the speed of sound at the speed of light. Many of you have brought up this incident, and collectively, all of you have got it right. Here's precisely what had happened.

The equipment contained a reservoir of water joined in a U-tube fashion with a straight vertical open-topped glass cylinder. If you moved the cylinder up and down, the water level would remain constant but the length of the air column above the water varied. You had to keep adjusting the length till you heard resonance when you placed a struck tuning fork at the mouth of this cylinder. The length of the column was used to derive the speed of sound using some formula. We had to get six readings over three hours, compare the six, find the average, and announce that as the speed of sound. I used the log table books to find that sound travelled at 333m/sec. I then used the same log tables to figure out the column length if speed was 333m/sec. I got six different column lengths in less than six minutes. I then decided that since I had the answer, I need not stand for three hours figuring out what I already knew. So I spent the three hours usefully. moving from table to table and gossiping with different guys about all important matters like Zeenat Aman's next movie, ITC's new cigarette launch, the centrespread in the latest issue of *Debonair*. I did notice the Matak frowning at me now and then. I didn't let that affect me. After all, a guy who spends five years studying engineering and then does another two year masters course cannot be all that harmful.

When we turned in our reading at closing time, Matak looked at my sheet and said, 'You got all six perfect and consistent readings. I have only seen you working on log tables and seen you disturbing other students. I haven't seen you even look at the equipment. Can you please show me one reading out of this six?' This got me. But I faked confidence and picked up the tuning fork. I was about to strike it on the table when I saw Fish motioning me toward a rubber lined wooden block on which one supposedly struck the damned fork. I picked up the block in the nick of time. I then took the vibrating fork to the equipment and looked to others desperately for help. They all stood there and laughed. Not even Fish signalled me on where I should place the tuning fork. I did a quick inky-pinky-ponky in my mind and wrongly selected the reservoir. By the time I held it on the reservoir, the laughter was deafening and the Matak murmured something about me not even knowing the most elementary step in the experiment and asked me to repeat the experiment on a Saturday.

This must have been the first re-experiment in IIT's recorded history. Fortunately, there was a different, more human version of the Matak on Saturday to supervise my experiment. With just the two of us in the lab, we shared some jokes, a cigarette, tea and some new friendship. He imparted some wisdom to me that day. 'Try to be honest and do not fake your way out in life. But if you have to fake it, do it intelligently. If you had written six different readings which varied from 312.6 to 340.83 m/sec, you wouldn't be in this soup. In our labs, neither the equipment nor the experimenter is perfect. A perfect result always arouses suspicion.'

I put the advice to very good use in my later life.

—*Bakul*

～

In our third year first semester (1979), the economics course was conducted by a rotund and portly Ms Kalpakam. She was a brilliant lady with a razor sharp mind and she was an extremely good teacher.

One day in class she drew demand–supply curves on the board. She must have realized there was some mistake in the diagram, because she stopped her speech for a moment, and said to herself, 'Oh fuck'. Unfortunately, she had a microphone around her neck.

On another day in the class, Ms Kalpakam drew more demand curves and supply curves on the board. Then, a little disappointed, she said, 'My curves are always bad.'

Half the 3rd-year students were taught by her while the other half were taught by a boring monotonous Sethuraman. It wasn't surprising to see that Kalpakam's class had 75 per cent of the students, some even sat in the aisles while Sethuraman droned laboriously to less than a quarter of the class. Kalpakam's class gave you an added advantage. You learnt good economics with a bonus lecture that sharpened your gaali competition skills.

—*Sunil Majgaonkar, '77-'82*

~

Doppler-gangbanger

Every hostel had its own intra-hostel gaali competition. The really fun ones were between adjacent hostels held on terraces in the dead of night. We would take on our neighbouring hostel and bestow the choicest gaalis upon them, and they, from their terrace, would return the favour.

H4 was positioned in such a way that H3 was our immediate neighbour and the wings faced each other in a gaali-friendly format. H3 was full of PGs (Post Grads) who spent no more than 2 years in IIT and often came to IIT after graduating from some tame engineering college somewhere. H4 on the other hand, consisted of battle-hardened warhorses who spent seven years to do a five-year course, and were coached in gaali giving by senior veterans from their first year on.

Deepak Patil aka Boss was a veteran gaali master whose imagination ran wild. The number and variety of things he could do in an H3's maternal receptacle was mind-boggling. He could do anything there. He once cooked chapattis, hosted a reception for an army, cultivated a pumpkin patch, engineered a short-circuit, all in one sentence and all in that very place from whence the poor H3s came into this world.

Sharookh Dara Lashkari (who unsuccessfully tried to rename himself Lashkari Sharookh Dara so that he could acronym to LSD) was high in MCs and BCs. But also, high in voice—he had a thin pipsqueak.

During a regular gaali spat with H3 from the terrace of the Central Wing, Sharookh, being a star gaali master was very much in attendance. Traditionally, we thrashed H3 hollow every time. This contest however, was different. The H3 guys had got hold of a mike and a loudspeaker. They generated enough decibel power to drown out our superior content. Champion after champion fell by the wayside—Manu, Pada (Anand Jain), Irani (another Bawa), Mondal. Sharookh, despite his 9+ content, could not shout loud enough, and soon, we saw Sharookh turn back and walk away. Just as we thought that Sharookh was abandoning the fight, we saw him turn, break into a rapid sprint, and run hard all the way to the edge of the terrace shouting 'H3 ke maa ki ...'

You might have heard of a physics phenomenon called the Doppler Effect. It explains why you perceive a noise emanating from somewhere other than its actual source. It is noticed generally in the case of aircraft and other fast-moving objects. By the time the noise reaches you, the object has moved away.

Sharookh should have known more about the Doppler Effect than most of us. Whenever you flunked a course at IIT, you

> either had to take a re-exam, or, you had to repeat the course during the summer vacation. If I remember right, Sharookh did a Physics course one semester and brushed it up again during a summer.
>
> Sharookh was certain that delivering a gaali while running fast would induce a Doppler effect and carry the gaali right into the courtyard of H3.

~

This was one competition that could happen at any time. This meant practising constantly. Some of us became so adept with our linguistic skills that it was hard to turn them off. The gaali became part of our normal speech. Of course, sometimes we were in situations outside the hostel, or outside IIT—in polite society. It all looks funny from where we stand now, but at the time, it could get hairy, to say the least.

One year, our wing mate Urvish Medh had just undergone a kidney transplant and was convalescing at a sanatorium in Juhu. Pinakin Patel and I went to see him. In the room were two folks who were obviously Urvish's mom and dad. Pinakin was one of the practitioners of gaali-linguistics, and his every sentence was laced with the B word, the C word, the M word, the F word and even some hitherto undiscovered G, H, and Q words. Urvish was squirming with embarrassment added to his discomfort and he motioned to me with his eyes to try and reign in Mr Patel. I kicked Pinakin on his ankle under the table as hard as I could, which led to a fresh torrent of F, C and M words from an enraged Pinakin who wanted to know why the fuck I was kicking him.

Finally, Urvish told Pinakin that these two folks were his parents. This led to an angry expostulation from Pinakin, 'Oh fuck! What a fucker you are! Why didn't you tell me before, you prick? Bakul, why the fuck didn't you tell me either?'

Later, we went to the airport to ostensibly see off my mom and granddad who were visiting Mumbai for a function, but the hidden agenda was to pick up some money to ensure my survival for the next month. I tried to keep Pinakin at a distance but he managed to come up just as I was receiving the loot and he wreaked further havoc by saying, 'Oh fuck, with this money, we can go and hit the rooftop bar at Taj.' I did not dare tell him that these were my granddad and mom for fear that he would say something further that would make them call the money back.

—*Bakul*

~

One summer during the holidays, Mad Rao happened to be in the Borivali area where Monty lived. So he called up Monty from a public telephone.

'Hello,' came a voice from the other end. It was Monty's dad.

Now Monty and his dad have an uncannily similar voice, accentuation and intonation, something Mad would learn the hard way. Obviously thinking it was Monty on the line, Mad, in his typical effusiveness goes, 'Hey Monty bastid, fucker. What the fuck are you up to? Move your sorry ass and meet me at so and so. And hurry up you prick, I don't have all day.'

There was a brief silence, followed by 'I'm sorry. This is Monty's dad. Monty is not at home. He has gone out.'

Mad was convinced this was one of Monty's typical pranks. So he gets more effusive. 'Nice try, fucker,' he says, laughing, dishing out more strings peppered with colourful expletives, and creative suggestions involving the use of certain body parts and choice orifices. He even dipped into the precious arsenal normally reserved for H3 life forms. Monty's dad, in his youth, must have been wild like Monty. He had a 'been there, done that, kiddo' attitude, and a sense of humour. 'No really. I am not Monty. I am his father,' he continued politely. This sort of exchange went on for a while until it finally dawned on Mad that this was indeed Monty's dad. He crapped. Nevertheless, being the astute diplomat that he is, Mad swiftly went into damage control mode, phasing out the expletives, and starting to discuss the Borivali weather, and so forth. After hanging up, Mad proceeded to where he had to go, shaken, sheepish and solo.

—as told to Rohan by Madanmohan (Mad) Rao, '81-'85.

~

Gaali fights were the kind of things that I normally had a fair chance of winning. But my most memorable one was one I lost, by quite a margin, actually.

There was this nice little bawa with Jimi Hendrix hair, Cyrus Vakil, who had joined 5-year M.Sc. physics, with a JEE rank of 222. And had he not been a bawa, nobody would have believed that he was not lopping off a 1 from the prefix of his rank and was indeed JEEAIR 222. Cyrus was a very soft-spoken guy, a thorough gentleman. He got bored with IIT and left after the first year—but that is another story.

So once during the ragging period, as freshers, Cyrus and I were pitted against each other—and I was quite confident of winning this one duel. So on the cue I started off by hurling all sorts of unspeakable names upon female members in Cyrus's extended family, then duly progressed to the male members, his anatomy, and everything that would have been private to him. I received absolutely nothing but a hurt look from Cyrus. Eventually as I paused to breathe, feeling a bit guilty at subjecting a fine bawa like Cyrus to such gutter treatment, Cyrus spoke.

He looked me straight in the eye and said 'Chutiya.' And man that hurt more than all my accumulated abuses. I was silenced. Cyrus was declared winner. And a deserving one at that.

—*Sandip Tarkas, '80-'85*

∿

Gaali fights for some reason bring forth a lot of nostalgia. Gaali fights were cathartic. They were great stress busters for people devastated by a tough quiz by Prof K.C. Mukherjee, a relief from being exceedingly bored from having nothing more illuminating to read than a Ted Mark book, something to do for anyone with nothing to do and no one to faat with, or just because you wanted to clear your nasal passages a bit. Any excuse, in other words, would do, to start one of these fights. You just stood in the corridor generally facing H3 and let fly a few B, F or M words. But that was only the opening salvo—just flexing the muscles of your throat to warm up. Because if your vocabulary was limited to only the generic B, F or M words then you didn't stand a chance of staying in the fight too long. You had to have a multi-lingual repertoire—certainly Marathi and Hindi but having a few Gujju B, F or M words provided an edge too. English was too tame, good enough only to start something. Just a multi-lingual vocabulary wasn't enough either. You had to be creative and imaginative with depraved situations, a menagerie of species intertwined in unimaginable scenarios, and you had to be able to describe them graphically.

If you couldn't construct a gaali consisting of at least eight words, you were an amateur learning from the masters. If you had a Bawaji in your team, that was an added advantage. No one—including Lukhha who was so fond of the B-word—could pronounce the B-word as effectively and with as much pith as a Bawaji can, and H4 had no shortage of them.

And then you needed to bring novelty and innovation in the brew by, say, translating common phrases into Sanskrit with which you could make people speechless because they would know that something bad was said but wouldn't figure out the meaning of what was said and therefore wouldn't know how to retaliate. I once won the day by shouting, instead of the usual B-word, 'Viparit Vilaskankshi'. My opponent didn't know what the heck to do.

How I miss the good clean fun of a liberating gaali fight. Imagine if I were to do it now—a pot-bellied, balding, outwardly respectable-looking guy standing in his balcony in a building occupied by other pot-bellied, balding and outwardly respectable guys and letting fly with some choicest phrases at no one in particular.

—*Satkya*

~

Bawanese

Talking about the advantage of having bawas on one's gaali team—there was Mehernosh Irani, whom NWFF folks fondly called Chavi (key) Irani. He would keep an eye on the papayas in the hostel garden. As soon as one was kind of ready, he used to chavi someone to pluck it, not giving the maali a chance to get to it first. Sometimes the maali got the better of him, and then Irani would retaliate by getting to the next papaya when it was still not quite ripe. Then he ripened it in a newspaper.

Irani had a foul temper and the requisite fouler mouth. Once, he was giving me a ride to town on his scooter. He told me how anyone not driving straight irritated him, and he would actually hit them on the back of their head while overtaking them along with generous references to the errant's mothers and sisters. He then instructed me that as pillion I should do the hitting and he would do the swearing. I tried an exchange offer which he didn't accept. And I didn't want to be hit and left stranded on the road. So, for the next sixteen kilometres, Irani slowed down his scooter alongside assorted cyclists and pedestrians and instructed me to 'just give the bugger one', which I did, and Irani then delivered his bawa trademark MC/BC.

We got to town almost an hour later than what a walk-bus-walk-train-walk-bus-walk combo would have taken and my hand smarted from assaulting so many errant Mumbaikars, not to mention that my Jain conscience pricked at practicing so much Irani-induced himsa.

—*Bakul*

~

139

By far the best exposition of our skills was reserved for the end-semester exams. Invariably during the run-up to end-sems, we used to have frequent power failures. At night, after grub, everyone would be engrossed in studies. There would be an eerie silence all around, when all of a sudden the lights would go off and complete darkness would descend on the hostel. After a few moments, though, someone would go to the end of the balcony in NWSF and shout a few gaalis to the inmates of H3. There would be return fire from H3, and soon the whole atmosphere would be electrifying in spite of the power failure. I remember, Satkya, Boss and Saheb would be so charged up that not just words but entire phrases with elaborate descriptions would be hurled at the opposite camp. H3 would soon lose the battle.

—Shyam (Shyama) Thosar, '76-'81

～

Time spent filling the air between with the hostels with vile words rather than studying for tests which would decide our fates proved detrimental to our fates. But we had skills other than the linguistic. We spent a fair amount of time and energy and thought and effort on our cogging skills too.

～

There was an endsem in progress, as they often were. There was this guy writing the endsem and we'll call him Punter for now. Punter, like all of his ilk who came ill-prepared for an endsem, was indulging in an act that was known as 'cogging' in IIT. In other words, he was copying. In still other words, he was cheating. He looked at his left neighbour's answer sheet, he looked at his right, he looked behind and occasionally, he got up and looked three tables away.

The exam invigilator was usually a prof, and this time it was Prof Gujjar. Punter's antics were not hidden from Gujjar. Gujjar watched him with an amused look and marvelled at Punter's audacity and brazenness. He decided to wait and watch some more. If he saw Punter getting totally out of hand, he would warn him sternly once. The next time, he would threaten to throw Punter out. And the third time he would actually execute the unpleasant task. Gujjar was wondering whether it was time yet to issue a stern warning or not. Just then, Punter's pen ran out of ink. Panicky Punter jumped from his chair and went rushing to other tables. 'Hey! Do you have a pen to spare? Do you?' He moved from table to table with the same 'Do you?' Midway through this routine, he ran to Gujjar's desk. 'Sir! Do you have a pen to spare?' This was Gujjar's moment. He took a pen out of his pocket, held it out and said to Punter, 'I'll give it to you under one condition. You will not cog.'

Everybody laughed and even Gujjar smiled at his own joke. Welcome Prof Gujjar to the cool profs' club. Punter did not laugh, and stared at Gujjar for a moment.

Then with a dismissive wave of his hand, he turned away and ran to the remaining tables, 'Hey! You got a pen to spare? Hey you! Do you have a pen?'

Gujjar, speechless, was left holding his pen.

⁓

During a workshop test, many of us sat around Sampath and cogged away shamelessly. Sampath was smiling mischievously (in hindsight, it was mischievous, at the time it was just a smile) while writing the test. Sampath, and all the rest of us who cogged Sampath's answers, got 2 out of 10 on the test. The instructor called all of us one by one and wanted us to answer an all important question. How did all twelve of us get the same wrong answer for every single question?

Sampath's mischievous smile now became a long hard laugh. He had set us all up. He did not care because he was going to crack his usual A anyway.

~

One who had mastered the skill of cogging was 'Mike Buddy'. He was also good at volleyball, field hockey and carom. Short, dark, wiry and soft spoken. Nice guy. The story was that he became too involved in hashish and booze to pay much attention to academics or to the non-stop stream of quizzes and tests. Once he showed up for a test still under the influence of one of those substances, and all he could do was copy from the guy in front.

Now the way people sat to give their tests, it would be very awkward to show the full page to the cogger behind. But Mike Buddy had mastered the art of copying the left hand half sheet first and then slightly shifting his position to copy the right hand side. The supervisor walking back and forth would look at his answer sheet in puzzlement and could not figure how he was deriving an equation in that interesting manner.

Mike Buddy was amazing at mechanically copying at breakneck

speed using this method, but once the guy in front was too quick and turned the page, and he suddenly missed a few steps. So against the next step that appeared to pop from nowhere, he provided the explanation—'My buddy told me' (instead of the usual—applying the binomial equation / or integrating both sides / or substituting z with e raise to Q).

Upon receiving his paper back, he was amused that he had got full credit. So he proudly put it up in the H4 lounge display cabinet for all to see.

Another way in which people cheated was the use of computer punch cards. The relevant formulae were neatly copied on a stack of punch cards and with a tack affixed to the bottom of the desk. As required, a card would by fanned out and looked at, and as the supervisor walked by, all the cogger did was slide his hand along the desk and the cards would disappear out of view—magic!

—*Ghoda*

~

Mike Buddy (Michael Alphonso) was my first Partition Partner (NWGF rooms 3 & 4). Brilliant guy, and not just at cogging. Also bit crazy about the corridor cricket.

—*Boss*

~

Corridor cricket. That was almost a normal extra-curricular activity. But H4 had to take it up—or down—a notch. Almost the entire NWFF played cricket-in-the nude. One of these times, an H8 freshy was sent to H4 to drop a leaflet in every room. The freshy was allowed to walk to the end of NWFF, and as he turned around to go back, he was faced with NWFF-ers playing galli-cricket in their skin.

He tried to run past them, but he was stopped by Rakesh Kapoor, Neil Elijah, Atul Mallik and the rest, and very politely, asked who he was, what he wanted there in H4, and other inane and mundane questions. He tried to keep his eyes to the ground, but he panicked, dropped his entire stack of leaflets, and desperately tried to run away, but he kept bumping into the naked NWFFers. They finally asked him, still politely, to join their team since they were a man short. Naturally, as a team-player, he had to wear the team uniform.

The scene was a riot, and soon gathered a small crowd—all jeering and cheering the freshy. I doubt that he ever returned to H4.

—*Dabba*

~

Maybe these skin bowlers took their took their cue from their cousins who came to live in H4 for a time. Four monkeys terrorized all H4 inmates by getting into their rooms and going on a rampage. They would take out calkeys, pull out the keys and chuck them all over the place. After roping in many monkey catchers, the council finally converged on the idea of a huge monkey trap which looked like a palanquin and was attractive enough for monkeys to venture into. Whether that worked or not remains unknown— the monkeys were still around in H4 when the 1982 monkeys passed out of IIT.

The Lit Sec (literary secretary) of the time Jiten Apte persuaded some of us to write a piece in Hindi for the H4 paper (Fourword) about this ongoing monkey menace. What follows is a loose translation from the Hindi piece:

Here's how the story ran 29 years ago—translated from the original Hindi.

One day, God looked down at the earth and felt very sad (atyant hi dukhi huye). *Murder, rape, violence, lies and a fall in moral standards everywhere. Even the bookstores sold mainly* Playboys *and* Rasvantis *and none of them sold even*

145

one copy of the Ramayana. *The anguished God decided that things must be corrected. The* Ramayana *must be re-enacted during this* kalyug. *And in order to re-enact a short version of the Valmiki original, he decided he would send Hanuman down to earth and let Hanuman find his own Ram. Now this Hanuman learnt on earth that all great men go to IIT and he would certainly find a compatible Ram there. Enquiries with the scrooty at the main gate revealed that while Ram was unknown in IIT, there was a Dashrath in H4 and maybe he could lead Hanuman to Ram. Hanu got to H4, enrolled as a student, dismantled his long tail and hid it in his room, and started living amongst humans as an almost human. Now this Hanuman guy managed to remain immune to all known kalyug vices. He miraculously managed to stay away from Panamas, RLC concoctions, bhang, pondies and so on. But there was one solitary vice that got him finally. Volleyball. So hooked was he on volleyball that he would play against a blank wall when there wasn't a Rajendra Laad or a Hari Singh to play with him.*

God was enraged. He had sent Hanu to find Ramu, not to fritter away his limited time playing volleyball. So God called four trusted monkeys from the vanar sena and asked them to descend on H4 and retrieve Hanuman's tail. These four faithful did as they were told. They went from room to room, they turned the beds and tables upside down in order to locate the missing tail, but their efforts yielded no fruit, and no tail.

Meanwhile, the anxious hostelites beseeched their council to take some strong action. Councillor Shenoy summoned an urgent council meeting. G Sec Fish could not attend because he was engaged in passionate loveplay with his cat Billee. Councillor Malvi(84) announced that he would seek a solution through his TM and went back to his room and his meditative posture. The brave councillor Manjunath Pai chased the monkeys but the clever monkeys ran past H10 and continued running while Pai stopped there and stayed stopped. (Pai aaj bhi daawa karte hain ki whey jiske peeche bhag rahe hain, woh vaastav mein, ek bandarni hai.) *Councillor Laad went to negotiate with the monkeys personally and the* vanar pramukh *told him,* 'Bhagwan ne hum chaar ko bheja hai. Tum beech mein kahan se aa gaye?' *Finally, the frustrated councillor Shenoy turned to Shashank Shah for help. Guys were flummoxed at this outrageous move by Shenoy. But the green pants-pink kurta wearing flute playing Shashank Shah told Shenoy that he had a plan. He would don the role of Ravana and do a Sita* haran. *That is, he would elope with Sita to Lanka. The monkeys would surely follow them, and H4 would be delivered from her misery. It's a different matter that while Ravana had ten heads, Shashank had none. And instead of the emerald isle of Lanka, Shashank headed for Manali and the monkeys stayed put in H4. (Those who know may smirk quietly. Those who do not, may derive their own conclusions.)*

Finally, the council has come up with a plan. They have ordered a palanquin (paalki) in which, Shashank will elope with a bandarni. This will entice the bandars away surely. All you readers mistakenly believe this paalki to be a monkey trap. The writers wish the councillors all the very best success.

～

Although H6 faced more monkey problems that we did, I never really heard of monkeys actually causing any harm to students. We would sometimes see monkeys in H4 for a couple of days and they would quietly go away. This time it was different. We had these guests for over a month. These guests, however, took over the house. Folks were missing bananas and fruits from the room. Sometimes the room would be in disarray, particularly if the window was open. The second floor was more accessible to the monkeys from the roof and SWSF was their favourite due to the trees that were so close to the windows. In fact, there was mutual suspicion and a bit of animosity among the inmates until we actually realized it was the monkeys, and not one of us, who was causing the annoyances.

Slowly these incidents increased. The monkeys gradually became bolder because people would run away from them. One or two guys were attacked. The monkeys caused so much fear that people carried hockey sticks and other tools for defence. It was soon clear that there was a female in the group who was pregnant and every monkey was protective of her. (We wondered who in H6 was responsible.)

We approached the zoo for a solution. As per their suggestion, we tried sedative darts. The monkeys threw the darts back at us. We tried sleeping pills in well buttered jam sandwiches placed on the roof of the mess. I don't remember eating such a well made sandwich (except the pill part of course) ever in my IIT life, not even during Friday dry dinner. The monkeys did not bother to eat them. Next we put powdered pills in the sandwich. We had our office boy try to catch when they dozed off. The monkeys went to the top of the trees and slept as they always slept.

After a few weeks, long weeks for us, The monkeys went away on their own. (Probably back to H6 to the father.)

—*Raj*

~

Simian terrorism had, at one time, heightened to alarming levels.

The boys were playing hostel cricket downstairs, and Monty hit a whopper that sent the ball to the terrace. In keeping with the rule 'he who hits it (to unfieldable zones), fetches it', Monty dropped his bat and made a slow trek to the terrace, only to encounter a bunch of ferocious monkeys. Although he managed to valiantly retrieve the ball, he did receive some nasty scratches and maybe a bite or two, which meant multiple hospi visits and painful injections.

Later that week, in the evening after tiffin, I was standing in the corridor between SW and CW, checking out the usual game on the H4 football field. I noticed a monkey family was chilling out along the terrace edge, checking out the footer game as well. It would have made quite a cute picture—papa monkey sprawled lazily, with his face resting on an elbow, mama monkey picking lice off one of her kids, and so on, all attention mostly focussed on the game.

The whole cricket ball incident came back to me. Kodak moment be damned, it was revenge I desired. I picked up a small stone lying by the side of the goalpost. Now don't get me wrong—I love God's creatures and all. I thought I'd chuck the stone near the monkeys and put a scare into them, merely to register my disapproval of their shameful

149

behaviour with Monty. Also there was considerable distance between us, and with an aim history like mine, statistically, I had to miss. I was wrong. Or maybe my inner desires were hidden from me. I did not miss. The stone caught papa monkey squarely on the back of his head. After a brief 'what-the-fuck' moment, he turned aggressively, miffed at the unexpected assault, trying to locate the source of the attack. He then saw me and seemed to back his gut instinct with some speedy trajectory computations. Clearly convinced that I was the culprit, he gave me the stink-eye, and there was menace, danger, and a 'I'll see to you later' vibe. I panicked and fled to my room.

I put away the blue checked shirt I was wearing, never to be worn on campus ever again, and may have also sported a moustache for the rest of the semester in a bid to escape detection.

The monkey did not get me, but I'm sure I picked up some bad karma.

—*Rohan*

~

I had just moved to CWSF (Room 239) and my partition mate was MegaWatt alias Meghawat who, at the time, was working quite intensely on a computer based simulation. MegaWatt was H4's Warren Buffett. He wanted to make his first million on the stock exchange before getting out of IIT. I had seen wrinkles on his forehead, anxiety on his face, and he worked hard day and night on his computer programme.

Those were the days when the Monkey Menace was at its peak. We were particular to close the windows while going out. One day I returned from morning classes (or rather a tea session in HSS canteen), and I heard some noises inside the room as I reached to open the door. I had heard many stories about monkeys messing with calkeys, and helping themselves to any booze in the rooms and creating even more havoc. There was booze available in our room. I cursed myself, and expected the worst as I opened the door. To my astonishment I witnessed 'Three Wise Monkeys' almost in that famous pose sitting on my bed. We exchanged a quick look, the monkeys left rapidly through the window. A quick inspection revealed nothing amiss in the room. Relief. I thought the visitors must have arrived just as I was getting into the room, and didn't have the time to cause any damage. MegaWatt arrived a few minutes later. He saw the damage they had done immediately.

The monkeys had arrived well in time, jumped over the partition to his side, had their party, and left his room in tatters. When I walked in, they had just jumped back and were posing for the prized photograph. The worst thing for MegaWatt was his computer simulation programme. The deck of computer cards were shuffled and scattered all over the room. We just collected the cards in the order in which we could lay our hands on them.

MegaWatt informed me that evening that he successfully ran that simulation.'Three Wise Monkeys' had debugged the programme.

—*Shailesh (Bridge bhadwa) Sabnis, '78-'83*

～

Mountaineer Monkey

V Square today is a certified instructor at the Alps and a fellow of Royal Geographic Society in London and something else in Edinburgh and he routinely delivers lectures in his capacity as a hot-shot management consultant under the aegis of his High Places Management Pvt. Ltd.

But back then, things were different. For starters, his name was Vasant Vasant Limaye (that still holds true), hence his nickname, V square Limaye. How he came to have this name is a small story in itself. Apparently, his coy mother, Mrs Limaye, would not call her husband by his name, and her husband Vasant thought that naming his son Vasant would force his wife to at least call her son Vasant, and in this way husband Vasant would have the pleasure of hearing his name pronounced by his wife's lips. Mrs Limaye, however, called her son Balya and Vasant was still missing from her lips.

It was not because of a lost key that Balya commuted through the toilet window. It was like this: one day, this intrepid mountaineer was watching a movie at the Convo. He liked the bench he was sitting on so much that he decided to dismantle it and carry it back to his room in H4. Unfortunately, a scrooty caught him red-handed. V Square was rusticated from the hostel for 6 months by the warden. The warden, in a public ceremony, sealed his room shut with a lock. After that, we in H4 were often regaled to espy a monkey-like figure swing from the terrace into a room late night and swing out with equal ease every morning. Warden did not take into account V Square's mountaineering skills which he used to enter his second-floor room from the terrace.

～

The Great Divide

Every hostel had its dominant share of Maharashtrians, uncharitably referred to as 'ghats' and a smaller number of 'elite', anglicized, upwardly mobile yuppies who were equally uncharitably referred to as 'pseuds'. Though they were of impressionable ages between 17 to 22, regional prejudices predated their entry to IIT and a kind of ghetto-ization was a natural corollary. Ghats and pseuds somehow coalesced into their separate existences in different wings. For a long time before 1977 when I joined IIT and for a longer time after 1982 when I left, the South Wing was traditionally referred to as the ghat wing and the Central wing was the pseud wing. Of course, in terms of numbers, the 'neutrals' formed the bulk but were inconsequential because of their silence. Neutrals, then, were the silent majority. Unlike the pseuds, they did not believe that Bhimsen Joshi was a constipated singer. And unlike the ghats, they did not think that an earring-wearing crooner who coiled pythons around his abdomen while singing was a case for a mental institution. Of course, there were a few cross-dressers. Pseud ghats were referred to as the 'western ghats' and occasionally, a non-Maharashtrian could be seen ghat-ing away. There were ample cultural and literary opportunities for both groups at the hostel level as well as at IIT level. There were magazines in English and in Marathi. There were plays in English and Marathi. There were quizzes, debates, what's-the-good-word, creative workshops, jest-a-minutes, different contests in both English and Marathi.

Somehow, the pseuds and ghats always appeared to be at war. They were deemed opposites and mutually exclusive. They formed lobbies which worked during hostel and IIT level elections. There was a clearly visible and unhealthy rivalry between the two groups within the hostel. However, and this is miraculous, the two groups always united during an inter-hostel contest of any kind. When attempting to beat H5 at football, the loudest 'Come on Mondal' came from Ghat Avasare. Ghats and pseuds outdid each other in melodrama when they had to jointly wrest the cultural trophy from H3 by performing their own respective histrionics on stage. By and large, the arrangement worked. There was an uneasy but a well working equilibrium that held the two groups and the rest of the hostel together.

This calm, however uneasy, was shattered by one unsavoury incident in early 1982, which created a deep rift in ghat-pseud relationships, and the outcome of this incident impacted all H4 inmates and brought shame and disrepute to H4. An attempt was made by some 'neutrals' to restore normalcy by coming out with a hastily cyclostyled 'magazine' called *The Hostel Scrawl* which attempted to take a humorous look at the pseudo-ghat divide, and the incident. Understanding and deciphering the innuendo in *The Hostel Scrawl* requires a bit of background and information.

The Scroll of Honour was the highest award given to any hostelite who distinguished himself in sports, cultural activities, academics and who had brought glory to H4. An award was given out each year to the chosen one from the graduating batch and his name was immortalized on a wooden marquee in yellow letters in the hostel lounge. Thus, in 1977, my batchmates and I knew names like Behruz Sethna, Homi Byramji, Uday Wagle, Dadi Ratnagar, Hemant Shah, K Rajaram, C Seetharam. These were some of those who had made H4 what it was. We were also fortunate enough to meet and spend two years with Gautam Barua who is currently the Director of IIT Guwahati. We read these names day in and day out in the lounge, and we heard stories about them from our seniors and respected them without having ever met them, simply because they were the recipients of that prestigious award which would perpetuate their glory long after we had left. Those yellow letters on the wooden marquee would be there forever, and everyone who sat in the lounge would read them.

The awardees were selected by a subjective decision taken by elected hostel councillors, but fortunately, each of the previous awards had gone to such clear cut deserving candidates that none could accuse any councillor of any subjective bias towards a particular person. However, in order to set up an objective procedure for the future, a committee was formed under the stewardship of G Sec Deepak Patil aka Boss to evolve a points system. Points would be added to each hostelite's name for participation and success in various events. The candidate with the highest tally would qualify for the coveted award. This was 1981, and everyone was fine with the procedure. But in early 1982, when the winning candidate's name was announced, disaster struck. Rajendra Fondu Laad i.e. RF Laad also known as Rough Laad was the frontrunner to receive this award. So what was the problem? The problem was that Rough Laad was a ghat. Pseuds thought that Laad was short and squat, and bearded, played kabbadi and khho-khho and wore a checked lungi with a striped shirt to the mess. The award should rather go to Mohan Giridharadas aka Mogi who played some good TT, and was tall, and listened to Pink Floyd. Ghats thought that although Mogi played TT, he looked and acted as if he played golf and indulged in skeet-shooting. He wore torn and faded jeans ostensibly in the name of fashion and spoke loudly, and worse, was loud in English. And thus began the nasty airing of regional prejudices about the two sides' socio-cultural backgrounds. Pseuds said Bhimsen Joshi sang with no lyrics, it was just Aaaaaaaaa and some more Aaaaaaaaaa and what was Malkouns or Bhairavi about it? Ghats thought that with lyrics like Pink Floyd's, it was better to not have lyrics at all. Where was the English in 'We don't need no education'? Do we need it or do we not? Why should one speak in three negatives and fox a listener? And why did guys dye their hair purple and orange and create weird sounds that could be heard during jungle treks anyway? This kind of back and forth went on. The pseuds demanded a GBM to discuss the issue of how not to give Laad the award. And in what resembled a political party's strategy of realigning forces to win a parliamentary debate, the level of snide politicking rose to a new high in H4.

Mogi's NWFF was a pseud wing, as was Sood's CWSF. Mogi's wing and Sood's wing worked as siblings in evolving stratagems to block Laad's candidature in a GBM and one originally-Kenneth-but-later-transformed-to-Gaitonde put up a notice which read like this (clearly, his name change did not change his affiliation).

We, the undersigned would like to clarify primarily three points regarding the system evolved for the conferring of the Scroll of Honour.

1. Is an untested system that has never been publically displayed a valid basis for making such an important decision as conferring the highest recognition—the Scroll of Honour? Further, can it be the deciding criteria in such

a matter or should the decision be a subjective impartial one referred either to the council or to the general body?

2. We would appreciate it if the persons involved in reaching this decision could explain it through some forum (e.g. GBM) to the hostelites.

3. We would like to understand why the council has forbidden the publishing of any article on this highly relevant and controversial topic in the current issue of *Fourword*. This is tantamount to stifling any form of protest. Any editor of any integrity has the final say in the article that he chooses to publish and NOBODY, not even the COUNCIL can force him to do otherwise.

We have written this letter to you to make you aware of the above points. We feel that a GBM is necessary to discuss the issue.

D-day came. The GBM was messy and attacks were personal. Decibel power won the day, and eventually, the council was bullied, the neutrals were sullen, and Laad was denied the honour. In an effort to lighten the situation and the mood, we came up with a magazine we called *The Hostel Scrawl*. 'Scrawl' was written in a scrawl. The graphic on the upper left corner was inspired by Russi Karanjia's newly-launched tabloid called *The Daily*. *The Daily* had a bulldog as its logo, with the words 'We are on your side' printed beneath the bulldog. We, that is Sandeep Shah aka Sandhya, drew the H4's gearwheel logo, a face within the wheel shedding tears and being crushed by a foot, and the words 'we're inside' beneath it. The price was 'Nil' to suggest that this magazine was priceless. All the keywords and puns were underlined to ensure that all the dramatis personae understood the references. 'Boreword' referred to the hostel magazine *Fourword*. 'RSS' referred to RS Shenoy who was the incoming G Sec. Mark Anthony's famous quote was attributed to Mark Anthony C, implying Anthony Coutinho aka Tony. Tony was also a frontliner Laad baiter who had initiated the demand for a GBM and was in Mogi's wing. The word 'honourable' was underlined to imply that it was about the Scroll of Honour.

The article that followed was titled, 'Will the tables turn?' It reproduced Gaitonde's notice word for word except that the Scroll of Honour was replaced with the sun mica table—the best table in the mess. An attempt was made to show that some hostelites were agitated over the allocation of tables for the hostel's valedictory function and there was a fight for the allocation of the best table viz. the table laminated with Sunmica-brand laminate. This was the spoof and the people signing the notice were made out to be the controversial RF Laad himself along with other names that belonged to actual winners of previous Scroll of Honour awards. And there was a note which said that references to real people was an intentional act. And another note which said that the tables had turned.

The second page featured a mock interview with Sanjiv Sood referred to as P. Seud and Ashish Khosla referred to as Hashish Khoj La who spoke in typical pseud-ese and talked about 'lards' and 'ruffians' and 'Pinky (for Pink Floyd)' and about 'grass' and roses and about occidentalists . There was also an interview with an AG hat, meaning 'A Ghat' who talked about the pseuds always being on a 'trip' and

THE HOSTEL Scrawl

we're inside a | VOL 2 NO 2 PRICE:NIL.

Editor's Note: We deeply regret that our priceless opening issue of the Hostel Scrawl Vol 1 could not hit the stands due to the sinister conspiracy hatched by BOREWORD,CIA and MSS.

Thought for the Day:

The noble Brutus hath told you that Caesar was ambitious
And Brutus is an <u>honourable</u> man.
—Mark Anthony C.

Et tu Brute- Caesar.

WILL THE TABLES TURN?

As it fits our high tradition of publishing the highest scrawls that rule over the times of the hostel,we have the privelege of bringing to our readers,the true story of the greatest controversy to hit our hostel since the days of the Athenian Oracle.The allocation of tables for the valedictory function must be of utmost concern to concerned hostelites and this most important issue is best exemplified in the following letter which we believe shall become eternal in the annals of our hostel literature.

Editors,

We the undersigned,would like to clarify primarily three points regarding the system evolved for the conferring of tables.

1. Is an untested system that has never been publically displayed a valid basis for making such an important decision as conferring the best table during the Val. function - The Sun-mica Table.

Further can it be the deciding criteria in such a matter or should the decision be a subjective impartial one reffered either to the council or the General Body, or to US.

2. We would much appreciate it if the persons involved in reaching this decision could explain it through some forum(e.g. GBM)to the hostelites.

3. We would like to understand why the council has forbidden the publishing of any article on this highly relevant and cotroversial topic in the current issue of the Hostel Scrawl.This is tantamount to stifling any form of protest.Any editor (integrity?) has the final say in any article that he chooses to publish and NOBODY not even the COUNCIL can force him to do otherwise.

We have written this letter to you to make you aware of the above points.We feel that a General Body Meeting is necessary to discuss the concerned tables.

- A.F.Lasi,Behrus Sethna,Homi Byramji,Uday Wagle, Dadi Ratnagar,Hemant Shah,A.Rajaram,Gautam Barua & C.Seetharam.

Ed's note:
Any resemblance to any person hitherto and hereinafter mentioned is purely INTENTIONAL.

L

LATE NEWS ...

According to reports received here from Western News Agency,and confirmed by our staff reporters, it was stated that

THE TABLES HAVE TURNED .

PTO

therefore away from the hostel. The V E L in the AG hat interview referred to Mahesh Velankar aka Velchya who was a prominent Ghat. Birjoo Mehta and I wrote this piece on a lazy Sunday after this GBM and we typed it on a stencil with Shashank's portable typewriter and I used a pseud-winger Arun Gupta to help me cyclostyle the mag in my room (on a portable cyclostyling machine) and I used a ghat-winger Sandip Tarkas to distribute about 50 copies in the mess during Monday lunch. Ashish Khosla was asleep when I went to his room the previous night to give him his copy and I left it in his window. Next morning, he greeted me with a scowl which did not wear off for a whole week. Later at around midnight on that Monday, I got frantic SOS-es from concerned hostelites that I visit Raghunath Iyer aka Radha's room. Apparently, Radha read the Hashish Khojla word at around 4pm and started laughing and was still laughing till midnight and there was no stopping him. Looking back, it could be said that this rag did thaw the ghat-pseud standoff to some extent.

—*Bakul*

~

About Blacky, initially there was confusion about whether he was a ghat or a pseud or a neutral. After one semester, it became clear going by the company he kept. He was Jack's closest buddy and therefore, an outright pseud. Even during breakfast, when he would position himself before a table and beg for an omelette piece by placing his paw on the potential donor's lap, he generally aimed for a pseud table. To complicate matters, the pseuds never woke up in time for breakfast and Blacky had to hunt for food at the neutrals' tables more often than not. During one such hunt, he was pestering Shashank Shah for an omelette while Shashank was discussing a profound doctrine of Advaita. Shashank was irritated and confused. He angrily told Blacky, 'Tikde jaa' ('go there' in Marathi). Now these were the only two Marathi words Shashank ever spoke in his life. Why did he single out Blacky for this rare distinction? Shashank's reply was more foxy than his expostulation of Advaita. 'Come on yaar! He is a dog. How do you expect him to understand English?'

But Blacky apparently understood. He scampered off with a sullen look on his face which seemed to say, 'Next MI, (Mood Indigo) come to the gymkhana grounds for the rock concert. I'll show you how much English I know.' Jokes aside, he attended every concert of MI-2 listening to Tull and Uriah Heap rendered by Nandu Bhende.

~

There were several extracurricular activities that took place in IIT to entertain and delight Blacky apart from Mood Indigo, the annual music festival.

In the '70s and '80s, two hostels were paired by a random draw of lots and were required to put up a variety show called the Entertainment Program. These were called the EPs. Thus, amongst ten hostels, there would be five EPs hosted, one every Wednesday from 8pm to about 11pm. (Today's EP is the PAF—Performing Arts Festival). EPs were hosted in late August and early September at the Convo. Preparatory work for all EPs was on a massive scale. Teams were formed to decide the format, theme and content of the EPs. Volunteers would work till late into the night making attractive posters and banners, and every wing in the hostel would reverberate with sounds of musicians practicing. The mess and the lounge would be taken over by wannabe dramatists, mimics, dancers and performers. The EP trophy put the winning hostel pair high up on their pursuit of the annual cultural trophy. This also served as a talent scouting exercise from among freshies, and the notable performers became potential Soc Secs (Social Secretary) and Lit Secs (Literary Secretary) of the hostel. The outstanding performers and the most tireless volunteers and organizers also vied for the highly coveted institute level post of GS-Cult. (Gen Sec Cultural for the Students' gymkhana which encompassed all hostels).

The standard of the performances was very high and most of the programs were hilarious. Understandably, the competition was fierce. In an effort to increase one's own hostel's chances, people would form booing gangs too boo all their rivals during their performances. The objective of booing was to demoralize a rival performer, but it was also to drown out the performers' voices so that the judge would not be able to hear them. To counter booing, people tried to enhance the visual content of their skits. There would be overly padded guys dressed up as women, they slipped in performances which showed aesthetic gymnasts, mobike riders, rope climbers and people resembling the Diro (Director AK De) or DOSA Isaac clowning around on stage. Sets and lights and special effects were to a higher standard than would have been necessary, had booing not been existent. Booing reached a feverish pitch in the 1978 EP. Booing squads now worked with the precision of a military outfit. Booers were selected based on the decibel level they could generate. They were all seated in a single block in predetermined and carefully selected seats. A maestro would actually stand up, turn and face his 'orchestra' and direct and conduct the booing in the manner of the most professional philharmonic orchestra conductor. Content used during booing had the mandatory swear words of course, and also just the plain good old-fashioned 'boo' which had now been developed into magical rhymes delivered as a jingle. These performances of the booing squads often matched those of the performers on stage. The H4 booing squad always belted out 'khushboodar antiseptic cream Boroline' in unison, picking up the lines from a TV ad that was prevalent on the sole channel of black and white Doordarshan. H5 was hung up on the ad jingle of 'VIP Underwear Banyan' (pronounced under-we-are and bun-yaan).

All EPs were designed around a theme. This allowed for a common set décor and tied up different styles of performances with a common thread. H4 was paired with H8. The theme we selected was *Rubaiyat*. For *Rubaiyat*, we created an Arab sheiks' abode, and a prosperous hookah smoking Arab invited various performers to entertain him. Edgar Dias twanged Beatles hits on his guitar, Soc Sec Ghoda directed 'ballet in prose' titled 'This is the house that Jack built' which referred to the MB (Main Building of IIT), freshy Sanjay Jagdale mimicked a funny politician. There was a humorous skit about Indian politicians with western songs playing in the background, Sakhardande mimed in a short play by Samuel Becket, Ghoda did his trademark mime performance in which he attempted to sit on a chair that keeps moving away from him thanks to some cunning engineering and light effects, and a retinue of highly practiced string pullers.

Preparations were elaborate and the EP was destined to be a super success. In the politician skit, PM Morarji Desai played by Ghatkopar was to go into a men's room with 'That's the way, aha aha—I like it, aha-aha' as the theme music. I was to play Charan Singh who fights with the whole cabinet while 'Everybody loves Kung-fu fighting' plays in the background, and finally, when Charan Singh is creamed and pasted to the floor, he (I) gets up and walks away slowly while The Beatles sing 'he's a real nowhere man, sitting in his nowhere land, making all his nowhere plans, for nobody.' Atal Behari Vajpayee's was well rehearsed by Viren Pathare to the tune of Cliff Richards' 'You are a bachelor boy and that's the way to stay'.

On the Wednesday previous to *Rubaiyat*, H7 and H10 had put up their EP, and as in any EP featuring H10, the booing was non-stop, not a single word or song could be heard and the visual was also obscured by the constant stream of booers who were on their feet more often than not. The possibility that H7 would hit back at Rubaiyat was accounted for. But we were caught by surprise at the strong presence of H10 girls all occupying the front row and we could also see hundreds of H7 guys armed with baskets that contained, as we were to find out later, rotten eggs and tomatoes. It seemed very clear—this was to be an all-out war. Everybody, even the girls of H10, were going to pull out all the stops.

Edgar had barely sung the words 'here comes the sun . . .' when one egg landed on his guitar and two tomatoes on his face and shoulder. The miming Ghoda was being avoided by the crafty chair but he could not avoid the missiles that erupted every minute. The politicians Morarji Desai, Charan Singh, Vajpayee and Indira Gandhi (Birjoo Mehta) were still in the make-up room getting their hair whitened and when they peeked out to see what was happening, a missile got Morarji on his lip. H4 spectators were in a quandary. How should we stop this guerrilla operation which had caught us unawares? That was when we saw politician in the making, Manohar Parrikar rise to the occasion. He had been forewarned about H7 and H10's impending attack and he had come prepared. He had rounded up all rotten eggs and tomatoes from the mess and a few potatoes and onions as well, to add to the flavour. Sitting in the audience behind the H7 gang, he engineered a parallel attack on the audience immediately ahead of him. This caused confusion in the H7 ranks. They cried foul. They said that Manu should be man enough to fight face to face and not from the back. In the confusion, and in a situation where things were fast spinning out of control and fisticuffs were just around the corner, suddenly, all lights on the stage were switched on. On the stage, leading a gang of dhoti-clad Morarjis, Charan Singhs, Vajpayees, and assorted guitarists, dancers and clowns, and also the Arab sheikh, was Nandan Nilekani from H8. Even before he became famous internationally as the co-founder of Infosys, Nandan was popular within IIT as the GSSA (Gen Sec Students Affairs). A hush descended in the Convo as Nandan walked and announced on the mike that current GS Cult Rajaram should come backstage.

Rajaram came. Hectic parleys took place. There was a temporary ceasefire as people anxiously awaited the outcome of the high-level backstage consultations. Rajaram warned the audience who were ironically from his H7 to desist from disrupting the EP. Raj Narain (Deepak Avasare) folded up his lungi to become Raj Narain again and the EP resumed soon after. But the missile throwers began again and Manu caught the miscreants by their collars and bundled them out of the Convo. Again, an exasperated Nandan walked on the stage and announced, 'We cannot carry on like this.' Rajaram came up and announced the scrapping of the competition.

The president of the students' gymkhana, Prof. Mathur got on the stage as the curtains went down and spoke to the aggrieved performers. He clamped his nose shut as Edgar walked up to him with a stinking egg still on his shirt. Mathur completed his conversation with all with his nose shut. An enraged H8 guy did not know who Mathur was, and told him in the middle of his lecture, 'Just shut up man! We need that bastard Mathur here on stage and he should tell us how he will stop this nonsense. Who are you?' Mathur told him that he was Mathur. The H8 guy bolted. The next day, there were arguments in every class between the H4/H8 team and the H7/H10 team. I gave a piece of my mind to Seema in the drawing class. Couldn't she have waited until after I did my Charan Singh gig? The H7 guys told me that Manu had behaved like a political goon. 'Ask him to join politics. He will do well there', they said. I conveyed their message to Manu. He obliged.

—*Bakul*

~

Debt

My friend Manu was highly respected, but also feared. People liked him for his altruism and respected his organizational skills, but were wary of him too, and sniggered behind his back sometimes. So, when he had to pick up his mother from Dadar station early one morning, (she was visiting her son for the first time after he came to IIT), he had just two friends accompanying him—his batchmate Anand Jain (nicknamed Pada), and me. The man behind the ticket window at Vikhroli station was deep in sleep, and snoring. All attempts to wake him proved futile. We had no choice but to board the first VT bound local sans tickets. At Dadar, as luck would have it, a TC materialized and asked Manu for his ticket. Manu begged, pleaded, grovelled but to no avail. Manu was fined Rs 10.40, 40p being the ticket price and Rs 10.00 being the new 'minimum' penalty. Understandably, Manu was cut up, and the disciplinarian in him decided to revolt. He travelled ticketless with impunity for the next two semesters.

One afternoon we walked into Manu's room and found him deep in an accounting exercise. According to his meticulous calculations, his ticketless travel until then was worth Rs 11.80. That made it Rs 1.40 more than he was fined that unlucky day two semesters before. I thought, 'So what?' But not Manu. Manu dragged me to the post office at YP. He bought postal stamps worth Rs 1.40. He then tore them up before a disbelieving postmaster. He announced that he was now *quits* with the Government of India.

Call it wicked irony or a trick of fate, but Manu (Manohar Parrikar) went on to become BJP's first Chief Minister of Goa and is currently the leader of the Opposition in the Goa Assembly. Considering that BJP was non-existent in minority dominated Goa, Manu's role in building up a party from scratch and winning elections on his own in the aftermath of the Gujarat riots is a commendable feat. From amongst all CMs who have ruled Goa in the last 20 years, Manu has been the longest serving CM of Goa and was much appreciated for his stellar achievements.

During his IIT days, he was seen as a rabble-rouser who was busy fighting with either the IIT authorities or the mess workers in order to ensure that students were not short-changed by anyone. He was tireless, he worked in the mess during his stint as Mess Secretary first and then General Secretary to ensure that mess bills were kept in check. He came down hard on any mess worker or student who indulged in any misdemeanour like pilfering or negligence, a trait that he carried with him to the Goa Secretariat. In his now famous speech made in California in the presence of Bill Gates during a pan IIT meet in 2002, Manu recounted how he was puzzled when he saw mess workers leave the mess with their lungis rolled up. When he insisted the garments be rolled down he was startled to see onions, tomatoes and potatoes roll out from the lungis. This, according to him, was his first lesson in vigilant administration, one that served him well in his duties as a CM. Manu was never afraid to court any controversy, was fearless in taking bold decisions and his revulsion to corruption led him to sack three of his ministers which he did at the cost to his own survival as a CM.

And when it was time to have fun, Manu was always game. He always brought back a bottle of cashew feni for all hostelites after his visits to Goa during vacations, loudly cheered H4 during EPs and other events and booed equally loudly when other hostels performed. During one EP, he countered an attack from H7 by using up all the stale eggs, potatoes and tomatoes from the mess which he directed at H7 performers. When the mess workers went on a lightning strike, Manu led from the front, walked right into the kitchen and got all hostelites to cook lunch and dinner, and people swear to this day that it was their best meal in IIT.

—Bakul

~

In 1980, we were paired with H8 for an EP which had Hitler's *Mein Kampf* as the theme. Normally, in most EPs, the structure remained nominally linked to the theme. This time, it would be different. Reason: Suresh Bhavnani aka Lallu, the Sindhi guy from IDC who spoke with a nasal twang was in charge of the graphics, banners, artwork department and was a creative guy with an uncanny level of fussiness. So, after mulling over whether it was *Mein Kampf* or *Mein Kempf* which remained unresolved even after countless visits to the library and whether Hitler's swastika rotated clockwise or anti-clockwise as some devout Aryans claimed, H4 witnessed an endless engagement amongst its residents over the finest detail.

For the publicity, Lallu had done a fantastic job with creating imaginative posters and banners which were plastered all over the campus. He had also created a giant billboard measuring about 18 feet wide and about 9 feet tall which showed four hostelites in silhouette form hoisting a flag in the ground. This was tied to the big hedge near the entrance to the Main Building and it was not possible for anyone in IIT to miss it. He had also created some great slides accompanied by sounds of war taped from several sources to show during the intermission of the Friday evening Convo movie. The publicity was well detailed and a guaranteed winner, yet Ashvin Sanghvi aka Ghoda went one step further. He hit upon a brilliant idea of organizing a motorcade of the Fuhrer which would travel all over IIT between 5.30pm and 6pm on Friday evening when more than 2000 campus residents could be seen trudging on the campus roads en-route to Convo for their weekly movie thrill. There was just one teeny weeny problem. From where did one bring a car for Hitler? It was already Thursday and how could this be done within a day? Ghoda took a lot of flak for not dreaming up this gem of an idea earlier. What followed showed IITans at their audacious best. G Sec Deepak Patil aka Boss and Ghoda went and met the Registrar and asked him to loan us an institute car for an hour since it was required for 'hostel work'. The kindly Registrar did not think of asking why the car had to be black in colour as demanded by this persistent duo.

The news that the car would arrive on Friday was met with a lot of excitement within the hostel. Teams were quickly formed to detail every aspect of the motorcade. Electronic whiz kid Raghunath Iyer aka Radha rigged a bunch of capacitors, transistors and resistors to create an oscillator which could be fed to my gramophone speaker to create a siren sound. Except, it needed to be turned on and off every few seconds by touching two wires to each.

The next day, when the uniformed IIT driver Devarde drove into H4 and saw a big crowd waiting for him, he enquired casually if H4 guys wanted to ferry a VIP somewhere. A hundred heads nodded their assent. Shri Adolf Hitler was certainly a VIP by any stretch of imagination. While Devarde went to the mess to grab a quick tea, hordes of H4 residents descended on the shiny black car that was IIT's best and reserved for presidents, prime ministers, heads of state and Nobel laureates when they visited IIT. The action that followed must have inspired the current crews at Formula One race tracks who quickly fuel, repair flats, change tyres and apply the whole treatment on their team's car within seconds. Surely, one of these efficient, well practiced and professional crew members must have been in H4 on that fateful day in 1980 to learn how a car can be handled by dozens of people in a neat, well-synchronized operation which lasted no more than the time Devarde took to drink his tea. There were people, scissors, cello-tape, gum, cardboard, flags, posters, stickers in strong evidence. The bonnet masthead now sported a swastika flag instead of the usual Indian flag. All windows were covered with black cardboard to simulate a tinted windows effect. There were German emblems and insignia plastered all over the car. Radha was already seated in the front seat testing his blaring siren. Lallu had shaved off his moustache Hitler style and was seated in the back. I was seated beside Lallu wearing a huge khaki raincoat that passed off as an overcoat and was wearing large gumboots because I was to get out of the car at the Convo and march up to the projection room with the slides and sound cassette in my hand.

Rustam Sethna aka Quack owned a Yezdi mobike which was as black and as shiny as the IIT car and it helped that a fair

Bawa Rustam looked like a fairer German and he was to lead the motorcade. Soumitra Banerjee aka Baps, another black Yezdi owner but fair only as much as a Bengali can get, was to be at the rear left flank and he had roped in his mobike mechanic Vasant to bring up the rear right flank. Many hostelites had two-wheelers but they all were generally scooters or tame toys like Mini Rajdoots which would have looked better in Mickey Mouse's motorcade. Vasant the mechanic was roped in because he brought with him a stunning array of black Yezdis belonging to his various clients who were led to believe that Vasant was on a test run with their vehicle somewhere in IIT. All the mobikers were packed in huge oversized raincoats to pass off as expensive German overcoats and they all wore borrowed crash helmets (except Quack who owned his own) and huge glasses. Swastika armbands were tied around their arms. A puzzled Devarde who was amused initially and panicky later, tried calling the Registrar to tell him that the car is 'looking totally different' and 'it is looking like some circus car' was quickly dragged away from the phone and bundled off into the car. Meanwhile, about fifty freshies were dispatched to the NCC office close by and each picked up a .303 bore rifle and ran to the Convo where they assembled in a troop formation. They were to click their rifles, snap to attention and reach their hand out in salutation and shout *'Sieg heil'* every time the car passed them. As expected, the motorcade was a showstopper and was a sensational hit. All the movie buffs congregated outside the Convo and did not go in for all the time that the motorcade raced in and around the Convo roads, leading to traffic snarls. A couple of times, Quack forgot that he was leading a monster of a car and he quickly U-turned on narrow streets leading Devarde to exclaim, 'Does he think this car is a rope?' Radha wore out his finger by keeping it pressed on the two wires that connected to emit the siren sound. Vasant's mobike ran out of fuel toward the end, but since the motorcade was running dead slow at this stage, he paddled his mobike with his feet which went unnoticed. There were a couple of faculty members who were overheard talking about whether there was a revival of the Nazi movement and about who allowed these hooligans to enter IIT and why the security was nowhere to be seen. The slide show was a hit too and the publicity raised the overall expectation level from the EP that was to be staged in the ensuing week.

After the movie, all the rifles were put in a wheelbarrow and five freshies wheeled the barrow to the NCC office. The strict subedar on duty checked every single rifle and found a rotoring screw missing from two rifles and a deep scratch on another and refused to accept the goods despite much cajoling. Finally, Major Radhakrishnan was called and he looked at the rifles and frowned at the freshies and some of us before accepting the rifles back.

The very next day, there was a notice from the registrar that was pasted in all departments and hostels The notice read, 'All campus residents are requested to note that no institute car will be provided to anyone for any private purpose and no requisition for any car will be entertained at any cost.'

~

Perhaps it would have been better for us if they had not allowed any sort of vehicle in IIT—we managed to have mishaps even on bicycles. And I suppose, if they had banned all forms of transport, we would have bumped into each other while walking, some professors and some of us were lost in thought and lost track of our surroundings sometimes. But we did have long distances to travel, so some of us did get around on horses, and two wheelers both man powered and gas powered. And so, we did occasionally collide with one another. But that's never the whole story in IIT, and a collision is never just a collision.

In HSS 201 (second year humanities logics course) we were taught a humanities course on logic which started with the usual:

All Sikhs are Punjabis,
All Punjabis are Indians.
Therefore, all Sikhs are Indians.

Maybe the logician did not know about Canadian Sikhs but that is an irrelevant detail. The ultra-logical IITan applies logic in his own inimitable way.

Vijjy was the reigning queen of IIT. She was pretty, smart and articulate. She was a talented badminton player and a sensational singer, and she was the Soc Sec of H10. Understandably, she set a thousand hearts aflutter, and was stalked by a few hundred suitors at any given time. One evening, Vijjy was cycling up the slope outside the Convo after a gruelling game of badminton. I was mobiking down the same slope after a gruelling beer guzzling session at RK. I saw that she was cycling in zigzags in order to beat the severity of the slope. I was going in a straight line, despite my recent activity. Just near the Convo entrance, Vijjy lost control and meandered straight into my path. My reflexes worked to jam on my brakes fast enough. But my tires were balder than Prof. Kamath's pate and I slid right into her bike. As I dropped, I saw her fly backwards in slow motion and land on her head. I got up quickly though I had bruised my head and forearm, and saw that she had passed out. I was struggling to get her up on her feet, and scores of guys materialized from nowhere. Odd, I never saw such an enthusiastic mob during my other numerous accidents. They began to fight among themselves about who would hold what while carrying her to the hospi. Her mouth was bleeding and her head appeared to be injured too (I found out later that she had chipped her tooth, and she still carries this reminder with her). I yelled at the 'perverts' and managed to get them focused on getting her to the hospi as quickly as they could.

Once there, the lone nurse Patil Sister administered first aid as even more guys materialized from nowhere—they were now flocking to the hospi in hordes. Fortunately, someone had the sense to call her friends, and almost everyone from H10 arrived there. I sat there holding my head and waiting for my turn to get fixed up when Vijjy started mumbling 'Main kaun hoon? Main kahan hoon?' It was temporary amnesia—very temporary—but long enough to scare me out of my wits. It was after all I who had an accident with her, and something told me that knocking down Vijjy in IIT was tantamount to committing suicide. There would be a lynch mob after me, I was sure of that. I must have said something in my panic, because the girls quickly came over and comforted me. They assured me that the tetanus shot Patil Sister was about to administer 'won't hurt at all yaar!

It's just like a mosquito bite.' They supervised as Ms. Patil cut my hair, applied ointment to my injured scalp, and bandaged my forearm and foot.

Vijjy was taken to Rajawadi hospital in Ghatkopar—all serious cases beyond the capability of our hospi were diverted there. This made me even more panicky. Fortunately, the mob of angry young men disappeared as soon as Vijjy left, and only a few girls stayed to see that I was properly discharged.

Patil Sister said, 'See Bakul! All boys are coming and everyone is asking Vijaya how she is but nobody is asking you. Boys are very bad, no?' I concurred silently. She continued, 'But I am not like them. I asked you first and I put bandages on you, no?' I mumbled something about her not being a boy, and I got a playful pinch on my cheek and a 'You're a naughty boy!'

Shashank, Vijay and Birjoo came to the hospi on Shashank's Bullet. I couldn't kick-start my mauled bike with my injured foot, so they did it for me. News of the accident had reached H4, of course, and I was overjoyed to see a huge reception committee at the entrance when we got there. I felt loved and cared for. I hadn't even gotten off my mobike when a mob of guys surrounded me. They asked me what she was wearing, how she fell, whether I carried her to the hospi alone, where she was hurt, where she was now, what happened to her cycle, whether I got to see any privileged sites, and so on and so on. Someone had handed me Vijjy's case of shuttlecocks at some point, and one of my numerous interlocutors grabbed it and inspected every last shuttle cock. He then gave it back to me and asked if I would be going to Vijjy to return her case and wondered if he could come with me, as my friend.

Vijjy returned from Rajawadi the next day. Her face was bloated and badly bruised. Her Dad came for her, to take her home to Baroda. Before Vijjy left, I went to see her. Manjunath Pai chauffeured me there on his cycle, my aching foot wouldn't even let me walk without a limp, leave alone start a mobike. Vijjy greeted me with a handshake and said that she was sorry, and that it was her fault, and that she felt bad about putting me through so much agony. This gesture touched me. I quickly agreed that it was her fault and told her not to worry. She was welcome to get knocked down as often as she liked and I wouldn't feel agonized at all, I said. The girls in her room went into paroxysms of laughter and I realized what I had said. I scurried out quickly while muttering my next blooper, 'See you next accident.'

Back at the hostel, there was another mammoth reception committee awaiting me. News had spread that *She* shook my hand. How? Pai was with me the whole time and had not stopped anywhere to make a call. There were some friends of Vijjy's from H1 in her room, but they didn't look like the types who could spread this news beyond their own wing. Anyway, this time, my hand was almost pulled out of my body. Every guy vigorously shook my hand. A few attempted to take that hand toward their face and neck, at which point I reclaimed it in disgust. They thought of a new method. They shook my hand and then applied the molecules of that second-order handshake to their faces, lips, neck and wherever else they thought they needed to. For the first

time, I felt I might have been better off in Vijjy's shoes—
her head injury seemed preferable to this mental torture
from these logicians. Their logic—

A girl shook hands with Bakul
Bakul shook hands with me.
Therefore, the girl shook hands with me.

—*Bakul*

~

Accidental Engineering

10th August 1978 was a beautiful day. It was the start of
our second year, we were designated seniors, we could
legitimately rag freshies, and today was Pagal Gymkhana.
All freshies from all hostels would be gathered at the
Gymkhana and be subject to participating in funny contests
like playing basketball with a rugby ball, wheeling three fat
guys around in a wheelbarrow, wheeling themselves down
on 'auto-pilot, playing hop-skip and squash in specially
prepared swampy mud and so on. To top it all, Soumitra's
dad had bought him a swanky new black Yezdi mobike with
a 250cc engine. The eighteen-year-olds among us would
take this Yezdi on a spin and vroom-vroom all over IIT and
experience the thrills associated with biking while attempting
acrobatics. This event paved the way for me to ask my folks
for a bike too, they belonged to the wait-and-watch-for-
who-else's-parents-are stupid-like-us school of thought.

After tiffin and before the Pagal Gym event, when G Sec
Manu requested us to run an errand, we did not need a
second invitation. Any excuse to race off on this Yezdi

monster was enough. And so, Soumitra rode while I pillion-
ed on this pleasant evening with a gentle light breeze
blowing through our hair and an expectation of a spectacular
evening blowing through our minds.

My last memory about this ride is that on this same
pleasant evening with a good breeze teasing our hair, I
could see the trees that lined both sides of this desolate
road near the Mechanical Engg workshops. The trees, in
their resplendent green glory, moved from front to back.
That is the way we had come to see things after two
semesters of instruction on frames of reference, where we
posited ourselves as stationary reference points and described
motions with respect to us. So there we were, assumed
stationary while the glorious trees on both sides of the
roads sped from front to back at a brisk 70 kph.

I am still hazy about what happened but I distinctly
remember Soumitra (Baps) swearing out aloud and jamming
on the brakes. Suddenly, the tyres were sliding on the road
and not spinning. The resplendent green glorious creatures
were now moving from left to right at the same brisk 70 kph
and not from front to back any more. There were two
parallel lines of trees. One moved from left to right in front
and the other moved from left to right at our back. There
was a sound of metal clashing with meek metal. Heavy steel
mudguards clashing with bicycle spokes. A sound of a kid
crying out more in fright and less in pain. The sound of my
entire right side sliding on a hard metalled road. Shoulder,
arm, thigh, knee and leg.

During the skid, I noticed Baps also skidding in front but
in the manner of an athlete who had a preview of what was

to come and had adjusted his posture so as to receive minimum damage. Despite the panic, the survival instinct in us made us quickly gather all parts of ourselves and jump on the still running mobike and head straight for the IIT hospital nicknamed Hospi and also referred to as a mortuary for a very good reason. And while driving to the hospi, we espied three girls from our class, Rita, Lakshmi and Gowri, out on their evening walk. They were walking on our left. This was a great opportunity to show off our bike and to show off the macho bikers in us. Even while we were wincing in pain, we vroom vroomed some more and waved at them with our intact left arms, hiding our ghastly mutilated right sides from their view.

This specific incident was the starting point of our fight in the hospi as we lay on our beds facing the same morbid white walls hour after hour for the next three days. 'How can you even think of waving to the girls while you are in this state?' Baps would ask. And I would quip that if he was man enough to vroom vroom in front of them, why should I not wave?

The kid we had supposedly run over but who, as it turned out later, got away with just minor bruises was the eight-year-old son of IIT bus driver Gaikwad. Kid was small, his cycle was huge and he was attempting to ride it with his legs going through the triangle of the bars instead of over them. Gaikwad himself had run someone over the previous year—run over and killed, actually, and IIT was defending the case that was ongoing. Be that as it may, this Gaikwad rushed to the Bhandup police station to lodge a complaint, and, soon enough, the cops arrived at the hospi with

Security Officer Singh, Warden Lakkad and G Sec Manu in tow. I was drugged and groggy and did not respond to the attempts to wake me up. In this sedated state, I heard the nurse telling the cops that I had been administered a huge dose of Calmpose and the doctor's advice was that my statement be recorded in three days.

The spirit of camaraderie within IIT was evident to us all through this ordeal. Throughout the day, we had a retinue of visitors checking up on us. Friends, wingmates, hostelmates, classmates on their way back from lectures, mess-workers, watchmen—just about anybody we knew in IIT came to look us up, and many even came with fruits, sweets and treats. So when Manu asked us if we wanted anything else, we got greedy and asked him to send three of the choicest freshies to our ward to entertain us.

Thus it came to pass that Gautam Mukherjee, Avinash Deshpande and Ashish Khosla came to us during lunch to entertain us and to get ragged. Ashish Khosla took our leave to go for a lab assignment but he arranged a replacement in the form of Shailesh Sabnis. Dr. Puniyani was not amused to hear Sabnis singing 'My name is Anthony Gonsalves' to the tune of *Jana Gana Mana* at two in the afternoon in a ward full of patients. But we argued that we were homesick and this is what we would have been doing at H4 which was our home. We were discharged three days later, and we thought our ordeal had ended. My wounds had not healed but my anxious parents had arranged for my anxious cousins to pick me up from hospi and take me to their home and see that I was properly repaired. On my return to IIT a week later, I learnt that we had a new complication. Gaikwad had been persuaded to withdraw his complaint but the cops had booked two cases and one of them was not withdraw-able. Baps would have to be arrested, produced in court, and sentenced. The only way out was to let the case slip-and-slide into the black hole of the archives, and be written off as 'unsolved'. Unfortunately however, a new SI named Naik took over Bhandup and came to IIT to arrest Baps. Baps was away at home for the weekend. So I had to step in. To be honest, I was deriving thrills from this adventurous bout of playing cop and robbers. So I gave the officer a 'solemn undertaking' and my 'word of honour' that I was 'singularly responsible' to ensure that 'the accused Soumitra Banerjee, s/o Dr. Satyesh Chandra Banerjee' would 'surrender himself to the law within 24 hours'. I remember Officer Naik smirked as I was reciting all this and asked me if I saw many Hindi movies.

Anyway, we all gathered at the police station next day and broke into an applause as Naik signed an order and said, 'You are arrested' and applauded again when he said, 'You are released' after another five seconds. Naik advised us to hold our applause until after the actual court proceedings were over.

What followed in the form of court proceedings was an education in the depth of disrepair, and of non-repairability the system of Indian legal jurisprudence had slid into. Here was an accused who said he was not guilty. The accuser Gaikwad said that the accused was not guilty. The cops said that everything was nice and fine and no one was guilty of anything. Yet, the court summoned Baps three times over a whole year to the Mulund court.

The first time Baps engaged a lawyer called Mamalde (appropriately named—he looked like a jar of marmalade with his puffed up cheeks and his multiple chins that wobbled every time he said, 'Your honour!'). Baps sat in the court from morning to evening and saw hundreds of guys coming in and going out. Different people stood up at different times and said something to the judge. The judge spoke off and on and generally scribbled notes in a paper. When court ended at 5pm and Baps walked up to Mamalde and asked what happened, Mamalde casually remarked that the 'matter was disposed' that morning and had been rescheduled for some date six months later. Six months later, when Baps went to the court and 'the matter' did come up, some lawyer told the judge that the proceedings could not continue because PM Morarji Desai was visiting Pune on Tuesday. The judge nodded and agreed. The bewildered Baps tried to reason with Mamalde: 'What does Morarji's visit have to do with this case? This is Mumbai, not Pune. Today is Friday, not Tuesday. I am Banerjee. Not Desai. Can we not finish this chapter here and now?' Clearly, logic and reason did not work in the Mulund court which posted the next hearing (hearing? Who was hearing anyway?) to a date in December, six months later.

I got urgent summons from Baps during the end of December vacations to rush to Mumbai because Mamalde wanted me to be a witness and depose before the judge. I was excited enough to cut short my vacation in order to participate in a court proceeding. What should I say? 'Objection your honour!' as they said in movies? or 'point note *kiya jaaye* milord'? and, should I angrily pace up and down before the judge or should I stay put in the witness

183

box? And should I swear on the Gita? Or should I find out the name of the holy book of Jainism and swear on that?

To say that compared to the exciting trip to Mumbai and countless rehearsals before the mirror, the reality was a damp squib would be an understatement. The case was announced and Mamalde got up. I got up too, to walk to a 'box' that I could not see. Mamalde pushed me down and said to the judge with all his rippling and wobbling chins, 'Your honour! My client is pleading guilty and I request your lordship to take a lenient view in the matter since the accused is a young boy,' and sat down, as a bewildered Baps and I stared at each other in shocked disbelief.

The judge was chewing paan, did not have the sedate and sober look that we were accustomed to seeing in movies and said something like, 'What rubbish you are talking man? It is matter of life and death and you are talking about leniency. Pay Rs 350. Next case'. Mamalde and his chins then tried to earn their Rs 150 per session. He asked the judge for a student discount. The judge warned him, 'If you try to bargain, I will increase to 400. Sit down. Next case.' End of trial. End of my dream of appearing as a witness for the defence. End of my dream of seeing India rise above myriad bureaucracy into an efficient well oiled machine. End of this very long story.

—*Bakul*

～

Sometimes our collisions were not vehicular, and ended us up at the dreaded hospi. There was a reason it was dreaded. And the reason was all the stories we heard, those of us who were lucky. Those who were not, were the ones who got to tell those stories.

This is a gruesome but true story. Those with a faint heart may want to skip it and move on.

There was a water-fight going on. Typically, one never knew when, where or how they started. The prudent thing always was to join the water-fight right away. If you did not, and locked your room door, buckets of water would come splashing in from above the door, drenching your books, bed and everything else in the tiny room.

Adi Asavaid came running round the corner on the top floor of the middle wing with a bucket in his hand, slipped on the wet floor and after a brief flight, landed heavily on the floor banging his head.

We ran to him immediately, and saw that he was bleeding. I put some newspapers below his head, and we started to work on stopping the bleeding from his forehead. After a couple of minutes we were confused. The more successful we were in taking care of the bleeding from the cut near the temple, the bigger the spreading red spot on the newspaper became. So we turned Adi over, and found a deep gash at the back of his head. It was time to rush him to the hospi.

We got to the hospi in less than five minutes and were in the ER. The doctor was available. He looked at Adi's head, and then at me, and said, 'stitching'. It took me a few seconds to understand, until he said again, 'Stitching. Required.' So poor Adi who was moaning and groaning in pain all this while, was flipped over on the table, and a nurse began trimming the hair around the wound so it could be stitched. Adi kept on pleading with me, 'Stay with me. Please stay with me, don't go away!'

The nurse was doing a good efficient job, when the doctor suddenly said, 'Stop. He will do it', and pointed to this young guy lurking in the corner. Hesitantly, I said to the doctor, 'Sir, this lady is already doing a good job'. But the doc said, 'No! He will do it. He must do it.' He even offered me an explanation. 'This boy interviewed at another hospital last week, and was rejected for being incompetent. How can we allow this? The reputation of the IIT Hospital is at stake. He needs practice.' Adi, in pain, would not let go of my arm.

So this guy loped over from the corner and took the scissors from the other nurse. This is when the gruesome stuff started. The guy's hand was so shaky that he kept on poking the scissors in the wound, rather than snipping the hair. This went on and on. I couldn't stand it and had to look away. Adi was bravely clenching his teeth tight. His grip on my wrist was so tight, I don't think any blood reached my right hand for ten minutes.

Now the doctor said 'OK' and brandished an evil-looking curved needle, with a thread through it. I winced. Fortunately Adi, having got relief from the scissors wielding guy, did not see the size of the needle. The doctor then proceeded with the stitching, going back and forth through the holes to make sure the thread went through. There was no local anaesthetic or any medication used. And then he appeared to tie-up the wound a little less carefully than what I do when I tie my shoelaces.

That was not the end of the story. When Adi went home for the weekend, he visited his family doctor, who said that the wound was infected, and Adi had to have the wound stitched all over again.

(Yes, Adi did recover, and he spent several exciting years working and travelling all over the US, and Central and South America. He currently lives happily in Pennsylvania with his wife Maria Elena.)

A week later, we were playing volleyball between the last two wings. Someone miss-hit a shot, and I ran way beyond the edge of the court, into the grass, to retrieve the shot. Some idiot had thrown an empty beer bottle in the grass.

It had broken and the bottom of the bottle was lying there, with its jagged edge pointing upwards. My left foot landed on it with my full weight of 60 kg.

So it was my turn to be taken to the Hospi. We met the same doctor, who looked at the huge amount of blood and the two deep bleeding gashes. Expressionlessly, he said the same thing he had said in Adi's situation. 'Stitching'.

A shiver ran through me, and I had vivid visions of what poor Adi had gone through. I said, 'No. No stitching. Just medicate and bandage.' The doctor warned me that I would need crutches and would not be able to walk for four-to-six-weeks. I said 'I'll stay on the crutches for six months, if that what it will take.'

—*Vikram (Vicky) Modak, '69-'74*

~

The nurses were sometimes helpful, though. And sometimes even pretty. Though for us this meant only that they had to be of the female persuasion.

Sometime in my second or third year, I developed a bad habit of scratching the inside of my ear canal with anything handy—a tightly rolled piece of paper torn from the corner of a newspaper was the best thing and really hit the spot. One day, after tiffin, I was waiting my turn to join a volleyball game between the middle and north wings. The attire in which people played was colourful, and mostly inappropriate for sporting activity. For example, Ghatkopar would always play with a lungi on.

Volleyball in those days was played mostly by amateurs, and the few professionals who knew how to bump, set and hit would get very frustrated. Shenoy was a good passer, Punter was a good hitter, Idi Amin served well. Limaye had his height to his advantage, but he would almost always come in the way at the wrong moment. That is why he got the moniker of 'Latkoo'. And there would be spectators for the game perched high up in the wings saying things like

'Service *hai!*'

'Latkoo net mein phir Latka hai!'

And for no reason someone like Chetan Shah would say— 'Ghaaaarpoooore!'

Fumbling was called out as *'Hugga hai!'*. And HK was a famous fumbler—and his permanent name became 'Hagoo Kumar' or 'Ech koo'.

Anyway. I digress.

So, as I was waiting, my inner ear began to itch. I looked around where I was sitting and found a perfect bit of dry grass. I plucked it and tried to satisfy the itch. It was a bit too pliable, so I doubled it up at the end and continued. Click—I let go one end and it opened within the ear. So I had the short end of the v inside and the really long one sticking outside. If I pushed it in, the pointy part of the V would pierce my eardrum and if I pulled, the short end began to draw blood. After a few tries, I panicked. So I asked Shenoy, sitting next to me watching the game, to help.

The next thing I know, the volleyball game stopped, and there were a dozen people around me, each trying to help get it out. And as they tried it got worse. The peanut gallery yelled out remarks thick and fast in the vein of 'oye horses eat hay with their mouths, not their ears', to make matters worse for me.

Finally Baps offered to take me to the hospi. So now here I am, on the back of the bike, racing toward the hospi with a two foot long piece of hay sticking out of my ear, waving in the breeze. We get there and the crazy doctor started pulling like a barbarian. He was making it worse. Thankfully for me, he was called away for a phone call (something about a med cert perhaps?) leaving me at the tender mercy of the nurse. I pleaded with her to do something before he returned. The nurse saved me. She used a pair of tweezers and efficiently solved the problem in ten seconds flat. Whew!

—*Ghoda*

~

Yes, nurses were among the few women in our testosterone filled lives.

Blood suckers, I mean the blood bank, visited hostels at least once a year. They would be in the lounge as we strolled back from classes in the afternoon for tiffin. Most students gave their blood. Once the crew had a pretty (I don't claim to be objective) nurse. We set a record for blood donation that day.

One year, a few of us were eating our Glucose biscuits after our donation (usual procedure: give blood, eat Glucose biscuits and drink coffee or tea). John (aka Dharma) finished last. He, however, fainted as he was getting up. He might have missed his lunch that day. We immediately put him on the sofa and the nurse came over to check on him. After a few minutes he came back to life. When he inquired what had happened, we told him he was out for quite a while and that they had turned his donated bottle of blood upside down and returned it to him. He was so convinced that he went to the nurse and asked her.

Those blood suckers were from Rajawadi hospital, and the nurse was huge, spectacled and middle-aged, and yet she sent the blood pressure high enough for the blood to flow out freely. Maybe John's blood overflowed while he looked at that nurse.

—*Raj*

～

We did go to the hospi voluntarily on occasion. When we needed medical certs. Medical certs were needed when we were about to face the consequences of missing lectures, not having the required GPA, not having studied for a test, and so on.

The hospi was a trading zone for medical certificates also known as med certs. It was well established that if you had a med cert from the hospi, it was a fake one. If you were genuinely ill and went to the hospi, it would have been unlikely that you would recover in time to carry a med cert back and submit it wherever required. So just like the stock market or any other commodity trading house, people queued up outside the doc's door, coughed unconvincingly when they went in, and asked for certificates. Most IITans have availed of at least one cert in their life and a few dealt in certs in a 'bulk' or a wholesale fashion including, I have to admit, me. The doc was the same, the patient was the same, the symptoms were the same, the cert was the same. It's only the date that changed after each fishing expedition.

In my first year, Dr Bilangadi was the head doc of the hospi. I was genuinely sick and I mistakenly thought that the hospi would be able to cure me. So I made my maiden trip there, stood in a long out-patient line, and watched as patient after healthy patient came out of the doc's room with a large piece of paper and a larger smile on their face. Surprisingly, many of the cert carrying patients were profs and not just students.

When I finally walked in to the doc's office, I was wheezing pretty badly, my temperature had risen to 103 degrees, and I thought I would faint. Dr. Bilangadi was an ageing but garrulous man. He glanced at my empty case sheet, read my name and said, 'Well, Mr Desai! I think we are getting late.

Let's rush. Will you take your certificate on the way back after the show?' Either my fever had climbed so much that I was hearing some gibberish or maybe Dr Billi-something was losing it. What cert? What way back? What show? Oh! Didn't I know that the Russian Ballet was about to start in the adjoining Convo hall and many students and many more profs had just taken lots of certs and walked out hand in hand with certs in their other hand to the Convo and Dr Billi-whatever was also rushing there and he would hold my hand and walk with me if I agreed to take the cert later.

This was my first experience, and last shock. Circumstances soon altered and made me a cert tycoon within IIT. So much so that my reputation (or notoriety) spread far and wide and my good friends helped spread it further. During a Navratri do at H10 three years later, I saw Niru and five other girls walk up to Ghoda. Niru pointed towards me and asked Ghoda, 'Shall we ask him?' and I saw Ghoda nodding. Niru and the girls (I remember Nina Wakhankar, Bhawani Laxman, Shobha Veer Raghav from amongst them) came up to me and told me that this Navratri function was going to stretch late into the night and they wanted to bunk the next day's test, and how should they go about getting a med cert? I was appalled. What made them think I could guide them to a med cert? Oh come on! They all knew. It was common knowledge.

The system had degenerated to such an extent that no prof was willing to believe any cert that originated from IIT's hospi. Prof. Shankar from the Elec department was teaching a course called EE 301 which every IITan had to take irrespective of their own department. Not only did Shankar generally set a tough paper, he was also an angry-not-so-young-man when it came to giving out grades. There was always a fear psychosis before his tests, and, understandably, as many as eighteen folks chose to duck his first test. Most were from H4. The hopeful plan was that there would be a re-test announced for all who produced a med cert, and hopefully, a re-test would be set by someone else.

When we checked with Shankar, he was clear that he would not conduct a re-test and would fail all guys who bunked his test. Satish Baliga protested that all were actually ill on the same day and yes, while eighteen folks falling sick on one day was improbable, it was not impossible, and that we would all have med certs to prove our point. Shankar reluctantly agreed to a re-test but his condition was clear. A cert issued by IIT hospi would not do. 'You know and I know that anyone can go there and get a certificate for any disease, even cancer', he said, and he was not far from the truth at all.

The solution to this new problem came from a pad of letterheads of one Dr R.A. Shah who was Shashank's uncle. Shashank had gifted me with this letter pad to deal with emergencies arising out of my lucrative business with IIT hospi going bust at some point. Just the kind of emergency, in fact, that we were faced with.

Finally, eighteen of us were seen writing the re-test as Prof. Shankar went from table to table collecting the certificate. When he had collected his tenth, he exclaimed aloud, 'This Dr Shah seems to be a good doctor. All of you are going all the way to Vile Parle to get treated by him and he has analyzed a common disease for you and has advised the same one week rest for all of you. Please tell me his address after this test so that I can also go some time and get treated by him.'

—*Bakul*

~

Keni needed a medical-cert for some Homo-exam he had missed. Homo was a notorious prof in the elec dept named MS Kamath. He was known as Homo because he screwed guys through his dangerous tests and exams. Homo was also wise to hospi-doc-certs. He did not accept them. After a couple of Thomas ek pachaas at RK (RK was an Udipi restaurant known as Hotel Radhakrishna across from the main gate of IIT and was a popular hangout, and later, served beer. 'Thomas-ek-pachaas' is code for a round of drinks. You tell a waiter generally named Thomas to get you ek pachaas—one round of 50 ml of brew), we went to see a lady doctor who was known to give out med-certs for a fee. We slipped in past her legit patients. She asked Keni what he was suffering from, and he admitted to 'very high fever and stomach pains'. She saw through him, and told him she didn't have time to waste and asked point blank if he needed a med-cert. She asked him for Rs 15. Keni fished around in all his pockets, emptied out all his change on her table, and since it wasn't close to the demanded amount, he looked at me for help. I explored and dug out what I had, and between us, we managed Rs 8.45.

By now the lady-doc was fuming, and when asked to accept all the change as payment and give us a cert she exploded. 'I am doing you a favour and you are asking me to count chutta-paisa instead of treating patients who are really sick?'

Unperturbed, Keni said, 'Sorry ma'am, but since it is only about Rs.10, could you sign off just high fever for that amount?'

We were kicked out of her office of course. But not before Keni had whacked off a page from the lady-doc's medical pad. We walked back to H4 happy. To this day, I don't think I have retrieved my share of the change that Keni had so deftly returned to his pockets when he saw where the situation was headed. He also got his med-cert for free.

I learned something about staying cool that day. One of the many 'Truly Higher Education' lessons we all learned while at IIT.

—*Dabba*

~

These 'Truly Higher Education' lessons came in unexpected ways. We just had to keep our eyes and ears open for them. And sometimes we were not at all sure what lesson was learned.

Bakul and I found out about an Institute employee in an important position who was taking bribes from students. His position affected all students. Neither Bakul nor I were jaded enough then to say 'Yeah so what's new.' Today, I am not so sure. But back then we were more idealistic, or so I like to think. In fact, we were outraged enough to do something about this man. Much as I would like to think our motivation was altruistic, I have a suspicion that we were, at best, concerned about students having to spend their cigarette and booze money on bribes. At worst, we were bored. Neither of us realized we were in IIT to study, and we needed to occupy ourselves somehow.

We decided a sting operation was called for. We had to find someone who would be unrecognizable by Mr. Bribery and Corruption. My friend Vish was a student in a different Engineering college, and Bakul and I used all our skills of persuasion (hitherto reserved for professors to give us re-tests or better grades) to convince him. He reluctantly agreed. We planned the sting operation and Vish's cover meticulously. Bakul procured a small tape recorder, which in those pre-open-market days, was no mean feat. Then we got Vish to call Mr B&C and say he had a private matter to discuss and could he come to his house to discuss it. Mr B&C predictably took the bait. probably guessing what this private matter was about. Bakul and I accompanied Vish to the vicinity Mr. B&C's house. Then we waited out of sight, delighted at the prospect of a successful sting which would shake the foundations of IIT.

Half an hour later, Vish returned. We are bursting with excitement. 'Did he take the bait?' we asked him.

'Oh yes!' Vish happily reported.

'Great. We can now nail the bastard.'

Vish hesitated and squirmed and said, 'Not really.'

'What do you mean not really? We have the tape. You have done IIT a stellar service,'

'Well, just as I was about to turn on the tape recorder in my pocket, his four-year-old kid came in.'

'So?' asked Bakul and I wondering why Vish was rambling about some damn kid when we had the scoop of the year in hand.

'He was adorable,' said Vish.

'So bloody what?' we said exasperated.

'So I did not turn on the tape recorder,' said Vish sheepishly.

Bakul and I were too stunned to say anything.

'I mean he would definitely be sacked over this and this poor kid would suffer. I did not have the heart to do this,' pleaded Vish.

'But he did agree to take the bribe?' we asked.

'Oh yes. You guys were absolutely right about that,' said Vish as if that would give us any comfort. I did not know whether to laugh or to cry. This seemed to be right out of a Wodehouse novel. All our planning and all our dreams of getting Mr B&C fired had come to naught because of the unforeseen twist that Vish was unduly fond of children.

Mr.B&C was employed for a few more years and embroiled in a legal battle with IIT. Probably put that adorable kid through college with all the money he earned on the side. What lesson we learned, I don't yet know. That bribery and corruption sometimes win out over altruism? Or that good does not always triumph? Or that our questionable motivations tainted the result?

—*Fish*

~

Unlike most professors, Prof. S Balasubramaniam, who styled himself as Yuss Balasubramaniam, was a tall lanky man. Like most professors, he wore specs and like a few others, he had a loud, booming and an imposing voice. Like all Balasubramaniams in the world, he was referred to as Bala. And totally unlike any known professor, Bala professed some lofty objectives and decided that he was a good Samaritan who would make time during evenings and discharge some social responsibility. Within his means was a short brisk walk to the hospi. Bala rightly reckoned, especially in our beloved hospi, that sick and ailing patients needed alternative medicine in the form of someone reaching out to them, showing concern, giving them a pep talk and engaging in some light banter with them. Bala had also learnt that prolific preachers like Buddha and Mahavira reached out to their followers by speaking in the language of the masses. Pali and Prakrit, not some tongue-twisting cryptic Sanskrit shlokas. His electrical wizard brain that delved on circuits and switches during the day had correctly deduced that Hindi was the language of the masses in these parts. Unfortunately, someone forgot to tell him that one needed to learn Hindi before one spoke it.

So on day one of his divine mission, Bala moved from ward to ward, smiled at patients, reached out for the case paper that was hung on a patient's bed, squinted through his glasses at the paper and exclaimed in the same loud booming voice. What he boomed was meant to convey, 'What has happened to you?' or in Hindi, *'Tumhe kya ho gaya hai?'* But his Tamilian Hindi actually boomed, *'Tumhara kya hoga?'*—'What is to become of you?'

A frail and an ailing patient is susceptible to what anyone wearing specs says, and even more so when he booms it so loud and clear.

It is rumoured that Bala managed to accelerate a few heart attacks before they were due.

~

To top off the horrors in our hospi, one day IIT decided to open a psychiatry department. The huge captive market for psycho cases in IIT were outsourced to Shushrusha Hospital in town. Some wise administrator decided to have a psychiatrist visit the hospi twice a week for three hours. When business picked up, and everyone was sure it would, they would open a full-fledged facility with the works, couch and all.

~

Fish on the Couch

Ashvin Iyengar aka Fish was convinced that he was in dire need of psychiatric help. And everyone he spoke to concurred vigorously with him. Fish was taking Dr. Rehana Ghadially's psycho class and figured out that all his idiosyncratic behaviour of touching walls and patting his own back with his leg and walking with a cat named Billee tucked under his armpit were signs of some deep psychosomatic symptoms which needed immediate attention.

So when Fish walked into the 'inaugural session' of the new doc-come-lately to IIT's hospi, the doc was overjoyed. The lanky specimen who stood before him looked like a research subject. His twitches, his callisthenic motions and his general demeanour were going to be a challenge to unravel and Dr Psycho loved challenges. Of course, he did not know that if anyone came to the hospi for a 'cure' and not for a free medical certificate (med cert), he definitely needed his head examined. In short, one went to the hospi for either a med cert or for committing legitimate suicide or because the patient was a psycho.

Not only did Fish have a problem, he also knew what the problem was. And thanks to Dr. Ghadially, he knew all the psycho jargon that described his ailment. So when the doc asked Fish to start talking, he had hoped to hear something about why Fish found cats so erotic. But our Fish was a man who had analyzed his own problems and wanted to share only the analysis with the kindly Doc. Hence, some Fish-isms which came to the fore were, 'I am certain that I suffer from obsessive compulsive neurosis. This induces certain behavioural patterns that lead to debilitating anxiety. If I could convert it into facilitating anxiety, them my anxiety would spur me to clear all my exams but the debilitation takes precedence over a potential facilitation on account of certain suppressed insecurities that overwhelm me. Dealing with these latent insecurities is possible only when I remove the shroud over the catalysts which trigger my obsessive and compulsive neurotic behaviour.' And it went on and on for a few more minutes. The amazed doc had stopped taking notes for a while now and he got up and moved to a counter in the corner of the room and took out a bottle and took out 2 pills from it. Fish was elated. The doc understood Fish's problem since he had described it so correctly and saved him a lot of time trying to analyze what the clever Fish had already done. And now the doc was going to prescribe two pills to Fish to shoot the anxieties and neuroses out of his bowels the next morning and suddenly, Fish would be a normal man. He would stop touching walls, he would stop humming melancholic numbers from *Pyaasa*, he would treat a cat like a cat and he would stop imagining that he was getting jilted by anybody and everybody and maybe, he would start attending lectures and maxing tests.

The doc moved slowly and silently to another corner of a room now and filled a glass with water. And just as Fish rose to receive the glass and pills and say 'Thank you', the doc quickly swallowed the pills, drank it off with water and rang his bell and called out, 'Next patient please.'

This was on a Tuesday. The next day allotted for the psycho was Thursday. On Thursday, the long line of waiting patients was told that the doc had not come and the psycho sessions were 'cancelled' until further notice. Fish had managed to drive the doc far away and maybe back to the medical college to do a repeat course in psychiatry.

~

Though there were not many Fishes who would voluntarily place themselves on the psychiatrist's couch, there were several who ought to have done so. They wouldn't agree of course. Swimmers who plunged into a lake full of crocodiles in spite of the threat of arrest, pigeon eaters and pigeon keepers, monkey impersonators—they all came into H4 the way they were. But some were surely driven to the couch by the demands of academia, the lack of plentiful female companionship, the daily culinary disappointments, to say the least. Sometimes corroboration about the mental state of IITans came from unexpected quarters.

In my second or third year, I was once standing in a queue at the ticket counter at Vikhroli station. Just ahead of me was Gautam Mukherjee from C83 (class of '83). He startled me by asking the ticket clerk to issue him 'one Vikhroli ticket'. Here was a guy asking for a ticket to Vikhroli from Vikhroli. A ripple of amused laughter ran through the queue. Those who hadn't heard Gautam were quickly updated by those who had, and soon, there was a lot of sniggering which clearly embarrassed Gautamda. What was more surprising however was the fact that the ticket clerk was totally unfazed. He just cast a deadpan look at Gautam and asked casually 'IIT student? Dadar or VT?'

When it was my turn to purchase a ticket I asked the clerk how on earth he had deduced that Gautam was an IIT kid. He wasn't wearing any IIT T-shirt, and he was actually wearing shoes and not the trademark slippers. The clerk was very candid. According to him, there were at least ten IITans everyday who asked for a ticket to Vikhroli. Clearly, he did not see an IITan in me because he went on to remark, 'People say, and I have heard, IIT students are walking brains. But I've never seen crazier lunatics, I can tell you that.' He also went on to wonder how can a guy be brainy if he uses the overhead bridge to go to a platform when he can easily do it by crossing the tracks.

Come to think of it, commuting in Mumbai was an unenviable task. We braved the sun and rains to walk from H4 to YP, waited in a queue and took a bus when and if it came, got off at Vikhroli and walked to the station, stood in a long queue at the counter to buy a ticket to travel like a sardine in a jam-packed chamber with dirty, stinky, sweaty bodies all the while thinking of an upcoming KD Joshi test, In this exhausted absent frame of mind, it is remarkable that we didn't ask for a ticket to Saturn and stayed sane enough to say Vikhroli.

—Bakul

∼

Manucination

Sometime in late '77, H4 was rocked by ghost sightings. This could be an indication of questionable mental stability within H4. Or maybe they were really visitations from another dimension. In any case, there were lots of rumours floating around but three guys in particular swore about the truth of their spooky experience. Mess worker More (the mental state of mess workers was never in question, if we go by what they considered fit for human consumption day after day) was temporarily occupying a room in NWGF left side. More said he was awoken in the night to find his door open. He saw a woman beckoning him to step out. More sprang from his bed and ran straight into what he thought was an open door and hurt his nose. He rushed into the mess and saw Manu there who claimed to have undergone a similar experience at the same time. Apparently, Manu experienced himself as a planchet object being pushed around in the lounge. Manu saw Satish Joshi sitting in the lounge, he tried to reach out and ask him to free Manu from the planchet where he was trapped. Manu was in SWFF, and his wingmate Datar said he had woken up to see a man sitting in his chair and staring down at him. All this supposedly happened the same night and guys were talking about it for many days and wondering whether to believe these stories or not.

I went to Manu to learn about his experience firsthand. Manu's said to me,' Look, I'll tell you everything. But if you come up with the same halwanation story as everyone else, I'll really be pissed off.'

'Halwanation? What's that?' I asked Manu.

'I have no idea. That bloody Ponga tells me every day, 'Manu! You have had a halwanation."

I laughed so hard that Manu refused to tell me the story. I'm sure it didn't help with establishing anyone's sanity. I had begun to doubt my own.

—*Bakul*

~

The ghosts were not the result of any of the substances some of us investigated during our H4 life. But there was a tradition of bhang at Holi time, and that brought on episodes and events whose memories are tainted by time and our altered states at the time. The H4 bhang was particularly awesome. The newly christened 'Dina Colada' was the 'Power Holi (or Holy) Drink' to begin with, first introduced by none other than Power Hiren in 1976. The Bhang Technology was transferred to Dina after Power left in 1977. Power used not one, not two, but three brand new one naya paisa copper coins, and God knows how much time he spent stirring the bhang. The bottom line was that after the bhang was all gone, no one could find a trace of those coins. It was more likely that we couldn't spot them after all that bhang than that they had assimilated into the brew, but, we cannot be certain.

I heard rumours but I don't personally remember whether anyone went to the hospital or threw up anything but one thing was sure—whoever visited NWSF (room no. 218) on that fateful Holi day between 1pm and 1am would never forget the miracle that took place in our historic H4.

The hill facing North Wing had been there for ages, is still there and will stay there. After lunch, Potty went back to his room and was lying on his bed relaxing and staring at it through the open door. Suddenly he focused on the hill and realized that he could read the hill's mind. He began to translate for us mortals what the hill was thinking, what the trees on the hill were feeling and so on. And then, his face changed. He went white, the face lost its gloss and Potty was shit scared.

The hill, he said, was actually thinking of coming to H4. He read its mind further. It had a reason to come to H4. It wanted to target H4. And then he had more clarity. The hill was not actually targeting H4 or NWSF or even room no. 218. The real target was Potty. The hill wanted to squash him. Poor guy was simply relaxing on his bed looking at the hill through the open door and giving us the experience of a lifetime by providing a glimpse of his Divya Dhrushti by reading the hill's mind, when he found out what the hill intended to do.

Potty, without getting out of the bed started pleading to the hill not to advance towards him. He was like a sick man lying on the bed crying out to the Yamaraj to go back. That didn't work, the hill was inching forward slowly but surely. With menacing looks it was telling Potty (or rather he was reading its mind because mortals like us couldn't see or hear anything when we looked at the hill) that was coming to his room to flatten him under its belly.

Potty's requests had no impact on the hill's intentions, and he turned to us for help. He urged us to stop the hill right away and tie it down firmly with tough iron chains. We said we couldn't do that, we didn't have chains and it would take hours for someone to go to Vikhroli or Ghatkopar to bring some in a truck. Plus we didn't have cash to buy chains, and who could lift them and tie the hill? Potty pleaded with us, saying, 'Guys, you don't know what you are capable of, you can actually move mountains.' Selva (Junglee), he said, could certainly do so. 'But please, please save me today!'

We wished what he said about us was true. One or two people tried to stop the hill but failed miserably. Potty came up with a brilliant idea (still lying on his bed and fearfully looking at the hill through the open door). He said, 'Guys, please get out of my room and close the door, lock it from inside and lock it from outside. close the window as well, and yes, take the keys away with you. Go to the lounge. This way, the hill can't reach me.' This solution was discussed and debated for hours, and scrutinized for any weakness . Many great brains of H4 participated and contributed to plug any holes and ensure 100% success.

Finally at 1am, it was decided that it was the best solution. Potty started breathing a bit normally then. We closed and locked the window and door of Potty's room and switched off the light as well so that the hill couldn't see him.

Only after that Potty got some peace and relief, and could go to sleep. When he awoke after God knows how many hours, he was greeted by the open door and open window. Hill was where it was, stripped out of its supernatural powers. Fortunately Potty had also lost his Divya Dhrushti.

We had survived the uncalled for and unreasonable attack from the hill to tell the story of this extraordinary once-in-a-lifetime experience .

—*Boss*

~

Sometime in March 1978: As freshies, this would be our first holi in H4 and we had heard enough stories about the famous bhang of H4 made by Dina which left a lasting 'kick' on the consumer. True to expectations, Holi was fun and the thandai spiked with bhang was tasty and kicked in after a couple of hours. While guys were laughing and some were dancing, there was one left unimpressed. Shashank Shah declared the bhang to be a big flop and he thought that all the dancers and laughers were actually faking it.

This was on a Friday, and after lunch, Shashank went to his Room 48 for a quick nap, after which he wanted to go home for the weekend and get back on Sunday night in time to attend the Monday morning test.

Shashank woke up 2 hours late. His watch showed 6pm. He still did not feel the kick that was promised to him. Unamused, he packed his bag and started walking to YP to get his bus. Somewhere near H5, he saw one H4 guy walking towards H4 with a bag. Shashank laughed and teased him for returning to the hostel on the day that he should be actually walking out. Along the way, Shashank met many more guys with bags. Shashank was delirious with laughter and wondered aloud if the guys had so much bhang that they were doing things backwards.

It was only when he reached YP and had crossed at least a hundred guys walking into IIT that Shashank suspected something was horribly wrong. He did a quick reality check and figured that his Friday evening was actually a Sunday evening for the rest of India. In other words, Shashank Van Winkle had slept for 48 and four hours. So much for Dina not knowing how to brew a bhang with a kick.

Shashank may deny this. Whenever we talk about it, he claims that I am exaggerating. According to him, Holi was on a Saturday and he woke up on a Sunday, after just 24 and 4 hours.

—*Bakul*

~

Of all the four years we were served Dina's concoction (81-85), in my memory '84 was the best vintage for this brew. We laughed hysterically for a whole day, and slept through most of the next two days—when not awake and laughing.

I have never seen an animal as drunk, or stoned, as our hostel cat, Billius (successor to Fish's Billee). He lapped some bhang, and lay flat on the mess floor. When I tried to pick him up gently by his neck, he gathered all four limbs in slow-motion, looked up at me with a really stoned look, meowed in ultra-slow-motion, and then plopped back when I let him go. That bhang affected all the 'cats' in H4 equally hard.

—*Dabba*

~

Blacky was stoned out cold and I remember that it was the source of many hours of hysterical amusement. It was the first (and actually the last) time that I have been stoned/drunk, and it was extremely surreal. We had a Machines quiz the next day and despite still being half-stoned, it was one of the very few quizzes that I cracked.

—*Srinivas (Pu) Ketavarapu, '81-'85*

~

Damnation Alley

Holi was not the only time we H4ites went about altering our perception by imbibing and inhaling. Nor was that the only thing we did for entertainment. We did that, as everything, with almost reckless abandon, throwing ourselves into whatever activity we had chosen to indulge in. Some of us had extra- curricular occupations bordering on obsessive. There were many among us who were physical. There was cricket, swimming and running, an H4 paper, political factions, animal husbandry, there were some who were so dedicated that their names reflected their occupation—like our Ajay Volleyball Singh. Some of our extra-curricular activities took place right behind H4. This one place was the setting for many of our activities of both the healthy and unhealthy kind.

There was something about the pipelines that ran behind H4. Two mysterious and magnificent black steel monsters six feet in diameter ran in parallel, encasing a narrow road between them. The mystery was compounded by the fact that the narrow road was out of bounds to the public. Anyone on that lonely furrow was a trespasser on property exclusively reserved for water works personnel who could occasionally be seen in fast-moving jeeps frowning at any of us who were not able to duck from their vision fast enough.

From the hostel, if you turned right, the road stretched eternally. Sometimes, it s-ed and other times, it l-ed. Not many had ventured beyond five kilometres on the road which spawned Ramabai Ambedkar Nagar beyond one pipeline and Savitribai Phule Nagar beyond the other. These two slum settlements were the reason one did not dare go too far down that road. You could be dispatched from this world in the most anonymous manner and none would ever know. For a few of us, the only thrill was to speed at 80 kmph on our mobikes and induce a girl pillion rider to clutch us harder as we took her on a journey into the unknown.

This was the place to shop for chills and thrills. The left turn from the hostel was more frequented and took us to the sleaze city of Chand Shah, where substances that could be abused were peddled. This forbidden road was once used by health-conscious joggers who wanted solitude, but their numbers petered down as stories of mugging and assorted crime were reported more frequently from these parts. Actually, one did not need much to qualify as a certified mugger while mugging IITans. Amateurs used this spot to test and hone their mugging skills on the easy prey of IIT joggers. A thick-spectacled student ruminating on the possibility of inventing a new rocket propulsion fuel while jogging, was not one who would go down fighting, kicking, screaming. In fact, most mugging victims began unclasping their wristwatches at the sight of a would-be mugger. In short, an IITan was mugger-friendly.

Enter into this story our intrepid hero Cyrus Gazdar aka Coover, who was a bird of a different feather—the bawa feather. Now this Cyrus was an unabashed adventurer. He routinely crashed his hang glider into hillocks. He braved arrest for indulging in prohibited swimming. He swam alongside crocodiles in Vihar lake. Hence, while almost all erstwhile pipeline joggers had migrated to the more secure tracks within IIT, our Cyrus continued his adventures. He

212

continued jogging between the two pipelines rather than use the gymkhana.

Expectedly, his turn came one day. He was accosted by a gang of muggers. The leader of the pack was a moustachioed giant in a banyan and lungi. His triceps glistened with sweat. He was thrilled by the kill before him. Clearly, this gora-chikna was an easy IITan and he even looked cute enough to take home to mama. He also looked rich. What Mr. Mustachio did not know was that while IITans were mugger-friendly, bawas were not. And Coover was more bawa than IITan. He gave the leader a bored look. And before anyone could say 'your money or your life', our hero deftly swung his leg at the giant and landed a sharp kick in the region where it would hurt most, making him yelp. This was a new twist, unheard of in the annals of any mugging incident all over the country. Unsure of how to handle this new precedent, the gang folded up quickly and bolted away to their own safety. And Coover continued his jog.

—*Sanjay Chavan, '80-'85*

~

The night of the last end-sem of the '82 batch, a huge gang of H4ites went to Chand Shah for a cup of tea (perhaps not just a cup of tea). Somebody peed on the wall of the darga, and we were chased by bearded men with sickles all the way to the lake. It is a sign of our supreme physical fitness at the time, that twenty-odd guys inebriated from the tea managed to run faster than a bunch of irate and murderous residents of Chand Shah. Some of us didn't stop running till we got to H4.

Needless to say, for several weeks at least, no IITans were welcome at Chand Shah—something several other hostels were quite pissed off about.

—*Arun (Jetu) Jethmalani, '78-'83*

~

Yes, runners—not those running from danger, but real runners, are a different breed.

Born to Run

Mangi was a low-profile guy. Well towards the end of his second year, most people outside his own wing at H4 did not know him. There were others like him but most of them managed to make a mark in academics, if not in sports or cultural events. Unfortunately for Mangi, he was bad at his studies, could not and did not play a single game nor could he even think of participating in any quiz, debate, drama or contest. He was not an artist either nor a writer, and did not even play rummy, leave alone bridge. He was short and fat and darkish. He did not wear any outlandish clothes nor had any odd distinct mannerisms like Fish that would draw attention to him. He was generally alone and never seen hanging out with friends or ever seen around the canteen involved in any cack session with anyone. All his social life was a handful of acquaintances with whom he exchanged a barely polite nod if and not much else.

This kind of a drab existence would normally have played havoc in a fiercely competitive environment such as IIT had. Many like Fish and me suffered from similar infirmities but there was a difference in attitude. Indulging in fun and being in the centre of action and in the thick of things made our existence manageable. We created adventure where there was none, we were forever courting danger, we were constantly experiencing new friendships and relationships in our quest for acquiring skills politely, and perhaps sarcastically called 'social skills'.

214

But what Mangi had and was not visible yet was some great resolute determination. His kind of a lifestyle coupled with his several limitations could easily have driven him to despair and destruction as happened with several like him. But Mangi decided to pick up one activity, one hobby, one passion that he would focus on and work on to the exclusion of everything else. Not so surprising looking back on it now, he picked up something that would be the most difficult for him. He decided to start running. It started off as a doctor's advice in order to knock some flab off his frame. Given his constitution, this activity would obviously strain him beyond his limits of tolerance. But it was precisely for this reason that he opted to excel in it. If something was difficult and perhaps out of reach, it would keep him all the more perseverant to achieve this goal and early failures would not discourage him from believing that he could not reach there or anywhere. Running, apart from being a biological necessity, would keep his mind and his spirit active and engaged, and defeat the feeling of emptiness that must have plagued him often enough. It was not important to run fast or with the right technique. It was supremely important to just run. What started off as an exercise at diverting his mind from boredom was soon to become his religion. He picked up books about and from famous runners. He bought the most scientifically correct shoes for the purpose. He read up bio-medical recommendations on the number of calories to be burnt, endurance levels to be maintained and how much sweat could be allowed leave his pores. Before long, his running began showing unexpected results. Physically, he was fitter and his face glowed with pride and an easy smile. Socially, he was a superstar. Everyone knew Mangilal Jain, the silent, resolute, perseverant runner who participated in cross-country races and aspired for the marathon. A visit to his room was now likely to be met with a preceding visitor who asking Mangi for tips and advice. Even athletes like Vasant Prabhu waited for their turn to run with Mangi and learn some pointers along the way. Mangi was famous, he was liked, he was adored and most important, he was respected for turning out a winner. For converting his drabness into something that made him a proud achiever. He still fumbled at academics and cultural activities, but it just didn't matter to him anymore. He stopped wishing that he was proficient at any of these other things. He had put his mind and heart and body into one thing, and excelling in it obliterated his need to excel anywhere else. Mangi was now bristling with confidence in spite of not having improved in academics or sports or cult activities and without having gone in for any plastic surgery. He was a changed man and all because he had the will to attempt something and persist till he succeeded. It is debatable whether Mangilal Jain learnt much during his seven years at IIT but he certainly did teach a lot by the sheer force of his own example.

~

I remember participating in the institute mini marathon once, preparing for a couple of weeks with healthy habits and appropriate dietary observances (Vishnu's canteen did particularly well during that time). The big day arrived and the race commenced near the guest house, with the path

circling around the gym grounds, then behind H4 along the picturesque Vihar lake, a bit of the pipeline stretch, and finally back again towards the gym grounds. I was full of enthu(siasm) and actually led the pack of serious marathoners initially. What a wonderful, heady five minutes of glory that was. But as we approached H4, the smell of the evening tiffin's batata vadas drifted to my nostrils, and with visceral determination I said fuckeet to the marathon, loped toward the mess and helped myself to a plate of vadas. Another plate (don't fret Mess Sec, I wrote it down in the extras book) and a couple of chais later, a feeling of guilt began to surface, and with number still on my back, I plodded along to continue the marathon, occasionally stopping (sitting) to check out the scenery.

I finished 157th, surprised to find organizers still recording results at the finish line, even more surprised that there were guys behind me arriving to finish. I shudder to think what sort of detours they may have taken.

And then there was Mangilal Jain on the other end of the spectrum—Mangi would easily crack any race, and then continue running, not even having broken a sweat, the marathon serving as a mere laughable warm-up to an otherwise everyday routine.

—*Rohan*

∼

A mandatory requirement of being in the NCC (National Cadet Corps) was a weeklong outdoor camp near a suburb in Pune (I think it was Dehu). The following story relates to this camp and it still brings a smile to my face.

After a ten-hour overnight passenger train ride to Pune from Mumbai (stopping at every single station), we boarded a large open diesel powered military truck. Just as I was enjoying the open air truck ride in the early morning hours of the Pune countryside we reached our campsite and by the very first look we knew we were in for a long hard week. The site was a barren piece of land next to their official training facilities. They asked us to get to work immediately. First, we were to pitch our own tents. Next, we were expected to dig a six-to-ten inch deep trough around the tent to keep the snakes out. Just as soon as we had finished building the tent and digging the trenches there was yet another task and then something else that needed to be done. Throughout the day we toiled in the hot sun to create the best makeshift accommodations for ourselves ('bathrooms' were open-air and beyond the fence—we had to walk there with a leaking 'tumbrel'—we were assigned one per tent).

After a very long and difficult first day our unit leader asked us to huddle together for a debrief and prepare for the next day's events. Our second day was to begin with an inspection of the facilities we had built for ourselves followed by a line-up and inspection of each cadet in the entire facility. The inspection would be done by the Commander at 6am and we were warned that this Commander was quite meticulous and detail oriented. We were given Brasso to brighten our belt buckles, shoe polish for our shoes, brushes for our NCC caps, oil for our rifles and so on, and instructions to ensure that we were in our best form for the morning.

Just before 6am a whistle signalled that we had to line up for the inspection. Everybody immediately got together their NCC caps and rifles, and in full attire we lined up in anticipation of this high-profile inspection.

The Commander made the rules clear at the very beginning. When he yelled attention, he meant attention. No snickering, no moving.

He then walked up to each one of us and inspected us from head to toe. The way our cap was positioned on our head, how well the shirt was tucked in, how we held our rifle. And he was very picky. As he came up to me, he poked his baton around to smoothen out some wrinkles on my shirt, straightened my cap, and after what seemed like an eternity, he was satisfied and he moved on to my neighbour.

He started with the same routine for my neighbour and adjusted his cap with his baton, shoved around his shirt and then slowly his gaze fell to my neighbour's shoes. And then almost instantly, his head jerked up to level with my neighbour's eyes and then slowly his gaze moved down again. He did this thrice almost to make sure that his eyes were not lying to him.

Since we had to look straight ahead and not move a muscle, I dared not even move my head to see what had bothered this Commander so much. I moved my eyeballs toward the Commander's face, and cannot forget the look of total bewilderment in his eyes. Now, it was clear to me that this commander had reached an absolute new low bar of incompetence within our group and could not make up his mind what to do next. I could not control my curiosity any longer. I decided to risk moving my head just enough to look at my neighbour's shoes, where the trouble seemed to be. I timed my glance right and looked down quickly and for just long enough to capture a mental picture of my neighbour's shoes. There was something wrong with the shoes but I had to examine that mental image for a while to figure out what that might be. The shoes were polished perfectly, laced correctly. Though, it seemed odd to me that the shoes were pointing away from each other. Just as it hit me and I realized what was wrong, I heard the fury in the commander's voice as he screamed at the top of his lungs in Hindi, 'Cadet, your shoes are on wrong! You are dismissed!'

Today, this cadet is fifty years old and I'll not embarrass him further. All I can say is that he was from Akola, Maharashtra and to this day he is a good friend of mine.

—Pol

~

Some of us found great delight in intensely physical treks and hikes we went on. Even here, IITans thought things through. There were two schools of thoughts and two ideologies concerning hiking. The Charvakists (who believed in the pleasures of the flesh—their own I mean) and the Masochists who didn't. For the Charvakists (which is the camp I belonged to, of which Sandeep Bhise was the gang leader) the hike itself was a pain in the ass, something to be endured to get to the top, with the ultimate pleasure being what you would see once you to the top. For the other camp (of which Balya was the high priest) the hike itself was the goal. Some guys (like Ajit Shelat) had one foot in both the camps. Some of us were extreme Charvakists who stayed on the plains and listened to accounts of guys who laboured up and laboured down and lived to tell the tale while we reclined in the comfort of our lounge chairs, smoking a full luxurious cigarette while you folks talked about how you lived on stubs.

Whatever camp you hiked with, there was a sense of camaraderie and adventure, and usually these treks were eventful. Some of them made lifelong impressions. And some of them actually changed lives.

—*Satkya*

~

We arrived at a small village in pouring rain. An old woman in the village yelled at me, scolding me for walking around in the rain like that. She took me to her hut and lit a fire for me and covered me in a blanket. I was very comfortable in the blanket in front of the fire. Several of the other trekkers had joined me, when there was some disturbance. The village chief had come to the hut and wanted all of us to move, either to his house or some of the other houses in the village. This hut was outside that small village. It turned out that the old lady was an untouchable and the villagers did not want us important city folks to stay with her. I refused to leave. The others with me did the same. We arrived at a compromise. Half our group stayed with the old lady and the other half went with the village chief. During the evening we found out that they were a childless couple and the blanket she had given us was their only blanket. She had lit that fire for us with wood they had collected over the past two days. I meditate on this experience every time I am depressed. How could someone who has so little in life be ready to give away so much to a perfect stranger? Is it something as simple as her seeing in me the children she never had? Or is there something more? Many times I feel as if God visited me in the form of that untouchable old lady. I have never felt more at peace in my life than I did in front of that fire and under that blanket that day. This is my most cherished memory from the IIT days.

—*Vijay*

~

When they joined IIT, most people joined a sport or pursued things like yoga or mountaineering. It seemed to me that the people who joined NCC were rarely folks fired up about defending the country—it was more the choice of last resort. On weekends we would see the most dishevelled NCC recruits. I had always loved rock climbing and trekking so, that was the natural thing for me.

One of the cool things we did every year was go for a week-long monsoon trek. You were issued gear (rucksacks, rope, flashlights, stove) from the Gymkhana, you collected some food, made some bus reservations and away you went. The treks typically took in a series of forts in the Western Ghats a day's journey from each other.

On one of the treks, I believe I was the rear admiral. We had a bunch of the standard folks on this trek (but for some reason we did not have veterans like V square). On this trek we had the usual die-hard trekking girls—Tara, Madhu, Meena (not sure if Seema was on it) and a couple of seniors. We also had some newbies like Baps. Baps used to admire

Tara from afar, joined in some exchanges with his mild mannered smiles, but that was about it.

Monsoon treks means it is wet and slippery everywhere, and you typically had two sets of clothes—a dry one to sleep in and a wet one you wore all day, drenched. Being the rear admiral, I had a great time looking at people's mud-caked butts after a fall on the first day. They changed my title to Rear Admirer. (By the way, my nickname Ghoda was from another hike where I ran ahead of the others.)

On the third day of the trek, early in the morning, we had to climb a steep hill. Being the rear admiral, I was the last guy climbing. Suddenly I heard a short scream, and I saw that a boulder the size of four footballs, was bounding down—it bounced off a cliff about 6 feet above my head and disappeared below. Split second later I see another form doing the same. It was Tara. She fell by me, just outside my reach, a completely dazed look on her face. She was neither screaming or crying—just could not believe that she was falling down the height of a few stories in the middle of nowhere. She disappeared from sight in the trees and shrubs below followed by complete silence. Next thing I heard was someone crying—no it was not Tara from below but Madhu from above.

I scampered down as fast as I could. I saw Tara lying flat with her arms and legs at awkward angles. She was staring straight up, white faced, so shocked that the pain probably had not registered. I asked her if she could move her neck and she said 'uhun', and her legs, and she moved them, and then the arms—that's when we realized she had fractured an arm. But it was a miracle that that was the full extent of the damage, given the fall. The trees might have cushioned it somewhat.

I was rapidly calculating, what would be the closest place where she could get medical attention. She stood up. What a trooper. I remember thinking that even then. We had a medical kit with some bandages. We found some straight sticks, and made a sling of sorts, tightly bandaging the arm. She mustered up courage to walk. Now we started off in a direction where we could catch a bus (it was a couple of days away!) and we asked the first gaonwalla we found where we could find a doctor. He sent us off in a different direction, as we met people along the way, they all pointed to a village where we would find the doctor. Finally we found the very respected doctor in a little hut. Turns out, he was a retired compounder. He looked at our handiwork and told us flatly that he could not do anything better! I was shocked, I have no idea how Tara was feeling at that time. But she kept a pretty good composure. Now she was on painkillers every few hours.

It took us a couple of days to get to a railway station. And once we got there, we found that the trains were very crowded . I was worried about people jostling her arm, and so quickly secured a couple of spots, and got her to sit and asked Baps to sit next to her.

They had a great time talking heart to heart during that trip, the painkillers probably helped. And I believe before they disembarked, they had fallen in love. I am not sure, about this, but I know that after getting to Bombay, Tara was in no rush to go to the doctor. She went to the hostel, showered, slept the night and then went to the doc. That could only have happened if love-endorphins were working.

On the train, I very well remember telling Baps, 'Take care of Tara.' To this date, I believe he has .

—*Ghoda*

~

I remember my version of it. I can remember that moment so vividly. The shock, the helplessness, the feeling of being totally out of control and the bewilderment and fear of what will happen next.

My mind was crystal clear. Kaushtub Bhadbhade was climbing ahead and suddenly some loose rocks came off. He was startled and yelled, but managed to get his balance back. I was looking at him and the stone fell directly on me and pushed me off the mountain. The free fall seemed so strange, the sky above, passing all of you, I remember Meenakshi's shocked expression, and yours also and all of you turned a hundred and eighty degrees and started running down. I bounced off at least three times and kept gathering momentum, it seemed so prolonged and never-ending and I wondered if it would ever stop. And when I finally stopped with a thud, I must have blanked out momentarily, because the next thing I remember was all of you shouting and rushing toward me, asking me if I was ok, pulling my legs, my arms, it was pretty confusing, and I was stunned at all the fuss, and I was stunned that I was alive. My right arm hurt the most, it was stiff, immobile, would not bend . You and some others got some sticks to support it and bandaged it so well, but it was so uncomfortable.

That night was bad, the pain was killing and I cried. More than me, Madhu cried. I still remember her being awake all night, giving me water and pain-killers, and crying because I was in pain. Those are moments one can never forget in one's life.

The X-ray at the hospi revealed a hairline fracture and my arm had bloated to twice its size, having been unattended for several days. I didn't want to get treated in the hospi. Just wanted to go home. With the stick supports gone, my arm was dangling like a log of wood and I had to hold it with the other. And the kanjoos that I was, I couldn't imagine taking a taxi—I changed two buses, and walked for twenty minutes to get home. My grandfather greeted me with a smile which disappeared when he saw my arm. I lied to him that I had tripped and fallen when trying to catch the bus home. I pretended to be fine, and only towards evening I told him that perhaps I should see a doctor, and slipped away with the X-ray. He had never approved of girls going on treks.

But Ashvin, though the 'Mills & Boon' ending in your recollection was very sweet, I have to protest that my memory here is better than yours. Soumitra was never on that trek and we were not that close either, at that point of time. As a rule, IIT boys are weird. Some days friendly, and some days they'd look through you as if you didn't exist. Soumitra was no different. Of course, things did develop but after almost a year after that.

—*Tara Banerjee nee Subramanian, '77-'82, speaking to Ghoda.*

~

Balya Squared

V2 Limaye (aka Balya) was one of those guys devoted to mountaineering. I went on a trek once with Prabhu and gang into the hills of Matheran. Late in the night we came upon a small tribal community up in the hills. Tired and hungry, we stopped for a while and talked with these folks. The moment they heard we were from Powai, and we knew Limaye, we were treated like royalty, including the pleasure of tasting their local brew. The reason for their affection and hospitality was a small dam Limaye had built for them to harvest rain and store rain water, which had transformed their lives.

—*Sanjiv (Sammy S) Samant, '77-'82*

Balya runs a leadership training institute in Pune. Some years ago he ran a programme for a company where a friend of mine works. There were about 12/13 senior execs from the company signed up for this programme—people had come down from US, UK, and so on. The programme was aimed at teaching team building through outdoor activities. Of course all of these attendees had no idea what Balya's notion of outdoor activities might be. They had come expecting perhaps a bit of a walk on a beach before retiring to a nice resort for a refreshing cocktail. Balya took them to Sinhagad at 5am, had them climb up by the most difficult route he could find, fed them zunka-bhakar with a refreshing glass of buttermilk, then took them down into the jungle on the other side, had them spend the night in tents with mosquitoes specially ordered to sing them a lullaby. The next morning, after tea was served in the tents, all these guys began to express some unease, and were told magnanimously by Balya, 'This is a jungle, you can *go* anywhere you like.'

—*Satkya*

~

I remember my hike to Harishchandra Gadh. The Konkan Kada—the top of Harishchandra Gadh—is shaped like a shallow pan. You can see a big rock fall all the way for few seconds and hit the ground. If you throw a piece of paper it will float back to you. We performed a little experiment. All of us made balls of paper, thus reducing the exposed surface area, and threw them over the cliff. We wrapped stones of increasing size in the paper, until they finally stopped coming back to us. As it turns out, the force of the air is so strong that you need a stone over a square inch in size to defeat those strange air currents off the Konkan Kada.

—*Raj*

~

Bhise led us on a hike to Harishchandra Gadh. The eight of us were members of a bicycle trip to Goa the previous summer. It was late June, and as we began our climb, a pleasant cooling drizzle came down. Harishchandra Gadh is not an easy climb. In spite of the cool weather, we all drank a lot of water to wet our throats on the way up. Since Sir Isaac Newton decreed a long time ago that what goes in must eventually come out, this created a problem. The coolness of the weather also meant that we didn't sweat very much, so there was only one other outlet available for the water.

As we stood on the Konkan Kada, a sheer drop of 2000 feet, our bladders were ready to burst. On the trip to Goa we had practiced how to stand in a row on a cliff and let go in parallel. So there were again the eight of us standing atop

Konkan Kada doing what must be done. However, there are cliffs and there are cliffs. The topography of Konkan Kada is such that the air swirls around like a whirlpool. Newton or no Newton, what gets thrown down actually gets buoyed up by the air currents. What should have splashed down in golden arcs floated up into our faces.

—*Satkya*

~

This reminds me of the malfunctioning urinals in the wing bogs. They would automatically start flushing when you were in the middle of your act. The CWSF bog in particular was the most lethal. Water would fill in fast, swirl up with golden hues forming a pattern in an eddy current of a swirl and start overflowing on your feet. This often brought out the agile gymnasts in us who moved their legs around in a ballet routine while holding a trouser in one hand and a trouser resident in the other and the feet doing a foxtrot to avoid the amber spillage.

And there's a typical Fish sick one-liner. Whenever you say 'YP', (Y-Point) he'd retort with 'Because I have to.'

~

We went further afield too, all the way to the Himalayas on treks. During our time IITB had a very active mountaineering club. Our club ranked at the top when compared with colleges, universities, and private hiking clubs, in terms of activities, member participation and equipment. Our activities included hikes in Sahyadri range, monsoon treks, rock climbing within IIT, and at Mumbra. We also had Himankan— expeditions over 20,000 feet in the Himalayas.

My first Himankan was Himankan 1982 in the Pahalgam region of Kashmir. From the base camp at Pahalgam the next camp was at Chandanwari—a six-hour trek. We left after breakfast, at eight o'clock in the morning. The weather was sunny and wonderful. Although we were on a dirt road, it was wide and well travelled. We were all very excited, this was our first trek in the Himalayas. We were enjoying the snow and ice-laden mountains, the gorges, the villagers, just everything.

After two or three hours of walking, tiredness began to set in. Although it was gradual climb, this was our first exposure to mountaineering. And then, all of a sudden, the sun disappeared behind clouds and it got cooler. The weather turned sour within next half hour. Clouds gathered fast, and snow came down. It was our first snow! We did all the things anyone does in their first snow. We collected it in our hands, some of us ate it, we had snow ball fights.

The snow turned thicker and heavier. There was a strong heavy wind on our faces. Visibility reduced to a few feet. We walked closely behind each other at snail's pace. We had a ways to go. Our leaders seemed to be looking at the map more often, they were as new to the route as all of us. We couldn't see landmarks, and they were worried we had lost our way.

At 5pm, we were cold and fatigued. Being students we had reasonably warm clothes, but it was unreasonably cold. The cold started biting into our fingers and one or two of us began to cry. We turned a corner, and we saw another camp leader with some people—they were worried since we were so late and came looking for us. We were so glad to see them. They injected new life into us. The camp was few minutes away, luckily we hadn't lost the way. This great camp team had hot chocolate ready for us. I was helping one guy along, and he was crying, 'I have a frostbite, I can't feel my fingers and toes.'

It can be quite cold in the Himalayas. It was so wicked cold at one of the camps during the '83 Himankan that I had hard time finding you-know-what in the morning. I also thought how fortunate we are to be hot-bodied mammals. At these high altitudes, one would otherwise get stuck to the ground with a yellowish ice stick unless the source was hot.

—*Raj*

~

In the summer of 1979, a bunch of us from H4 went on a YHA trek in the Himalayas. Vijay Desai, Shashank Shah, Idi Amin, my brother Kaushik and I. We took the Jammu Tavi express to Jammu, a bus ride on mountain dirt roads that collapsed left and right, to Kishtwar. Kishtwar, a small town 7000 ft above sea level on the Jammu side of the Himalayas, was where we met up with our fellow-travellers, and acclimatized to the altitude for about three days. Then we would begin our twenty-one day loop which included crossing Margan pass into the Himalayas and Synthen pass back to Jammu. Every day we would be sleeping at a camp already set up by YHA volunteers, they would give us dinner, breakfast and pack us lunch (which was never enough). With these arrangements, there was not much to carry.

I took my brother along only because my parents insisted. But Kaushik turned out to be an asset. He was the first to get into camp, befriend the cook, even adjust the menu if needed. We would ask him what was for dinner, and he would say something like 'It was peas pulao, papad and achar, I asked them to add tomato soup and add some pieces of cheese to the pulao.'

The base camp, at any given time, had a few hundred people living there. Some, like us, on their way to Margan-Synthen, some on their way to base of a nearby peak, and some on their journey back. These last were all sunburnt, blistered, but in a euphoria, full of camaraderie and with stories to tell. Every night the residents of the camp gathered around a huge campfire. In this far away place, among hundreds of people, amid the gathering crowds of people at the campfire, we found someone special. A middle-aged, slightly paunchy guy, dressed in non-trekking clothes (woollen pants, dress shirt, high-heeled shoes) and a jacket, with a Dev Anand-type cap, and two babes on each arm, having the time of his life.

Actually, he found us. He took one look at our IIT B H4 shirts and yelled, 'H4, IIT B? No way!' He took out a flat whiskey flask from his jacket breast pocket—'Lets drink to this!' He was not only an IITB graduate from the sixties, he was an ancient H4ite. He regaled us with H4 stories from his days—to us they sounded like ancient times, but for sure, he was an H4ite, one of our own ancestors, and his stories confirmed it. He told us, for example, that the wooden sign marking a certain house in Bombay's red light district was created by them in the IIT workshop, and even has a small indicator saying on it, 'With compliments of H4'.

—*Ghoda*

~

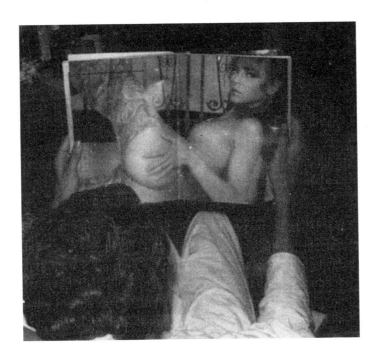

Interruptus

Fish and I were always trying to outdo each other. The latest contest between us was about who would bunk the most number of lab assignments, which were always post lunch. About bunking lectures, we were on par. We knew because each of us saw the other waking up groggy eyed around 1pm just before the mess would close. But about bunking labs, each of us thought that the other was sneakily snaking his way to the lab, and so, we decided that post lunch, we would both park ourselves outside the warden's office and discuss earth-shaking issues such as the average number of drags it took to finish a cigarette. We also spent our time imagining that if the word CAPSTAN was an acronym, what it was an acronym of. And we went further and tried to devise a reverse acronym. This was to add to the prevailing ruling acronym and reverse acronym that went, Can A Prick Stand Twice A Night? The reverse one was also an answer to the first—Not All Though Some Pricks Are Capable.

So and such, at around 2pm, while indulging in our soul-searching answers to tricky questions, and long after most of the hostelites had left to explore scientific truths about atoms and molecules, Fish and I were startled to see a girl walk up to the hostel entrance and ask the watchman to call Ram Chopra from Room 2. The girl was Manju and Ram Chopra was the type of guy whose middle name should have been Kanhaiyya. There was a lot of speculation about these two, and while Fish and I wondered why Manju and Ram were not in labs and whether they wanted to conduct private experiments, we winked at each other and moved out of sight. We were itching for a prank and these two provided us with the opportunity. Our lives suddenly took on new purpose. There was suddenly work to do for our unemployed souls. Work that would test our ingenuity, our creativity, and, though we didn't know it then, work that would create the script for a story that would be told three decades in the future.

Thus it came to pass, that about fifteen minutes after Ram escorted Manju to his room in the faraway section of the hostel, Sonaji the hostel maali knocked on the locked door of Room 2. The door was opened by an irritated Ram. He was handed two red roses by Sonaji the maali who stammered,

'*Saab! Aapne* order *kiya tha, woh phool laaya hoon.*' Per Sonaji the maali, Ram grabbed the roses, threw them inside the room and barked a 'thank you' at him in a tone that sounded more like 'Get the hell out, you creep.'

Fish and I asked Sonaji the maali to go to the back garden since we did not want him to meet our next decoy and alert him about what to expect. The next assignee was mess worker Dina who carried a tray and two glasses of tea and knocked on the same door of room #2 and offered hot tea to a hotter Ram with the same 'aapka order' line. Dina did complain about use of unparliamentary language and we assured him that he would have ample opportunities to return the favour to Ram. We gave Ram 20 minutes to conduct a few more experiments before sending the next messenger to his room. Hostel sweeper Kalidas. The few people still in the hostel were puzzled to hear loud shouting erupting from Room 2. Kalidas had arrived there with a bucket and a broom and a bottle of Phenyle and told Ram he had come to clean the mess just as he did everyday an hour after the 'chokri' walked in. Kalidas went one step further. He looked at Manju and said to Ram, 'I see, today you have some different chick.'

Soon, it was 5pm and guys were returning from the lab one by one only to be told by Fish and me that Ram 'is looking for you urgently because he has an important message for you'. I think it took about sixteen guys knocking on Ram's door at intervals of one minute to finally cause Manju to bolt and return to saner surroundings. Ram decided to hammer/clobber/slother Fish and me. Fish escaped to the safe haven of H7 for a day. I braved out Ram's attempt to pour a jug of ice cold water on me in the mess, and in a contest that lasted three minutes, I managed to push the jug away in the nick of time. Ram could not however prevent the jug from disgorging its contents on about twelve hungry guys who were in the middle of their meal. End result: Ram got hammered/clobbered/slothered.

Ram had vowed to take revenge on Fish. He waited for almost a year. But, true to his word, when the opportunity came, he struck like a vengeful cobra. Fish was entertaining two girls from town in the mess over lunch. When the group dynamics had settled down to nice funny conversations, and a lot of laughter and joy emanated from this session, a watchman walked over to Fish. He handed him a packet of condoms with a not-so-unfamiliar line: 'Saab! Aapka order.' A bewildered Fish turned to see a triumphant Ram Chopra grinning at him from the adjoining table.

—*Bakul*

~

Well, some of us were lucky enough to have visitors of the opposite sex. Some of us were not, and we did sometimes entertain ourselves by scuttling their plans. And for some of us there was the beauty queen of H4 that several generations of H4 guys lusted after—The Dhoban. We heard that she woke up at four in the morning and came into the NWGF bathroom to take a bath. So the story goes that for three nights V Square hid in the gap behind the bogs and the first room. Unfortunately, each night he fell asleep, and the rumours about The Dhoban's bath were never proven.

~

There was a strong rumour always floating around H4 (I wonder who used to create these rumours and how, with all their intelligence, folks kept falling for them) that every night around 10pm or so the Dhobi and Dhoban had their dinner and thereafter spend the next hour in fun and frolic of a kind that a husband and wife (not necessarily from the same pair) are expected to indulge in. And, this rumour went, if one happened to be in a particular corner of the NWSF terrace, and one had particularly sharp eyesight, then, it was said, one was rewarded with some interesting views. For the next several nights you could find not less than forty seven guys patiently sitting and waiting on the terrace in a line like a line of crows on a overhead electrical wire.

—Satkya

~

My Beautiful Laundress

The obsession with The Dhoban lay heavy on this one guy. Lean, thin beard and thick spectacles, generally nondescript. For some reason, he was referred to by one name and one name only, which was not very complimentary and neither was it parliamentary. Nobody, and that means nobody, knew his real name.

There are many stories about him, most of them about his name, and a few about his focusing Birjoo's telescope on the dhoban's window at night. This telescope was old school. It showed objects upside down. This did not matter if it was used for the purpose it was built for, since most heavenly bodies are round. You can't tell the upside from the downside of, say, the moon. But the heavenly body of The Dhoban, and her gyrations occurring upside down, was another thing altogether. Most IIT

237

minds would reset the mental frame of reference and perceive the dhoban on a bed which was on the floor. But our friend, who for propriety's sake we shall call Sharma, could see a dhoban suspended face down on a bed which was suspended face down from the ceiling. And how did he correct the visual defect? He played contortionist and turned his head downwards and stuck his leg in the ledge to synchronize with the dhoban's reference frame.

Birjoo's telescope focused more often on The Dhoban's heavenly body than boring Saturns and Jupiters. L**d had a vantage room which was closest to The Dhoban's so the telescope was always parked outside his room. One early morning, someone from NWSF saw The Dhoban from the terrace. He went running down to L**d's room and knocked on the door and said urgently, 'L**d, you bloody idiot L**d. Hurry up and let's have the telescope. There's a chick out there.' The door opened and there was L**d's father. He had come to see his son for the day.

There were several stories of how people had called him by his unmentionable name in the most embarrassing situations. Satish Joshi called him *that *in front of his (Sharma's) wife. Hiren shouted 'oye L**d' at a busy Dadar station in the presence of thousands of commuters.

We keep running into guys from the past and we do call each other by nicknames and swearwords when recognition dawns. We always wonder what we'll do when we run into this guy with the unmentionable name. There is a fleeting recollection that his last name was Sharma. Because when his dad came once to H4 to look him up, he asked KV for Something Sharma's room. KV told him there was no such person in H4. Dad then said that Something Sharma's room was 21 something, and KV immediately told the poor man, 'Oh, you mean L**d. Go straight to the end of the corridor and go up to SF.'

Sometime in our final year, PG L**d got engaged, and of course everyone speculated on what his fiancée's name could be. Was it likely to be the obvious? A milkshake was offered to whoever would be bold enough to ask L**d the million dollar question. After some fuss, one of us volunteered and asked L**d the question amid a lot of sniggering. If L**d understood the motive behind the question, he did not show it and answered that her name was Neelam.

While the prize milkshake was being devoured, Soumitra Banerjee (Baps) opined that Neelam was perhaps short for 'Neel'. He paused for a few seconds for what turned out to be dramatic effect, and then added, 'kanth'. The milkshake was passed on to him for delivering the punch line of the day.

It was only recently that we scanned IIT graduation records and figured out L**d's real name.

～

This verse about the above unmentionable should be appreciated for its mechanical rather than poetic attributes:

There was a young fellow named Dick,
Who had, poor fellow, a corkscrew prick,
He spent his time in a lifelong hunt,
For a woman with a spiral c**t,
His search ended in far Glamorgan
Where he found a woman with such an organ
But alas! On his wedding night, he fell down dead,
Because his wife had a left-hand thread.

(This was narrated by Punk (Aditya Srinivasan) during an EP in 1977 called Cantata in which we were paired with H5.)

～

Yes, a lot of plotting and planning and energy and thinking did go into arranging encounters with the opposite sex. It didn't help that the ratios were stacked against us, nor that the opposite sex were all ensconced in their own hostel, with rules in place that made it even harder for us to socialize normally. Fortunately, the ladies felt the same way we did, if not about us, then about the authorities and the rules.

Ladies' Night Out

The late 70s and early 80s were turbulent times for a group of inmates of 'Ladies Hostel' who campaigned for their hostel to be called Hostel 10 like the rest of the nine numerically named boys' hostels. Leading this pack of feisty feminists was the duo of Sandhya Gokhale and her junior Revathi Kasturi who believed that the 'Ladies' Hostel' name was discriminatory (and who defied the curfew rules by entering and leaving the ladies' hostel via drainpipe). They were also up in arms about the fact that while a girl could visit any room in any of the boys' hostels, male visitors to LH were restricted to a meeting room near the entrance. The treatment was unfair and many girls felt chagrined enough to do something about it. Initially, as all movements are, this one too was met with sarcastic digs and derision. But the movement grew into a popular groundswell of supportive opinions, and things settled down to a new equilibrium. Hostel 10 was now H10 and decidedly so. The LH label was dropped for good and forever. Surely and steadily, things were moving positively forward. To complete this fight for parity and to protest the still unfair visitation rights, the girls invited scores of boys to their hostel one evening to mingle in the lounge upstairs and the mess downstairs. This event, needless to say, was a great success. During Navratri, the girls invited some boys to their hostel for a dandia and garba do at their hostel in the same manner that boys' hostels hosted Navratri celebrations to which girls were invited. This event was to take place in the courtyard within the wings which formed a three sided U shape.

Girls were dressed in nice traditional dresses, the guys wore the trademark slippers which had become a compulsory part of an IITan's attire, but had at least turned up with their hair combed. There was a dholi who turned out some melodious foot-tapping fare when the time came. The atmosphere was festive and there was a sense of triumph for the girls who had launched yet another crusade that was bound to succeed and make way for more permissive times ahead. But for a reason that has been widely speculated upon since, there was no electricity in H10. Surprisingly, there was power all around and even immediately outside H10. People were seen working on the mains to establish and repair the cause of the blackout. And while people moved around in darkness trying to identify others and figure out how much longer they would have to wait, my urge to light a cigarette was killing me. I was sans matchbox thanks to Fish who had pilfered it earlier during the day and I was soon to learn that asking for a matchbox in the dark of H10 would not yield any results. In this pandemonium caused by the mysterious darkness, I could see a girl moving towards Shashank, and, after she correctly identified him, she announced herself as Bhavna. With some hope and half in jest, I asked Bhavna if she could point me to a woman who smoked, so that I could borrow a light from her. Bhavna answered, 'Actually, there's a woman who smokes. But I will not tell you her name. Just yesterday, she threw her cigarette and it landed on her bed and she didn't realize that her mattress caught fire and after the mattress was half burnt, she let out a scream and all other girls came to her room and said, 'Oh My God Mona! Your mattress is burnt'.' Oh my God Mona? So would Bhavna be kind enough to identify Mona Singh in this darkness and take me to her? Bhavna was shell-shocked. How on earth did I know that Mona Singh was the smoker? Shashank and I used the cover of darkness to stifle our giggles. And while I went hunting for Mona, there was a commotion near the entrance. A shortish man wearing a raincoat (it had rained earlier) and wielding a flashlight stormed into the courtyard with four security guards in tow, all bearing candles.

The shortish man was none other than Director AK De commonly referred to as the Diro. Diro was livid. 'Who is the hostel secretary? This is a ladies' hostel. Power is out and the boys are in. What is happening here? Don't you know that it is not allowed?' And then he asked all boys to immediately get out of H10. This sparked off angry protests from all present. Revathi was the G Sec of H10 and she asked the Diro to be polite and not behave dishonourably with her guests. The Diro retorted, 'I know how honourable your guests are. Just a few minutes ago, I got a call from Lamington Road police station that three IIT boys were arrested in a brothel raid.' All hell broke loose when he said this. Indignant girls demanded that Diro explain the connection. Unfazed, Diro mentioned something about him knowing what 'kinds of things happen in girls' hostels'. Amongst the active protestors, the loudest and most vociferous was the left-leaning Sudheendra Kulkarni, a well-known rabble rouser and Diro-baiter in IIT who became more famous later as a BJP bigwig, Officer-on-special-duty in Vajpayee's PMO and LK Advani's man Friday, and is now believed to be an aide of Mamta Banerjee and her Trinamool Congress. The conversation in the courtyard was turning acrimonious and there was promise of more to come. At that stage, my urge to light up was out of control. I walked up to where the Diro was lecturing from and leant over to a candle to light up. This induced some applause and laughter from the amused girls and enraged the Diro enough to ask Security Officer Singh to 'take down' my name. Seeing that I could flee quickly enough in the cover of darkness, I announced my name as Isaac Newton and left. While still in flight, I could hear Michael Faraday identifying himself in Ghoda's voice, Albert Einstein in Vijay's voice, and then Rutherford, Galileo, Watt, Edison announced themselves and followed me out.

The next day, Ghoda narrated this incident to some friends from H8. They seemed squirrelly when Ghoda came to the part about the call from the Lamington Road police station. Finally, one of them—Nadkarni aka Nadu—began laughing uncontrollably. He wondered aloud how the Diro could have fallen for the call he had made, and not only that, but raided H10 within minutes and use Nadu's call as an excuse to justify his raid.

—*Bakul*

⁓

Soumitra Banerjee was among the lucky ones who had female visitors. And then there was Ajay Volleyball Singh who was meeting prospective in-laws.

Shooting Star

Ajay Singh makes it seem as if some guys in our wing were created by God specifically to become an important subject matter of our book.

Ajay Singh's prospective bride's parents came to visit him in H4. I remember a big dowry was at stake. Junta had to cover all the pictures on their walls. When the potential in-laws came, everything was covered except a leg sticking out behind a *Times of India* page in one of the rooms. Some felt that Ajay Singh should pay us all a cut from his dowry earnings. It was not easy to present ourselves as devout Ram Bhakts and live without smoking for a full one hour.

Ajay Singh wore only undies when he was in the wing. He wore shorts and a banyan when he was playing volleyball. (He wore 'pant-shirt' when the prospective in-laws came from his native Jaunpur.) When he played volleyball in the wing, against the wall, he was confused and alternated between undies and shorts.

One day, Soumitra Banerjee was entertaining five girls and three guys in his Room 247. Ajay Singh was walking from the bogs to his Room 255 in his trademark undies. Naturally, Soumitra's room door was open and Ajay Singh heard laughter and cacophony coming from Room 247. He stopped short of the room and called Soumitra outside and requested him to shut the door so the girls wouldn't see him in the buff.

Soumitra was an innovative man, full of ideas. He told Ajay Singh not to worry, he would think of a way without closing the door. He was doing a psychology course with Rehana Ghadially and would put one of her principles into practice. He told Ajay Singh to quickly run past his room when he heard the words 'shooting star'. Soumitra then went into his room, pointed to his window and shouted, 'Shooting star!' Everyone turned towards the window to see it, and Ajay Singh sprinted away with his modesty intact.

Soumitra was elated with his success, and related the whole story to his guests. After ten minutes, Ajay Singh again called Soumitra out. This time, he had to take a pee and needed to go by the room again. Ajay Singh told Soumitra, '*Junta ko phir se* shooting star *dikha dena.* My bogs *jaake aata hoon.*' Soumitra dutifully carried out Ajay Singh's instruction. When Soumitra said 'shooting star', everyone turned towards the door. This time they did see the shooting star.

~

In spite of all the variety of people who inhabited H4, our hostel was devoid of any religious symbols. This was in a stark contrast with most students' houses and with the world right outside Powai. It was as if there was an unwritten rule banning display of religious symbols in the hostel. Overall, that was a good thing. It provided a neutral ground for students of various religions and sects to interact with each other freely. There were intense debates on topics ranging from whether there is a God, who created this God, what is the purpose of life and so on. After all, there was no proof about God in Kreyszig's calculus tome. Some students ventured into exploring new intellectual approaches such as EST, but old time religions were pooh-poohed.

In this barren agnostic world, a few individuals openly pursued their quest overcoming the ridicule from the rest of 'prove it or else it doesn't exist' techno crowd. Kocharekar was one of them. He was in my wing, and also my class mate in Computer Science. He got into reading Hare Krishna books and visiting ISKCON temples regularly. He then decided to invite the ISKCON group to H4 for a discourse.

So on one fine evening, about twenty saffron-robed ISKCON devotees and their Swami descended upon our hostel. In those innocent days, no permission from any authority was required.

The ISKCON folks set themselves up between the central and south wing. Students began to gather around them. The visual contrast was fascinating. On the one hand there were clean-shaven (head and face), clean-robed ISKCON folks and on the other hand were students with their ragged, unkempt, some unwashed assortment of clothes. The session started with a kirtan—sung in an odd mixture of accents. Some ISKCON folks were from Western parts of the world and pronounced Sanskrit words in a strange way. However, what they lacked in diction, they made up through their sincere efforts. The kirtan was followed by a brief lecture from the Swami. Finally, he invited students to ask him questions. Questions were initially polite but soon degenerated into a typical IITan cross examination. Although the questions themselves were perfectly logical and intelligent, the tone became more and more insulting. Eventually a few of Swami's well-built disciples, upset and provoked by the treatment of their leader, stood up in an aggressive stance to stop the barrage. But the Swami calmed them down, listened patiently and tried to address the onslaught. On one hand were sceptical students demanding logic/proof and on the other hand was faith/intuition/experience. As typically happens when two sides have diametrically opposite yet firm views, the night ended up in a stalemate.

—*Shekhar Bhide, '80-'85*

~

ISKCON. We had among us a brilliant mind, in 1980. Manjunath. He and I were both freshies then, and partition mates in SWGF. He was a staunch ISKON follower and a topper as well. Unlike Kocharekar, however, I think he left IIT in his first year itself and joined ISKON full-time, and changed his name to Swami something. He used to say 'I will care for God, and God will care for my family'.

Talking of spiritual experiences, I have not had any, so, really cannot comment. But last year in H4 during the Mood Indigo and alumni celebrations, I had the 'privilege' of listening to some detailed explanations of the spiritual experiences of Asanka Sen. I could not tell how much of it was driven by spirits that had gone down his throat.

—*Rajeev (Jora) Jorapur, '80-'85*

~

I met both Manjunath and Kocharekar last year (2009), and though I don't know whether they discovered 'I' or not, they definitely discovered something. In my view these three guys: Manjunath, Kocharekar and Madhusudan have achieved more than anyone I have known since they left IIT.

Madhusudan now heads ISKCON Bangalore, Akshaya Patra feeds approximately ten million kids every day. His company produces a TV show, 'Krishna'. He has built theme parks, and is in the process of building perhaps the biggest theme park in India. ISKCON Bangalore is under construction too. Kocharekar heads ISKCON (minus ISKCON Bangalore). He too has dabbled in software, import-export, and has a textile unit. ISKCON is no longer a cult where crazy swamis abduct you and you sing and chant until you either get bored and drop out, or decide to stick with it because you burned all other bridges. Now ISKCON is a regular religious movement. These guys have built better, bigger temples to visit for pujas. They have relationship managers who bring prasadam to your home and schedule puja timings. A friendly clean temple experience you always wanted.

Last year I was in Mathura and visited old temples. I was afraid of pickpockets and was accosted by random guys who quite threateningly demanded alms. Then we went to the ISKCON temple. It was a calm and clean place. I did puja, got prasadam which I knew wouldn't make me sick, I even went to their guest house and freshened up before heading back to Delhi. That is thinking and planning I have never seen anyone else do in India. So hats off guys, I am proud of you.

—*Sanjay Kohli, '80-'85*

~

S. Madhusudan (Sivashankar Madhusudan) graduated as a Civil Engg from IIT Bombay. He is now known as Madhu Pandita Das and is the head of ISKCON Bangalore, Chairman of Akshayapatra Foundation (Harvard case study example and winner of several prestigious awards focusing on child literacy and mid day meal schemes), and Chairman of The India Heritage Foundation. Madhu, operating from a temple built by him at a cost of 40 crores, is spiritual guru to millions. He is involved in a controversial succession battle with ISKCON Mumbai.

He has done pioneering work in organic farming at Mysore. During his stay at Hostel 4, he was seen as a rebel. Toward the end of his stay, he, along with Vijay Govindan, Manjunath and Joseph, had embraced the ISKCON movement.

~

Chinchpokli Reprise

Madhu wanted to go to Lucknow to visit his sister. He asked Gogate about the departure time of Lucknow Express from VT. Gogate said *dus pachis*. Madhu, with his Mallu Hindi interpreted 'pachis' as 'pachaas'. He got to VT at 10.30 to catch a train he thought would depart at 10.50. Unfortunately for Madhu, that was a golden day in the history of the Indian Railways because the train actually departed at the scheduled time of 10.25. A dejected Madhu decided, rightly, to return to H4 and wrongly, to chant Krishna bhajans in CWFF.

Krishna however did not smile upon Madhu. What followed is this:

Madhu caught a local at VT. It was a long way to Vikhroli, and as people do, he dozed off . When he awoke and looked out of the window, he saw that the train had stopped at Chinchpokli station. It was still a ways to Vikhroli, so he dozed off again. After a while he awoke with a start, praying that he hadn't missed Vikhroli. The train had stopped, and there were only railway tracks outside his window. He looked out on the other side. The station was still Chinchpokli except that now it had moved to the other side. Krishna alone could have moved the station from the left to the right. And since Krishna did not perform miracles during Kalyug, Madhu correctly deduced that he had slept through the up journey and a good way through the down journey. His suspicions were confirmed when his train headed toward VT, and then back toward the elusive Vikhroli. I don't think Madhu was in the CS department but he was practicing the do loop—because he dozed off again, and awoke again at Chinchpokli. By this time Madhu had wised up, and he decided that he would simply not close his eyes anymore. He would stay awake all the way to Vikhroli. True to his resolve,

249

he stayed awake, and wondered why everyone in the compartment alighted at Kurla and a whole new herd got in. Only when the train started toward VT—again—did Madhu realize that it was a Kurla train he was in. At great cost to his life and his baggage, he jostled his way through the crowd and jumped out of the moving train.

Enough was enough. Madhu decided he would now catch a train to Vikhroli which was just three stops away and he would not even sit, and therefore would stay awake and reach H4 in time to tell Krishna how much he doted on him. But not for nothing is Krishna known as the natkhat Kanha of Brindavan. Krishna had put Madhu in a train that did stop at Ghatkopar. As Madhu was making his way to the exit, he watched with horror as the train, instead of stopping at the next station which was Vikhroli, hurtled past it, and Kanjurmarg, and Bhandup, and Mulund, and finally came to a stop at Thane. This was a fast train, and clearly, events were happening too fast for Madhu that day. He found solace in the fact that he was aspiring to get to Vikhroli, and this time, he had managed to go far beyond, all the way to Thane.

Madhu now prepared himself for his next mission: He would find a train that was not a harbour line train, not a Kurla train, not a fast train, and one that would deliver him in one piece to Vikhroli. He found such a train. He heaved a sigh of relief. Already stressed out and fagged out, he—yes, he did doze off again—and awoke. Yes, at Chinchpokli.

Nobody is clear about what happened after this because we all were in splits by the time Madhu's narrative reached this point. He told us all this because we saw him walk into H4 at midnight with his Lucknow bag in hand, and we wondered aloud how he got back from Lucknow so fast. Did he take a flight to and fro?

~

Excitement of the unknown, curiosity to know, creativity using limited resources, desire to explore beyond known boundaries and experiment with life. Stuff IITans think and do—stuff that explained the tremendous variety that hit you when you walked into H4.

I invited my girlfriend (now my dear wife) to my hostel one day, and she was shocked to witness an ISKCON off-shoot. This small group had literally given up pursuit of technology and had dedicated themselves to the pursuit of Krishna. They had by this time created their own 'temple' and were down to flowing robes and regular chants and prayers. One side of the wing- you could hear Ian Anderson belting out *Thick as a Brick* and from the other side the chanting of *Hare Ram, Hare Krishna*.

—*Sammy S*

~

Although there were not many religious symbols in the hostel itself, there were temples right outside the gates of IIT. The Devi Padmavati temple, which was Prof. Gadgil's pet project, and the Hanuman temple, to name just two. But not many of us had religion or temples on our minds, as the treasure hunt incident illustrates.

Many IITans tripped over each other to outfox people in contests like 'What's the good word' and treasure hunts and other such mind-bending games. The annual Gymkhana treasure hunt always enlisted a decent level of participation. It usually began after dinner at 10pm and carried on till the wee hours of dawn. The format was the same every year. People assembled at the badminton court, formed teams, received their first clue and went about solving the clue. Then they would go to the place or the person referred to in the clue and receive the next clue. Clues got progressively tougher and when the event finished late into the night, more than half the teams had dropped out.

In one such event, the organizers devised an innovative way to give out the first clue. Rather than give text written on a computer punch card, we had IIT's own rock star'Ouch' (Shrikant Awalegaonkar) perched on the high referee's chair in the badminton court with a guitar in hand to deliver the clue in song. He sang a'Kinks' song that went,

I'm an ape man, I'm an ape ape man
I'm an ape man I'm a King Kong man I'm ape ape man
I'm an ape man
'Cos compared to the sun that sits in the sky
Compared to the clouds as they roll by
Compared to the bugs and the spiders and flies
I am an ape man

This was the first clue and it was meant to be easy. Surely and expectedly, hundreds of participants rushed out of the badminton court in unison. What puzzled the organizers thoroughly, though, was the fact that not a single participant turned left towards Y-Point to reach the Hanuman temple just outside IIT where they were supposed to go. Everyone turned right. When realization dawned, the organizers recoiled in horror at what they had failed to anticipate.

In Hostel 6 lived 6-foot 3-inch tall and 3-foot 6-inch broad and dark Kenyan Ambrose Otieno who was also IIT's star basketballer and star athlete. It was too late for the organizers to rush to H6 and prevent a catastrophe. The first to reach him, H4's treasure hunt stars George Verghese, Patrick Kar and team, had poked a sleepy and a stunned Ambrose in the ribs and said, 'Hey apeman! Give us the next clue.'

Within the first fifteen minutes, there were at least half a dozen casualties. Bruised lips and bleeding noses decided the organizers. They set up a camp outside H6 to direct all participants to head to the Hanuman temple.

~

In a similar incident two years later, one of the clues—the third or fourth—was 'Sociable queen getting cross.' The intended target of the clue was the Civil Annexe building because according to an IITan's typical logic, sociable meant civil, queen was Anne and getting cross was symbolized by an X.

Unfortunately however, the participating IITans didn't think like the clue-setting IITans and instead, chose to make a beeline for H10 (the Ladies' Hostel), and seek out Medha Gore who was the Soc Sec. To make matters worse, people believed that she sported a cross look, and many were therefore convinced that the clue referred to her.

For once, it was fortunate that the rules in H10 did not allow people (male people) to go up to a girl's room. After a few initial failed attempts to call her out of her room, the scrooties got tough and managed to ward off insistent contestants who were later diverted to Civil Annexe by the distraught organizers.

~

H4 games. Dumb charades had become popular 1980 onward. A team member was given a written clue, generally a movie name, and he had to act this out before two other teammates without speaking a word, and the time taken to crack the clue was noted. The total aggregate minimum time decided the winning team. In H4, it became clear that the trio of Birjoo Mehta, Ashvin Sanghvi and Vijay Desai were the reigning monarchs. They were far ahead of anyone else. No clue, it seemed, was even remotely difficult for Birjoo to act out and for Ghoda and Vijay to decipher in record time. They had evolved all kinds of conventions amongst themselves. The number of words in a movie name were first identified. Easy words were acted out straightaway. Difficult words were truncated into multiple parts. Each of the parts was referred to by acting out and calling out its Hindi or English synonym. There were signals to denote opposites, exchanging syllables, rhyming words and even names of actors in the movie. After days of practice, Birjoo had converted his clueing technique into a fine art. He could convey an 'Albert Pinto *ko gussa kyon aata hai*' in six seconds. 'Arvind Desai *ki ajeeb dastaan*' could be delivered in five seconds.

Thus, when the time came for an inter-hostel competition, H4 was upbeat. And true to expectations, the trio coasted to the finals effortlessly. The finalists also included some tough nuts from H9 who were also good. But our stars had a clear edge, it was easy to tell. When it came to the last clue, we all knew that if our team would crack it in less than ten seconds, we could go home with the prize. Birjoo walked up to receive the clue. He glanced at the clue and smiled triumphantly. This one was a piece of cake and nobody could now separate H4 from the coveted prize.

The clue was *'Aakhri Daku'* and Birjoo wondered why such a clue was given in the first place. IIT clue setters always devised extremely difficult if not near impossible clues, and this one was certainly not. The apparent reason was perhaps the fact that *Aakhri Daku* was an unknown movie. *Aakhri Raasta*, yes. Maybe *Aakhri Dao* or even *Aakhri Khat*. But the Daku word was foxy and the organizers must have thought it would be elusive too. Not for Birjoo though. He would quickly clue in Aakhri and for Daku, he just needed to point towards KV and presto! Daku would be home and so would the trophy.

Birjoo started off in right earnest. He gesticulated.

'Two words,' said Ghoda and Vijay. Birjoo nodded and gesticulated again.

'Hindi.' A nod again. More action.

'First word.' Nod. Action.

'One.' Action.

'In Hindi? OK. Ek'. Action.

'Expand it? OK? Pehla?' Action

'Opposite of pehla, is it?' Nod.

This was when Ghoda went through an identity crisis. Was he the winning horse for H4? Or was he a Gujju first before anything else? Ghoda decided that he was a Gujju and before Vijay could remember his Hindi lessons and recall the opposite of pehla, Ghoda moved his Gujjudom into the contest.

'Opposite of pehla? Simple. It is Chhella. OK, got it. Movie is *Chaila Babu*.'

Before the stupefied Birjoo could even act out 'No you donkey! You idiot! You monkey! You rascal! This is not Bhavnagar', Ghoda quickly collected himself and his victorious smile, got up and moved over to the H4 entourage to start shaking hands and saying 'thank you' to those who would tell him 'congrats'. By the time he realized his faux pas and ran back to his seat, many seconds had elapsed. Crestfallen Birjoo looked as if he would strangle Ghoda and his entire neighbourhood in Sion who must have influenced him to think in the 'Chaila Babu' school of thought.

The loudest laughs were from H9-ers who were saved by some queer Gujju logic.

~

Around 1980 a game called Anti-Chess became a craze. The object was to get all one's pieces killed by one's opponent, the player with all pieces off the board first was the winner. The craze caught on so strongly that Sports Sec Phule had to conduct an Anti-Chess championship in the hostel. And guess who the winner was? It was a surd called Surd. What else did we call them? His name might have been Ajit or Rajeev, and he played TT too. Initially, his presence near the chess board attracted the usual and obvious PJs about a Surd playing chess, how could we resist? But when it was seen that he was playing Anti-Chess and that he actually won, suddenly the fact of Surd winning the Anti-chess tournament made a lot of sense and it wasn't funny anymore. How could he not win?

~

We were provided passive entertainment every Friday night, in the form of the Friday Night Movies in the Convo. These contributed significantly to many pleasant memories of IIT. Over half the hostel would empty, because the locals—those with homes in the city—went home. The campus descended into a soothing end-of-week tranquillity. The silly Hindi movies enhanced this experience. H4 junta had their regular seating area, a spot on the front right of the Convo entrance. The movies were entertaining, but not always in the way they were intended.

Some seniors before our time had a kind of a bet that one of them would go up and kiss the heroine on the screen while the movie was on. Let's assume that the heroine was Zeenat Aman. In order to help this intrepid hero, a few guys walked up to the screen with him, formed a human pyramid like we used to during Krishna Janmashtami celebrations, allowed him to climb up on the shoulders of three layers of guys to reach Zeenie's lips. But by the time he reached the top, the scene changed and our hero was rewarded with Pran's lips when the kiss materialized.

One of the Friday movies had a famous Gujarati actress in the lead and Garam Dharam was the hero. The scene shows the heroine in a temple talking to God with a small wish in her mind 'Bhagwan! *Meri ek chhoti si aas hai . . .*' The entire Convo erupted with peals of laughter at this request, and some cried out that this lady was extremely ungrateful. Everyone remembers how well stacked she was there, and yet she had the cheek to call it *'chhoti si aas.'*

~

VCRs became available in the early eighties and it opened up the possibilities of watching certain educational kinds of movies in the privacy of a lounge. Much earlier, a few unsavoury incidents resulting from watching 8mm flicks in a cubby hole of a room had led to the closing down of that option. In 1982, H4 awoke to the possibility of watching two cassettes, *Deep Throat* and *Private Nurse* (which were borrowed from Rajiv Kohli, H7), on a VCR. We were unsuccessful in renting one. Then TNT (a tall, lanky, wiry guy with prominent features, did funny dances and his real name was Tarang N Thakkar) offered to borrow one from his dad's electronics stores if we sprang for the sixty rupee cab fare. We sprang, and were finally watching Linda Lovelace perform oral calisthenics in the lounge whose doors were shut tight and entry was controlled tightly too, through the narrow door on the wash basin side of the mess. The flick did provide initial thrills as expected. But a few engineering minds got impatient after a while and started wondering if what they saw was physically possible or not. Some opined that it was trick photography. On insistence from many of these engineering minds, a rewind was ordered to check the trueness of the act. The rewind process provided us with a view of said acts taking place in reverse motion and that turned out to be hilarious. For instance, a reverse ejaculation induced the comment, 'he is going, he is going'. This must have been the only instance in recorded history where the blockbuster *Deep Throat* was seen backwards and enjoyed more as a comedy rather than forwards and . . .

⁓

Q: What do you call a dashing Malayali?

A: Debo Nair

Right. Along with the mess bill, we collected money for the Amenities Fund which was used for upkeep of the lounge, maintenance of the lawn, sports equipment and so on. Part of the lounge upkeep involved magazine subscriptions to all the magazines that were available at that time.

One of these magazines was *Debonair*. This was a singularly useless magazine except for one feature—the centrespread. By today's standards, the centrespread was pretty tame, but in those days educational material of that nature was rare. The problem was that within minutes of the magazine being placed in the lounge, the centrespread would be gone, causing considerable distress among the sex-starved inmates.

A solution (no pun intended) was devised. The magazine was delivered to the Literary Secretary who would remove the precious centrespread taking utmost care not to harm the model. He would pin it up in a locked glass covered notice board in the lounge, for all to enjoy.

Now, when I was the G Sec, I had merely inherited this tradition, but I saw every reason to uphold it (pun intended). But this tradition inevitably met with some conscientious objectors. Some students complained that their visiting parents were offended by this. I blithely replied that the hostel was for students and not for parents.

The commies, for some reason, decided to take their focus away from the plight of the mess workers and being champions of the downtrodden, and ganged up with the feminists to tread on our horny inmates demanding that this fine tradition be brought to an abrupt end thereby giving new meaning to KLPD. Yours truly hid behind democratic principles and refused to budge.

Later in my G Sec career, I would have occasion to ponder on the philosophical differences between democratic principles and mob psychology. But at that point, I was thinking with two heads and in retrospect, two heads were not better than one. All the accusations of promoting the objectification of women were brushed off summarily as inconsequential to the interests of the inmates I was representing.

Looking back, I don't think I could have done anything different, but I could have seen some merit in the arguments against the practice and been more sympathetic to people whose sensibilities were outraged. But back then it was literally a case of, the penis mightier than the sword. Or rather, the penis mightier than the dhoka.

—*Fish*

~

H4 put it all together when it came to a common purpose. Especially when it involved entertainment and entrepreneurship.

Black and Blue

Ajay Shah went back to his room to change into a clean H3 t-shirt and dab on some Old Spice (there might even be some girls at the H4 fete). Then he walked out toward the music blaring from the lawns. He smelt the chat masala in the air, and was tempted to head over to the bhel puri stall, but decided to try the Lucky 7 tables first.

He was soon engrossed in the game, placing one rupee bets and losing steadily, when he was startled by a thick, hairy arm on his shoulder. 'Don't forget to check out the movie in the third wing,' the senior who had ragged told him, 'remember the time we first met? It'll help you, man.'

Ajay blushed, the memory of that incident still strong: he'd been forced to demonstrate his most private actions, and had felt humiliated. It was only later that he felt liberated of the guilt associated with the act—the seniors, led by a large hairy-chested fellow who asked to be called V-Sir, had laughed at his hand motions—but when the ragging was done, assured him they all did it, too!

He frowned at the reference, but decided not to dig. 'OK, V-Sir, I'll go there if I have money left.'

'Well, stop gambling and go now.'

261

Ajay took the advice, stopping first to buy a cold Arlem Pilsner, very conscious that he would be broke the rest of the month, and then joined a serpentine line winding down the staircase into the corridor. Every fifteen minutes, a bunch of laughing young men would come down the staircase, and the queue would jerk forward. Ajay had to wait nearly an hour, and was wishing he'd not come alone—there were no girls around, anyway.

The movie was running in the corner room of the far wing. H4 had rooms in pairs, separated by the partition. They were really packing the audience in—after he'd paid the five rupee fee, Ajay was told to stand on a bed and look over the partition. He soon forgot the discomfort of perching on his toes to get a view, enthralled by the moans of lust and the flickering blue tinted celluloid from the 8mm projector, absorbed with detail of anatomy and action he'd only imagined: at first it was revelatory—and then Ajay thought it fitted well with the Ted Mark novels lying under his mattress.

His mind reeling with the images of those sleek Nepali women, he went off into the dark corner of the ground floor to finish his beer and dwell on the pleasant arousal. When he tossed the empty bottle over the wall, he saw the glowing tip of a cigarette, and leaned over to find V-Sir and Sexy talking to a tall student. The senior noticed him, and waved him over.

'Enjoyed the show?'

Ajay was glad the darkness hid his blush, 'yea—it was ok. What are you guys doing here?'

'Reviewing security,' Sexy said. Ajay knew he was the Social Secretary of H4. 'The projector and reels will get lowered from the window if we hear the Warden is walking around the hostel—and Janjua will grab it and head over the hills to Chand Shah Darga.'

'Impressed!' Ajay said, quite awed by the forethought and planning.

'Come get a drink with me,' V-Sir said, as he jumped the wall and headed over to the second wing.

Ghoda Sr. and Punk stood at the door of the corner rooms, counting cash. 'Hey, man, unbelievable success! Check out the crowd in there, and the line for the movie. We'll make the target for the new music system easily!'

'Cool. Two whiskeys with soda,' V said, paying Ghoda Sr., 'just be careful no one gets too drunk and makes a fuss.'

'We have the Fiji footballers on stand-by,' Ghoda Sr. assured him, 'Jai and Satkya will keep anyone who makes trouble locked in an empty room till they sober up.'

Punk took out his tobacco pouch and rolled a cigarette, and the senior lit up a Wills. Ghoda promptly took over Punk's drooping fag, much to Ajay's amusement.

Ten days later, Ajay walked into the Electrical Engineering Department for a viva voce with Professor Malkani. He knocked and had to wait a few minutes, when the door opened with a bang, and a red-eyed and unshaven V-Sir brushed past him. The retreating figure wore a rumpled black shirt streaked with ash, and seemed to be talking to himself.

'Sorry about that. I guess he's a little upset.' Prof Malkani was composed, and Ajay thought there was a glint in his eyes. 'He just heard the H4 General Sec has been called to the Director's office over a small incident, and thought I should have stood up for him.'

'That's the guy they call Punk?' Ajay asked, digging.

'Yes—I like the young man. He's a go-getter. Came up with an idea for raising money for the hostel, and the Students Council helped execute, and they pulled it off. I'm not sure it's to do with factionism—but some of the students thought some money was siphoned off.'

'Wow! What will happen to Punk?'

'It's for the Director to decide—my take is Punk's clean—if any wrong doing was done, it's not him. Now the project itself was misguided—but there's nothing but youthful zest for life to blame for that!'

Later, returning to his hostel, Ajay saw an unusually dapper figure—almost formally dressed—walking ahead of him, and hurried to catch up. Even the drooping moustache had acquired a certain grooming.

'I heard you were called to the Diro's office?'

Punk smiled, 'Yes. Survived, man. My CPA is down to the 7s. If he had called my parents in I would have been in deep shit. But he just lectured me for a half hour and let me go.'

'You guys have a good warden.'

Punk paused, 'yes—you're right. We never give Malkani enough credit. Anyway. We did get our music system. Come on over tonight. Homi and gang will be playing 'The Doors' till morning, and there'll be some maal from Chand Shah.'

—Aditya (Punk) Srinivasan, '71-'78

~

One day, before we had our own music system, there was a prominent notice on the board put up by Ravi Tilak and Viren Pathare. The notice announced that there was a top quality ghazal singer named some Dhar who was going to perform exclusively in H4 that evening. Dhar, according to the notice, was an accomplished ghazal singer who had given performances in several cities and was also aired on Radio Srinagar and was going to feature in an All India Radio concert at Delhi. This was a once-in-a-lifetime opportunity for music enthusiasts all over IIT and not just in H4. Hype was tremendous and expectation levels for that evening were unprecedented. All day, Tilak personally supervised the setting up of a 'stage' in the lounge and he also roped in several tabalchis, tanpura-ists and mike turning, sound adjusting, speakers fixing sideys. Viren supervised the floral arrangement and oversaw the chairs placement at the periphery while the centre was cleared for placing rented durries, of course red in colour. Atmosphere was festive to say the least.

Mr. Dhar arrived finally in a taxi. He was fair, balding at a furious pace and carried telltale signs of a handsomeness he must have once possessed. He was dressed in a long silk kurta and wore tight chudidars and mojdis and looked as if he would surpass the expectations folks had from him. Out of the taxi, he flashed the smile a seasoned performer flashes to those who welcome him with expensive bouquets as did Viren, who by the way, never presented such a bouquet to his sweetheart Meera despite his calls to her at an hour per day for 5 days in a week for 52 weeks in a year for the fourth year running. Dhar beamed several smiles at the throng of admirers, some of who were from the Datar family of musicians. This was before Tilak went on to marry Vandana Datar and much before Tilak would get her to perform in the Convo. True to expectations and the established convention in the Indian music world, Dhar fiddled with the harmonium, 'adjusted' the taal with the tanpura, got the tabla guy to match the beat and fussed and frowned till the setting was right after a gruelling 35 minutes of 'adjustments'. It was then that the performance started and the audience followed the protocol expected from them. They nodded their heads in appreciation, they hummed in accompaniment, they said 'wah wah' whenever it sounded like a punchline delivery within the ghazal. Dhar was impressed with the turnout of the fairer sex, never before and maybe never again seen in H4. The women were the invitees of eager folks who wanted to score brownie points by inviting their potential dates to a happening do. Ghazals were certainly in and in a way, quasi-intellectual. They were like the clues to a treasure hunt or to a 'what's the good word' where you had to decode a sound byte to arrive at the 'hidden meaning'. In a cloud, you were to find Dhar's sigh. In a star, you could seek a spark from his heart. There was pain and melancholy in his voice and in the text. Dard and Gham. Her 'nigaah' wounded his heart as no bullet from Sean Connery's pistol ever did. And while Dhar was on a roll and the women in the front row murmured a demure 'wah wah' and the guys in the back pronounced the performer as 'damn good', Pinakin Patel walked in after having listened to Jethro Tull's *Locomotive Breath* in his room, and he too was moved by Dhar's rendition of '*Aye dil mujhe aisi jagah le chal*' of Talat Mehmood and Pinakin finally gave his stamp of approval. 'This Ghazaler is good.' Ghazaler sounded like Guzzler and it did evoke the expected laughs.

And then came the climax. Just as Mr. Guzzler rose his pitch to an exciting and a feverish crescendo, in walked Rupert Desouza, braces and all. Rupert had kicked his daily 6-7 shins in the football field that day and walked into the lounge with his pock marked face and his fearful steel braces and exclaimed . . . 'Arre! This bastard is in my tutorial batch.' Most people laughed. A few thought that Rupert was confusing this outstanding performer with a lookalike in his tut batch. Only when Rupert started swearing on his mother and his God, a few people started taking him seriously. They all shhh-ed him when he was going ballistic but many eager minds wanted to wait and watch. Finally, after polishing off a lavish meal of specially ordered chicken with Tilak, Viren, Warden and the women, Mr Guzzler walked to the same taxi that was made to wait for him all this while. While bidding adieu, Tilak was seen giving the cabbie Rs 100 and Mr Guzzler was given Rs 600. Rupert walked angrily to Mr Guzzler and asked, 'Aren't you in my tut batch in the CC (Computer Centre)?' The smiling guzzler was still smiling while nodding a yes. And to a question of where he was heading for, he replied that he was heading back to where he came from. To Hostel 1, a hostel reserved for PGs and which was a ghazal throw away from H4.

Guys were appalled. He was one of us and he had fleeced us. Tilak and Viren did take a lot of flak but all attacks later were targeted on the guzzler. He would be seen walking from the MB to H1 several times carrying a 'jhola' and he would be greeted with comments like, 'Hey Guzzler bastard! Want a cab?' or 'Want a chicken up yours?' or 'What happened to your silk kurta? Did you return it?' The expression on his face told us that he finally started experiencing *'dard'* and *'gham'* and not even H1 was interested in promoting his talent any more.

～

Fleeced. By a PG. From H1. It can't get any lower than that.

—*Rohan*

～

That got everyone riled—that a H1 PG could outfox us. To Viren's constant question, 'Forget where he is from. Was he not good? Was he not worth 600 bucks?' we said, 'Yes, he was.' But the truth is, none could stomach the fact that Guzzler had pulled a slow one on us. He had performed in Srinagar and his resumé was good. But taking money from a fellow IITan was considered sacrilege in those days.

As Rupert told Viren later, 'You should have told me about him. I would have kicked him in his shins and got him here to sing for free.'

~

Occasionally, we would have visitors. Uncles, aunts, parents, prospective in-laws would arrive. Some brought much needed and very welcome funds. Some brought food from home or treated us and a few friends to dinners at restaurants. Some came to calm their nerves when memories of their own wild youth and desire to experiment with all things good and bad overwhelmed them. Sometimes these visits were unannounced, but usually they gave notice, and we had a chance to clean up our act according to their expectations, as much as we remembered them.

My father (one of the coolest guys I have known) decided that he wanted to join the twins on one of those final-year hostel graduation dinners. Having been forewarned about my parents planned visit, I wanted to give them a good impression.

The first task at hand was to clean my room and make sure there was no evidence of any of my extracurricular activities. This did not take too long since I had very few belongings.

The few unwashed undies lying on the floor, I pushed under my bed. The bed sheet which had not been changed for a couple of months I flipped upside down in the hope that the bodily stains were not visible. I emptied the pockets of my (only) spare trouser (to make sure there was no maal). I arranged textbooks neatly on the study table.

The second job was to make sure that the rest of the gang in the wing knew in advance that we were having some visitors. Chavan worried me—he was absconding as usual. Chavan had this nasty habit of walking down the wing (after a shower) in a skimpy towel, and in front of total strangers, in one swift Shivaji-drawing-a-talwar-like-motion, taking the towel off his meaty Bheem-like thighs and rigorously drying his hair. Nothing wrong with that, but he never wore underwear when he did this. Luckily I found Chavan in the mess and told him to be on his good behaviour.

My father, true to his character, since we were graduating, came with a bottle of whiskey. He insisted that we join him for a drink, which we did very reluctantly. My mother kept telling him that he was spoiling us and that we seldom drank. Our parental party was underway in Chavan's room since, despite my gallant effort in tidying up my room, the ambience of Chavan's room was much more hospitable.

After a few drinks my father decided to check out my room to which I reluctantly agreed. Having cleaned my room I was quite confident that there was nothing incriminating that he was going to spot. He spent a minute or two, commented on the fact that there were no books in my room. And just when we were about to return to Chavan's room we both heard birds chirping. He looked around and asked what is that.

I said, 'Nothing, Papa, some pigeons.'

He said, 'Where did they come from?'

I said, 'I am raising them.'

He said, 'Really I didn't know you were fond of birds.'

I said 'It's good to have some company when I am studying late.'

Then he asked me 'Where are these birds?'

I had no choice but to show him. So I stood on my bed and pointed to the top of the closet. There it was, a big nest, built over a period of few months, and in the middle a few young squabs and few un-hatched eggs.

He looked at me and said 'Good to see that you have developed some interests other than engineering. I was getting worried about you.'

—*Sammy S*

~

One day Fish's kindly parents dropped in unexpectedly. We saw them from the lounge and I invited them, and when that didn't work, pulled them into the lounge and pretended that Vasu had taken away Fish's room key by mistake. Vasu and Gilfrou aka Harry hurriedly cleaned up Fish's room, they removed all the cigarette butts and arranged his stuff neatly. They also kicked out the billie that Fish slept with.

Eventually, when we 'found' Vasu, he said 'Oops, here's your key', and we all trooped into Fish's room with his folks and I got a jolt. Such a clean Fish room (was always a fish market), I had never seen. Shows what a clean-up master Vasu was.

Sadly, I could not avail of his services when my uncle came directly to my room. I had to pretend that this was Ajay Singh's room, and I walked into Ajay Singh's room and called it mine. Uncle was surprised that I had a calendar of Lord Ram, and he looked disgustedly at Ajay Singh when I introduced him. I had my wall plastered with centrespreads.

—*Bakul*

~

Parents and family were justified in their worries. Many of us did of course experiment with anything and everything, sometimes to excess. The drinking, for one, led to all sorts of hairy situations, and we got out of most with only stories to tell. Looking back, they were funny stories, but it could well have turned out otherwise. And these booze binges needed booze, of course, so we had to turn on our business brains before we could turn them off with the liquor.

When the first Mood Indigo was being organized in 1973, I thought it would be great to have a Disco during the event. The committee accepted.

The venue was a huge hall, a sometime cafeteria, with one wall of windows facing the Gym building. Thirty or forty guys happily volunteered. For our Egyptian theme we pasted sheets of white paper along the one long wall, and artists from H4 drew and painted pyramids, pharaohs, sphinxes, Egyptians, palm trees, etc, along the whole wall. Anil 'Neelu' Vaswani, was kind enough to lend his super-duper Akai dual-deck, and taught two guys how to operate it. I stayed away from the contraption. If something went wrong with it, it would take three years of my tuition, hostel rent and mess money, and even that wouldn't be enough to cover its cost.

We got multi-coloured flashing lights and mirrors, and created a dancing area. The cafeteria counter was turned into a bar. On one side of the room we placed several gymnastics mats from the gym and hung a separation net. This was for people who smoked a variety of exotic smelling concoctions from Chand Shah's Darga.

We got approval to sell beer. Complex calculations by a bunch of experts from H4 concluded one hundred cases of beer were required. A contact would supply Arlem Beer at a greatly discounted price (or so we thought). We needed several thousand rupees. We were assured that if we bought it with our money, the committee would reimburse us in a couple of days. And of course, we were so enthusiastic about our disco that we believed it. Several guys chipped in and we got the beer.

We had a bunch of 4-5 Iranian students at IITB at the time. These guys were rowdy, belligerent and always looking for a fight. I worried that these guys would create trouble. I talked to their leader (I think his name was Saeed), and put him in charge of all security and safety at the Disco. He was totally thrilled with this 'responsibility', as if he had made the rank of general in the Iranian Army.

The opening night at the disco was a blast. The music was great. There were actual girls there. The beer was selling well. And there was a huge smoky and hazy area behind the net, on the gym mats. (It was also the first time for many of us to see pot-smoking, staggering-drunk girls.) The Iranians, full of self-importance, were walking up and down patrolling. They would come to me every ten minutes, and ask me seriously if everything was going OK, and I would tell them that they were doing a terrific job.

The problem started sometime after 10pm. There was this Kashmiri guy who hung around with the Iranians, who walked into the disco with a whole lot of liquor in him. He started dancing and banging into people and generally making a huge nuisance of himself. Arguments broke out. There was pushing and shoving. And the Iranians tried to calm him down and stop him from getting violent.

In the middle of all this, 'Gidu' from H8 declared, 'I know how to handle this, I've read about these situations. Watch me.' And before I could do or say anything, Gidu had balled up his right fist and hit the guy really hard on his face, and turned to me and said, 'That should sober him up'.

Well, it didn't. He went crazy, and so did the Iranians. All hell broke loose. More people got into the fight. So now Gidu was running around and these five guys were chasing him through the crowd. In desperation, Gidu went to the edge of the terrace and jumped to the ground. I don't know how he didn't break any bones, but we did see him running away in the dark.

Then the authorities stopped us from selling beer, although our beer had nothing to do with the incident. And now there was no money forthcoming to pay for the beer. Although the Disco was still running, we were stuck with eighty cases of beer. We couldn't drink that much beer ourselves, even over several weeks and months. And even if we did try that, we didn't remotely have the money to pay for it. We had to figure out a way to get rid of it for cash.

I managed the canteen in the lounge in H4. We had a mess boy running it and selling toasted sandwiches, baked beans, Coke, etc. (Incidentally prices were deliberately kept low. The intention was not to make profit, but to serve as an occasional alternative to the mess food. It seems unimaginable now, but we would buy a two-dozen case of Coke for Rs 5.80, and sell each chilled bottle for 25 paise). We had a storage room to keep supplies for the canteen. It was the last room on the ground floor in the first wing. And that is where we stored all the cases of beer that we were stuck with.

Whenever we got news of a hostel having a fete, we would get there first and sell them the beer. We got rid of ten cases at H7, which they did not manage to finish. Before they could off-load them at the H5 Fete, we sold H5 ten cases. Some of our guys from the wing sold some off to a restaurant at Vikhroli station.

We still had some forty cases left when some unhappy souls complained to Warden that there were guys storing evil stuff like liquor on the hostel premises. I found out when the 'inspection' was to be carried out. We hurriedly got two cars. The cars were parked on the road between H4 and H3, going towards the pipeline and Vihar Lake. We had a human chain pass the cases of beer from the room, over the wall, and into the two cars where they were put in the front seat, back seat and trunk. The cars then drove away. The whole operation hardly took fifteen minutes.

Then we hung around the Warden's office looking innocent. Inspection time, I unlocked the room and expressed utter shock that we could be accused of doing such things. The room of course, was empty, except for Coke and baked beans.

It took us several months to get rid of the stock, which was snuck back into the storage room. When there were just a handful of cases left, they had been in that hot room for a long time. We decided to open one. It was barely drinkable, so we threw the last five cases away.

* OK, so how many nerds divided 5.80 by 24 to figure out the cost of each bottle?

—*Vicky*

~

There were times when we would have mass booze parties which were open to everyone in the hostel. I forget where the funding for these parties came from, but it only allowed for the cheapest alcohol. In those days, the cheapest legitimate alcohol was government certified country liquor. Ratna Country Liquor was right across from the YP gate. Country liquor came with fruit names—mosambi, narangi and so on, but they were all clear. Since the liquor was pretty strong and most people with the exception of me could not drink it straight up, it had to be mixed with something. For our hostel parties, we mixed it with gallons of sherbet and served it in buckets with serving ladles.

On the day of one of these parties Bakul and I had gone into town for a reason that I will not divulge. When we got back, there was pandemonium coming from the lounge. Pandemonium in the lounge is not abnormal, but Bakul and I were curious. What greeted us when we went to look was a whole bunch of guys staggering and singing and rolling on the ground. Staggering pleasantly drunk was the norm at these parties but these guys were clearly out of control. We investigated. The buckets labelled mosambi and narangi and other such fruit flavours, since they were mixed with sherbet, were taken to be just sherbet. People who had never touched a drop of liquor had ingested massive amounts.

Neither Bakul nor I are the Florence Nightingale types. But there is a camaraderie among drunks and maybe that's what moved us to help people to their beds. We found Anil Bansal in dire straits rolling on the lounge floor and actually frothing at the mouth. Bakul and I tried unsuccessfully to stand him up. We got a guy in slightly better shape to help us carry him. Luckily his room was on the ground floor and in the south wing so we didn't have to carry him very far. We changed him into his pyjamas and tucked him in.

As we were leaving, Bansal suddenly got up and reached for the alarm clock on the table. Bakul and I both thought that Bansal for some reason wanted to smash his alarm clock. I was an avid P.G. Wodehouse reader. I was thinking, 'Bansal reached for his clock with hostility, for some inexplicable reason'. Bakul and I held him back. Bansal again tried to get up and again Bakul and I restrained him with a 'Bansal, no!' marvelling at how strong he seemed despite being sozzled.

Bansal again tried to get up and again we restrained him. And Bansal let out an exasperated yelp saying 'I just want to see the time, yaar!'

Bakul and I felt sheepish and told him the time and asked him to sleep.

—*Fish*

∿

Bansal was quiet, meek, diminutive and a restrained freshy till that day. He spoke mostly Hindi being a Delhi resident. He came from an affluent family of jewellers and was the youngest amongst seven brothers. And in his drunken stupor, he stupefied us by stammering, 'Ritu Mehra! Where art thou? Don't mar thy beauty by being so inaccessible.' He spent his remaining four plus years in IIT feeling sheepish about this incident and still recoils with embarrassment if we talk about it.

—*Bakul*

∿

Piggy and Fish of the Flies

The hostel mess closed during vacation time. Sometimes during this time, hostels would compete with each other to provide catering services for various events like the Inter-IIT Sports Meet and various industry conferences held on campus. Mess workers were paid extra to work instead of having paid vacations for four months a year. We made a profit which went toward the Hostel Amenities Fund for upkeep of the lounge.

One such December we catered for two big events. The Inter-IIT Sports Meet and a high-budget Civil Engineering conference. Fifteen student volunteers ran the show. Among others, there was Waghamare, Pai, Vasu, of course Bakul, and a guy I am going to call Piggy for reasons that will be soon apparent. Slaving day and night, we made a net profit of about Rs. 31,000. That was big bucks in those days. To put it in context, it was close to twice my first year's salary in Tata Burroughs. The Warden readily okayed a budget of up to Rs.1,000 for celebrations. On top of it, the sponsors of the Civil Engineering conference were very pleased at the work we had done and asked us what beer we would like. We said Haywards 2000. Whiskey? Peter Scot, of course. We were happy recipients of four dozen bottles of our preferred beer and two of the whiskey.

We geared up for a night of unbridled celebration. Snacks were bought. We assumed that only the guys who drank and the guys who were cool would join us. Poor Piggy was neither a drinker nor was he cool and just did not fit in. Neither had he touched a drop of alcohol in his life. But Piggy wanted to drink and party with us. This was like rain on our victory parade. We conferred secretly as to how to solve this problem. I was called upon to live up to my nickname, Fish. The plan was that I would challenge him to bottoms-up a full glass of the potent Haywards 2000, put him to bed, and continue with our party. To my discredit, I agreed wholeheartedly to this plan.

I poured my glass and Piggy's glass and said, 'Piggy, let me show you how to drink This is called bottoms-up' and proceeded to do it, the strong beer burning my throat despite all my practice. Piggy followed my lead, bottoms-up. But he did not go bottoms-up as we had hoped and planned for. Piggy kept chirping happily on, casting a damper on everyone's mood. I received cold stares, upon which I asked Piggy to join me in another bottoms-up. Piggy gulped it down and kept on babbling. Enough was enough. So I poured out a third glass for Piggy and me and said, 'Piggy?' Piggy happily followed me again and continued talking. Then finally, mid sentence, he stopped, rocked, and fell backwards. We carried him to his bed and we continued with our party until morning.

I don't recall feeling the slightest twinge or remorse that night and as a matter of fact, we were all very amused by the whole incident, but almost thirty years later, as proud as I am of the 30,000 we earned for the hostel, I am horrified at what we felt justified in doing to Piggy. He had worked with us day and night and had every right to be part of the celebrations but we felt justified in our plan just because he did not fit in. As Wooster would have said, 'This is the kind of stuff that William Golding would have gotten a three volume novel out of, eh Bakul?'

Levity aside, Piggy, I am sorry.

—*Fish*

~

Two Guys One escape

In our second year guys were just learning the power of booze to make them look cool. Our friend Sanjay Chavan decided to show his moxy to his seniors, had a little bit too much booze and puked all over the wing. Initially everyone was amused and watched him with smiles—he had leaped too high and hurt himself landing. But as time went by he got worse instead of better, and then passed out cold. We had no idea what to do, some seniors suggested we take him to the hospi.

Bhaiyya, Rod, Gujju and I called the ambulance. They took one look at him and pronounced him a drug case and sent us to the state hospital in Ghatkopar. In the ER (Emergency Room) we are not the most serious case; we have a guy sitting right next to us bleeding from a recent knife wound. The nurse asked for the police report. He pleaded that he was alone and bleeding, but nurse wouldn't have any of it. He had to produce the police report. A policeman happened to be in hospital, some money changed hands, the police report appeared, the bleeding was taken care of.

Our turn. We told the nurse our boy had a little bit too much of the drink. She wanted to know what drug or poison it was. We filled in a huge form. All we wanted was a bed and an IV (probably just water). The bed was in a big hall with hundreds of patients, and they could not let all of us in. I bullied and begged and got to stay with Chavan for the night. A good thing too, five minutes of IV fluid, and Chavan's whole body began to shake.

I called the nurse. She was unimpressed. She asked me what I wanted to do. I told her we should do something to stop the shaking. She said she could remove the IV, if I signed the form that gave me complete responsibility in case Chavan died. Now, I did not get Chavan drunk. I was not even present when he imbibed and effected his temporary departure. I had known Chavan intimately for a few months, but didn't feel close enough to take on his death. So I declined, and waited a while. The shivering did not stop, and then his hand ballooned up at the IV site. I summoned the nurse again. She took one look and summoned the doctor. They both realized that they had to remove the IV. They said they would remove the IV but Chavan would now have to move to the floor, like most of the patients in the

281

hall. The floor smelled like urine and we found most of the people had brought their own beds. By this time Chavan had gained some consciousness and he could probably hear my conversation with the doctor. As soon as the doctor left I asked Chavan if we should just return home to the hostel, and he agreed.

With Chavan semi-conscious on my shoulder and no footwear on, we began our jail-break from the hospital. We made our slow way toward the exit, and the nurse saw us and shouted for us to stop, adding that we could not leave unless the doctor signed release papers. The staff was slow to respond to her, and we ran and literally fell down the stairs, and then rolled out of the hospital. We could hear commotion inside the hospital, they were still looking for us inside. And as luck would have it we found a taxi parked right under the stairs and the driver for some bizarre reason immediately agreed to take us to IIT.

We were back in our beds in the wee hours of the morning and we both slept through breakfast till lunch time. We had lunch together, other guys in the wing came and helped Chavan out and he was better by the end of day.

—*Kohli*

I remember Kohli, Gujju, Rod appeared. I was told that I was taken to the IIT Hospital where the nurse refused to admit me. I have a faint memory of the scene in IIT Hospital but nothing clear—a group of boys pleading for their passed out friend. Then it was dark.

Next I was on a bed somewhere and in extreme pain. The pain was due to someone pressing his knuckles hard in to my chest and turning them in a crushing action. It was a doctor with a stethoscope around his neck and this surely was a hospital and not the IIT Hospital. Next I heard him telling someone 'he is ok'. This someone was Gujju who looked worried but now showing some relief. I saw also Kohli and Rod. Then it was dark again.

Next I remember Kohli talking to someone—it turned out to be a nurse. I was seeing and hearing a bit and Kohli seeing me asked how I was. I said 'OK' I guess. This was about my swollen hand that was receiving a drip. The drip had already changed hands (no pun intended) and Kohli explained to the nurse and also to me that I had been shivering and that the hand was swollen like the other had been. Kohli was asking the nurse to take off the drip. The conversation was not simple—Kohli spoke to the nurse in Hindi, the nurse translated into Marathi for another person who replied to the nurse in Konkani, and then the nurse translated that to Hindi for Kohli. I could make out that Kohli wanted my IV to be taken out, and the third person wanted him to sign a form in case I died. In case I died!

Hell, at that point I was completely back to my senses. It was just a little drink that got me there, so it had pretty much worn off, but talk of my passing on brought me back entirely. I looked around, the place was filthy with bodily smells, dingy with 25 watt lamps located in alternate rows of beds, patients and visitors dozing, floor littered with sheets, slippers, people and other things I did not want to think about. At this moment of awareness I was having, Kohli made the proposal that we go back home. I was overcome with relief. If I was so close to my permanent departure, H4 seemed a much sweeter point for departure than this hell hole. After this I experienced a logistic exercise and show of courage and compassion that few would experience and fewer would demonstrate. I still feel great love and gratitude for my dear friends when I think about what they did next.

Kohli asked me if I was ready to leave. I said 'Yes'. 'OK.' Kohli told me 'I will make the arrangements'. He went to organize a taxi. Soon I heard the nurse was shouting 'somebody shut the door'—Kohli had left the lift door open to facilitate our escape. As Kohli came running in I began to get off the bed only to realize that I was only mentally alert, the body was refusing to accept any commands. Kohli saw this and lifted me up on his shoulders and ran to the lift. Kohli ignored all the shouting—different people shouting different things to different people in different languages— 'he is running away', 'stop those guys', 'call the doctor'— and carried me into the lift, shut the door and we were going down. That's when I realized that we were on a higher floor. All along, I had thought we were on the ground floor and all we had to do was run out. Being a runner, that did not seem such a task. If I had known how weak I was and that we were on a higher floor, I am not sure to have agreed to make a hospital break. I did not realize till then what Kohli would have to do to get me back home.

The cool IIT breeze made me feel that the world was how I remembered it and I knew I would be fine. I was back in H4.

—*Sanjay Chavan*

~

One of these parties we had organized really had a lot of booze. Seven or eight vodkas, twenty or thirty santra/mosambis and umpteen beers. Even so, all this booze was gone by midnight, and I went to Ghatkopar on Nagarkar's (H9) mo-bike to buy more. I drank very little, I had to remain sober all night to make sure everything was alright. A couple of fights were broken up, and the party went on until 3 o'clock in the morning.

Arvind Baliga from H2 drank continuously the whole time. At around midnight he started throwing up. I told Baliga he had enough, but he said, 'The night is young. I can drink whole lot more, this is nothing. I'll eat something I'll be fine' I tried to take the glass away from him but was unsuccessful. I advised him to be careful and moved on.

After the party, we cleaned up and went to bed. At 7am the watchman called me for a phone call. Cursing the caller, I went down to the lobby. It was Baliga's friend from H2. He informed me that Baliga had been admitted to Sion hospital. Shocked, I asked for details. It appears that Baliga was totally out by the time they went to the hostel. When he tried to put Baliga to bed, he fell off and was a little hurt and was shaky. They took him to the IIT hospital. Since IIT hospital could not give him an IV, they sent him to the Sion hospital.

Pai and I went to the Sion hospital. The ward was full of patients. There were patients on the beds, there were patients on the floor, and there were patients everywhere. After looking for Baliga everywhere, we finally asked. The nurse looked up the register and gave us XY co-ordinates. Pai and I went to that location. No Baliga. We looked around again, no Baliga. Last resort, we shouted for him. A person at Baliga's co-ordinates made a drinking action. We nodded our heads and he said, 'The drunk's friend came for him and they ran away without discharge papers.' Pai and I ran away immediately as well.

—*Raj*

~

On weekends, those of us whose home was in the city would go home, to rediscover the delights of our mothers' cooking. I'm sure mothers and fathers were happy to have this weekly visit to evaluate our progress, or even just to see we were still intact in body if not mind. But, eventually, H4 became home to such an extent that some Bombayites (sorry, Mumbaikars) became part of the gang that stayed back on weekends.

In our group was Rod. Klein Rodrigues. Rod was famous and infamous for many things, I will mention only three : This was the guy who had half his moustache shaved during the ragging period, this was the guy who famously told Hats 'Hopefully' when informed that Hats would pass out of IIT in a couple of years and this was the guy who was involved (yours truly being the main culprit) in ragging a freshy called Mahabaleshwarkar who was 'hospitalized' allegedly on account of the ragging session but in fact because he choked on his own name. So Rod: As the months in H4 progressed, Rod began to return earlier and earlier from his weekends home. Monday morning, Sunday evening, Sunday afternoon, Sunday morning and so on, and leave later and later for the weekends. Friday night, Saturday morning, Saturday afternoon, Saturday evening and so on, till he started to stay the weekends altogether. It was a nice time because we could then play footer, mug together and have wonderful outings in and out of the campus. The best were when we all went to his house for such wonderful meals, or when his father came to see him in the evenings and took us out for dinners to wonderful places.

I am sure there are others preferred to spend part of the weekend at H4 not because they loved their home less but because they loved the hostel more.

—*Sanjay Chavan*

~

I went home Friday evenings and came back Monday mornings during the first semester. The time I spent at home got shorter and shorter, because I lost track and never realized when it was already a weekend. I was always on or around the carom board. We would sometimes play carom days and nights without a break, have breakfast at 7:30 and then go to sleep. Vashya and Ganpya would be around most times. Someone would be playing various LPs. I never paid any attention to the songs. I had never heard any Western (rock or country or any other style) music ever in my life before IIT and hardly any after IIT. But the music playing in the hostel seeped into me without my knowing it. Recently I found myself singing along with a rock song I didn't know I knew.

When I did go home some stray weekend my father would ask me whether I was home to scrounge cash. He was right.

—*Sudhir Bapat, '76-'81*

~

While 'home' for me at Tardeo was just an hour away, I'd rarely show up at home even on weekends, preferring to hang out in H4 instead. That didn't go down too well with my mom.

One weekend I was home. It was Saturday evening, as mom kept calling my dad, brother and me to the dinner table, and she was getting tired of reminding us to come eat. Eventually we were seated. She served us some really delicious stuff—a warm '*bhakri*' (you have to be a true Maharashtrian to relish a warm bhakri). As I munched my first delicious morsel of home-cooked food, she asked me— I detected a slightly upset tone—'Tell me honestly, do you come home just to eat good food?'

Loaded question, but in my sheer joy at dining on her delicious cooking I dropped my guard and got a little too honest in my response.

'Well, I have a lot of clothes to get washed as well,' and kept on eating.

—*Dabba*

~

Keith Rebello left for home with his trademark red bag. He used the same bag for all the five years he was in IIT. Come rain, hail or sunshine, Keith would leave campus on Friday evening and return on Sunday evening. Keith was a man of systems. I should know, I was his room partner for most of the time. I would know Keith was ready to sleep, not when he wished me good night but when I smelt the strong smell of kaju feni from across the partition. Every night, two

288

capfuls of Goa kaju feni before bed. No more, no less. In five years I never ever saw Keith get drunk even though he loved his feni dearly.

On Friday evenings, the town guys like Ashish, Jetu, G, Keith, would leave for home. Primarily I suspect, to get their dirty clothes washed at home. No such luck for guys like me who had to stay behind on the weekends. My Saturday mornings were spent washing clothes. It seemed pointless to spend money for washing clothes when it could be put to far better use like cigarettes and booze. Bakul would also be found in the hostel on weekends. But, I never saw him wash any clothes. Eventually my curiosity got the better of me, and I asked him how he survived without washing. His explanation was simple: Use one set of clothes for fifteen days or so, dump them under the bed. It helped that he came from an affluent background and had enough clothes to last him a semester. I do hope he changed his undies more often than his outer garments.

Subra had a fixation about others' undies. Once Subra made freshies wear undies over the trousers, and all freshies from that batch went to lectures with this Phantom attire.

Subra described the Sammy twins' undies habits: On Monday, both twins wear their undies the right way. On Tuesday, both wear their undies inside out. On Wednesday, they exchange undies and wear them the right way. On Thursday, they wear those each other's undies inside out. Friday is a no undies day. Sat and Sun, undies get washed at home. Monday, the routine repeats.

—*Sanjiv Sood, '78-'83*

∼

What I remember about the Sammy twins' undie method is slightly different:

Mon—wear undies right side out.

Tue—wear them back to front.

Wed—wear them inside out correct side on the front.

Thu—wear the inside out and back to front.

Fri—no undies day.

—*Arun (Bevda) Gupta, '77-'82*

~

Being a Mumbaikar, during my first semester I thought I would take all my clothes to my parents' home and have them washed there. The first few occasions my mom was very happy to accommodate me, and had my clothes washed along with the home bed sheets and tablecloths that she got washed over the weekend. I am sure the bai (no machine washers back then) was not very happy with the big pile. I think she decided to teach me a lesson. One fine day, she delayed washing my clothes until a couple of hours before I was to leave and consequently, I had to lug a very heavy load of wet clothes through two BEST bus changes and a train ride and then finally the walk from Y Point to the hostel. I cursed the bai all the way back to my room, and I never took dirty clothes home again.

After trying to do some washing myself, I solicited advice from my wingmates. It was Benoy and Shaky who introduced me to the dry cleaning technique which saw me all the way through my bachelor life. They advised me to drop my clothes (undies and all) in the dry bucket (we each had a colourful one we had purchased on our first day in IIT). The next day reach into the bucket, pick out a pair of clothes you want to wear and off you go. Dry-cleaned.

—Pol

⁓

There was a more efficient and environmentally friendly method employed by a guy some years senior to me who shall remain nameless because my memory isn't what it used to be. He was from somewhere in Karnataka (Gulbarga, Bijapur some place like that, and no this was not Thomas Mathews from H4). Every new semester he would come back sporting a spanking new pair of jeans and T-shirt (one on his back and one in his backpack). Through the whole semester he would wear the two Jeans + T-shirt combos on alternate days but never wash or even 'dry clean' them. What he did for undies I was too polite to ask him but I suspect he never wore them. By the end of the semester his clothes were black and fashionably grimy. On the last day he threw one set in the garbage, he needed the second set for his trip home. Story has it that his mom buried that set under a banana tree in his yard and the tree bore the most fabulous bananas in all of Karnataka.

Since the jeans and T-shirt were made of bio-degradable materials and since he never wasted any water in washing them, I must declare him a pioneer of the Green Movement. Although looking at his clothes one should probably call it the black-and-brown movement.

—Satkya

⁓

There was another movement in H4 that became a cult. The cult of The Balaji.

First, some myths, legends, and facts that grew around The Balaji:

~ Never missed a class in his 5 years at IIT. Except when someone locked his room one day.

~ Never had tea. Ever.

~ No question of alcohol.

~ Or cigarettes.

~ Or any alternate intoxicants.

~ Never gambled.

~ Invariably began studying for tests more than 24 hours before the test time.

~ Never studied beyond twelve at night. Regardless of his preparedness for the test next day.

~ Never missed meals.

~ Never had rice. Ever.

~ Never gave gaalis.

~ Never discussed 'chicks'.

~ Never missed weekends at home.

~ Always caught the train at the same time: the 6.14pm fast local from Vikhroli to VT. The train was rechristened in his honour, 'The Balaji Superfast'.

Now all this may not seem unusual to some, but remember that he lived, out of choice, among some of the worst degenerates to have occupied the Madhouse at that point, some of whom indulged in all of the above-mentioned vices, sometimes simultaneously. However, he took every jibe and taunt we threw at him with a smile. And believe me, there were many.

—*compiled from contributions from Sanjiv Sood, Jetu, Ashish Khosla, G.*

~

About the origins of The Balaji® concept, this is how it started: Soon after the successful staging of *The Court of the Crimson King EP*, Balaji put up a notice on the notice board which read:

To all concerned
Here's a big THANK YOU for a great EP
Balaji

Maybe Balaji wanted junta to add their signatures to this notice, because the notice was on a foolscap sheet and there was a lot of empty space below the message. A few days later, there was an issue—the institute would not release funds due to us for running the inter-IIT sports mess during winter vacation. All of us put up a big fight with the Diro—Fish, Vasu, the entire council, even Manu who came down from Goa to fight for us, and of course, I-don't-give-a-shit warden Suresh Dixit. We got the money eventually. 30K, a colossal sum in those days. For kicks, Vasu and I put up a notice which read:

To all concerned
Here's a big THANK YOU for recovering money from the Diro
Balaji

Many guys thought that it was the newly conscientious H4-ite Balaji on the loose again. The next time there was a notice, someone scrawled below:

I support this
Balaji

Sometime, circa 82-83, mysterious notices appeared on hostel notice boards, ostensibly signed by The Balaji, now followed by an encircled R. Soon, some avid disciples starting approving notices with the 'The Balaji' sign. In short, nothing of note in H4 happened without the blessings of The Balaji. Notices not signed with 'The Balaji' were ignored, torn off or defaced. Freshies were now convinced that nothing in H4 moved without Balaji's (sorry, The Balaji's) sanction.

Very soon, every notice was splattered with I agree-Balaji, Thank you-Balaji, keep it up-Balaji.

As with so many other issues in H4, this one too spiralled out of control until 'Balaji' became 'The Balaji' and then 'The Balaji ®'.

For IITB's silver jubilee celebrations in 1982, Governor Air marshal Latif was chief guest. We decided to put up a banner which would say

'BALAJI WELCOMES THE GOVERNOR'

Security officer Singh told us we would have to get permission from the protocol attaché of Raj Bhavan. Vasu and I met the attaché. When we were negotiating with him, one of his guys suggested that if Mr. Balaji Raghavan came himself and made the request, it would help (we had told them that Balaji knew the governor personally and wanted to put up his own banner). After a lot of pleading the attaché finally agreed, but he wanted to confirm with the Governor's ADC first. He tried to get the ADC on the wireless set but the signal wouldn't go through.

And I did find Balaji in the library eventually, but by that time, the project had been abandoned. Very unfortunately,

H4 was denied one episode that would have been another sensation in IIT.

—*Bakul*

~

Thanks!

I had no idea at all that The Balaji was going to welcome the governor in 1982.

—*Balaji*

~

One day at a football match: H4 was playing H5, and as usual doing badly. We were a couple of goals down at half-time, and most of us die-hard fans were quite dejected, to say the least. Many of us were wondering whether we should hang around for the second half, or even start booing our own team. Suddenly, Balaji (The) arrives, with his usual big smile, and a 'what's the score guys?'

A bunch of guys let out a manic cheer (anything to forget the dismal state of the match), and started chanting variants of 'Balajiiii', 'Baa Laa Jii', 'Jay Balaji' and such like. A few freshies got even more enthused, hoisted Balaji on their shoulders and carried him down the sidelines, chanting and screaming maniacally. They couldn't do this for too long as the only fit guys in H4 were on the field—so he was brought back to earth. By this time the second half had begun, and believe it or not, H4 scored a goal.

The crowd went berserk. But instead of cheering Tony or Mondal or one of the usual soccer heroes, it was all Balaji. Once again, he was hoisted up and perilously carried around. And this continued for the next forty-odd minutes. Whenever H4 did well, or there was a slack period, or H4 played badly, or whatever, The Balaji was invoked and paraded.

I'm not sure whether we won the match or not, but after this episode, the legend of The Balaji was firmly established. And at all matches, gaali fights, or drunken sessions, whenever there was something to commemorate (or not), cheers of 'Jay Balaji' rent the air.

But what really made the legend was The Balaji himself. He never, never lost his cool, and though he protested (frequently), he always took it like the sport he is.

A small correction—there are only two recorded instances of The Balaji losing his cool. One when he was locked into his room forcing him to miss a lecture, and the other, when Khosla lost Balaji's precious notes.

—*Jetu*

~

Once, when I had to pee, I saw Balaji at that infamous pee pot which would auto-flush at the wrong time. I stood a polite distance behind Balaji waiting for him to finish his job. When Balaji went on and on like a never-ending waterfall, I had to ask him if there was a problem. Apparently like all other things with the systems freak Balaji, his peeing routine also followed a system. He peed once in the morning and once in the evening. That's it. Pee at a standard fixed time twice a day. No more and no less. I had to move to the adjoining wing to relieve myself there.

Balaji's sister was getting married and the wedding time coincided with one lecture. Balaji went to the prof to request him to cancel the lecture.

—*Ashish Khosla, '78-'83*

~

One evening, we were all playing bridge as usual in my room in CWSF. Khosla came in grinning. He said he had just met Balaji in the bogs. Now when Khosla takes a leak he pulls his left pyjama leg all the way up to make room. So there he was, his left leg bare, when Balaji crept up behind him. That year Sood was contesting a Councillor's post. Balaji whispered to Khosla, 'SWGF is in our hands'. Now Balaji could not have chosen someone less interested in wing and hostel politics than Khosla. So Khosla, I don't think he turned around, said, 'Well done, Balaji.'

—*Kenneth (G) Robertson, '78-'83*

~

Khosla was clearly one of the brightest in our batch. So, he and I did not have much in common. I remember after one summer, we were back for the next term. I asked him, 'Khosla, how was the last sem?'

He said, 'It was good, did not get a single B. How was it for you?'

I said, 'I did not get a single B either.'

And we just smiled and moved on.

—*Pradeep Fulay, '78-'83*

~

Ashish was the one who introduced us to the most intriguing game of cards—bridge. This game took some of us by storm for the rest of our H4 lives. We could hear the shouts of 'Banaa De' at varied times during the day and night, signalling the start of a rubber. We would have quick rubbers as early as breakfast to as late as three in the morning.

—*Bridge Bhadwa*

～

Bridge is a curable addiction. But I remember Ashish getting hooked onto what looked incurable at that time. No, it's not what folks may think. It's the Rubik's cube. On one rare day that I was up at 7am, I saw Ashish walking to the bogs, sleepy eyed, but working furiously on his Rubik's cube. He taught me how to solve the puzzle by using a combination of Sampath algorithm and Shenoy algorithm. Once, when one of the pieces in my cube became inversed, I took it to Ashish who quickly solved the puzzle first, and then identified the offending piece. He prised it open with a chisel, put it back in the correct orientation and also oiled it as a bonus. He had a full-fledged maintenance kit to look after his cube. After several months of seeing Ashish at all times of day and night furiously working his Rubik's cube, came an announcement by him. He was organizing a Rubik's cube competition. He was announced the de-facto winner of the competition as no one else signed up to challenge him.

—*Bakul*

～

Ashish Khosla had a genuine stint in the advertising business after he graduated. But before him, another duo had an idea. Or hare-brained scheme. Me, and KK.

'Let's start an ad agency.' Krishna Purswani, aka KK. KK, brilliant topper for whom consistently getting a CPI of 9.5 was not challenging, he wanted to be an entrepreneur. Why he chose me as his partner, I don't know. KK had this crazy idea that we could go cold calling around town and get some contracts to design ads. I thought I could try my hand at writing copy for the ads.

And this is how I came to meet Merwyn Pinto.

On one of our trips to town, we were approached by a bum at VT Station saying, 'Can you spare a buck?' I had never before had anyone beg for money in English and I was curious. Surprisingly, I did have a buck on me and I was intrigued enough to also offer to buy him a cup of tea. KK was also curious and we had tea together and the bum, Merwyn poured out his troubles. He came from a middle-class family in Bandra and had rich relatives all over but had self-destructed and had gotten himself disowned. In those days, getting myself disowned seemed extremely attractive, and I wanted to learn Merwyn's trick. KK's eyes lit up when he heard rich relatives. 'Fish,' he said to me conspiratorially, 'Merwyn's relatives can help us with our ad agency and looks like Merwyn can use some money too.' I was sceptical but having gone along with Bakul's crazy schemes in the past, my sense of discernment had been severely dented.

It was vacation time and there were plenty of open rooms in the hostel and I invited Merwyn to come and stay with us. In retrospect, this was probably misuse of my powers.

But back then, this didn't occur to me. Merwyn happily accepted. KK detected a hidden agenda and said, 'Fish, don't get any idiotic ideas about rehabilitating this guy and effecting a father-son reunion.' Of course, that was exactly what I was going to attempt to do, but I saw no reason to tell KK about it.

I went to visit Merwyn's father in Bandra and he wanted nothing to do with Merwyn.

'Why?' I asked him puzzled.

'He killed his mother!' exclaimed papa.

'No!' I said shocked, I had certainly not expected anything like this.

'How?' I ventured to ask.

'She died of cancer,' said papa leaving me totally nonplussed as to what this had to do with Merwyn.

'Killed her with worry, he did,' explained papa.

I was speechless. This had to be the mother of all the crazy guilt trips I had heard.

All my reports about poor Merwyn hanging around VT station begging for a buck and that too from someone like me who didn't know where his next cigarette was coming from, fell on deaf ears.

'That boy is no good and I don't want anything to do with him,' said papa with a finality.

I shrugged and said, 'Can I at least take him some clothes? His clothes look dirty even by hostel standards.'

Papa reluctantly parted with some of Merwyn's clothes. KK and I then tried his rich relatives. KK, to get some ad contracts, and me, to try to get someone to rescue Merwyn.

'You are a Hindooo?' asked Merwyn's rich uncle in Nariman Point. I didn't know what that had to do with the price of cigarettes and brushed it off summarily proceeding to implore him to adopt Merwyn. Uncle refused and said he wanted nothing to do with Merwyn. I never learnt exactly what happened to provoke this kind of reaction from his relatives and obviously anything Merwyn himself said could not be relied upon. I gave up my efforts at effecting a last scene in a Bollywood movie kind of family reunion and decided to enjoy Merwyn's delightful company. Merwyn and I roamed around town—I wanted to see Bombay through this bum's eyes. I had often wondered what it would be to sleep on a railway platform, and I did some vicarious living through Merwyn. This was way before movies like *Salaam Bombay* had made the camaraderie of Bombay street life common knowledge, I learnt it from Merwyn. He introduced me to hawkers who gave him freebies—leftover pav bhaji and ragda pattice—and he knew which ones would chase him/us away. He showed me brothels where he could get laid for free (and no I did not avail of any such free services) and my heart felt very warm that even his sexual needs were taken care of, which is more than what I could have said for myself. My neighbour in Ghatkopar wanted to buy a gun, and my thirst for new experiences overcame my dislike for guns, and Merwyn arranged for my neighbour to meet some thug who would get someone to sell him a gun.

KK realized at some point that priming Merwyn's relatives for business was not going to work and gave up the crazy idea. I lost my bicycle one day, and Merwyn too was nowhere to be found. Maybe he sold my bicycle for money and vanished. I don't know. But I am sure that hostel life was too tame for him and he was probably more comfortable on the streets. A bicycle was a small price to pay for the Bombay seen though his eyes—experiences I vividly recall thirty years later. Merwyn, I hope you remained a free spirit, but I hope you took better care of yourself. I worried about you.

—*Fish*

~

Bakul's crazy ideas, which, by his own admission had severely dented Fish's sense of discernment, had not always failed. We had achieved our elephant on campus, thanks to one of them. One of these came at the end of his time in IIT. With contributions from many of the stars, Bakul tells the story of his last EP contribution.

In 1982, H4 was paired with H7 for the EP competition. It was early August and I was to bid adieu to IIT soon, but remained enthused enough to offer some 'parting advice' to my juniors, most of whom had become my good friends. As it happened with all previous EPs, most of the initial ideas came over some lazy off-the-cuff remarks made in jest during tiffin time, when the organizers supposedly congregated for a serious brainstorming session. I had reasoned that our 1980 Hitler's motorcade and the elephant had been sensational hits and H4 should carry on the tradition. I said we should rent a helicopter during Friday evening Convo movie time and throw confetti on the guys walking to the Convo. As usual, this was greeted with jests and barbs and a 'let's see you try to pull this off'.

The elephant-renting success made me believe I could whistle 'chopper' and the rotor-ed version would soon be hovering overhead. Soc Sec Sameer Vijaykar sanctioned a budget of Rs. 500. The chopper company guy (I think the company was Pawan Hans) asked me lots of questions about why IIT needed a chopper and why they need to throw confetti from the air rather than from the ground and if there was 'nothing fishy' in the deal and whether we would get the Police Commissioner's permission 'at our cost'. After answering his questions satisfactorily, he quoted a figure of Rs. 6000. Fortunately, this was on the phone, so he could not see my eyebrows aiming for the sky and neither did he catch my 'oh shit'. I decided to at least compensate myself for the princely 50p I had paid for this call. I asked him if he had paratroopers to land near the Convo. I asked him if his aircraft could skywrite H4. I asked if he was willing to negotiate his figure 'a bit'. Sure he was. How much was the bit? Could he look at Rs 500 all told including the confetti? He was incredulous. Surely, I meant five thousand and not five hundred, right? 'Wrong,' I told him. It was five hundred I wanted to pay him. The answer was the click of him hanging up. Clearly, he was not a bawa. I was half hoping that he was, so that I could reply to his inevitable swear words with what I had learned from my friends Sharookh and Irani.

One evening and one more tiffin later, amid guffawing and more jests and barbs, I was selling my new idea of the day. Instead of showing the customary slides that we generally did during the intermission of the Friday movie, why don't we film a ten-minute trailer and run it during the intermission? In those days when video cameras were not even heard of, thinking of renting a movie camera and a projector was more ambitious that getting a helicopter. I waited for the next series of barbs.

Surprisingly, there were serious and silent faces all over the table. Jetu spoke up finally. 'Why should we spend money and make a trailer for publicity? Why don't we make a movie and run it as a feature in the main EP?' Ideas started flowing soon after this and it took us another evening and another tiffin to start discussing specifics with Photography & Fine Arts sec Sheshgiri Rao aka Shesh from H7. Shesh could and would borrow a 8mm movie cam from his friend. A ten-minute reel would cost us Rs 350 and another Rs 150 if we wanted it with soundtrack. Brilliant IIT minds decided that they would beat the soundtrack system by dubbing the vocals on a cassette which would be played synchronously with the movie and we would spend the saved Rs 150 on beer to celebrate what looked like a clear cut box-office silver jubilee hit the moment Shesh said yes.

I left for Hyderabad soon after but returned within barely one week when an excited Sood and an equally excited Vijaykar called me in Hyderabad to say that the movie deal was through and that we were going to film it on so and so day. I got to H4 early on that so and so day. Vijaykar ran the oral script by me hurriedly. It was going to be Bollywood masala all the way. Two lost brothers. Villains with dens, goons and molls. Car chase. Comedians. Dubbed songs. I was to play a guest role. I was to drive the mobike with the hero in tow to rescue the heroine from the villain's clutches. But before that, I was to milk a cow when the hero comes running to me asking me for help and I was to stop the milking and jump on the nearest mobike to take the hero on the chase.

Vijayakar had already talked with head sweeper Kalidas who was going to loan his favourite milch cow for the scene. Kalidas had assured Vijaykar and team, 'Saheb! I will give you such a cow, fountains of milk will spring forth from her teats.' And the rascals had conspired to get me to be the comedian discovering these fountains. I had to make a hurried and secret trip to Kalidas's dwelling just north of the north wing (which also housed The Dhoban). Kalidas was washing and scrubbing the cow while his family members babbled excitedly at the big day in their cow's life, little realizing that I was about to play spoiler. I reasoned with Kalidas that I was appearing in the fillum too with my cow i.e. my mobike, and I had carried an ironed pair of my favourite striped shirt and cream trousers for this momentous shoot, and would he please leave his cow where it belonged and would he please tell Vijaykar that she had taken suddenly ill? Kalidas apparently remembered a few lucrative deals with me in the past, including a bounty of my discarded clothes which I shamelessly made a big deal about, and dejectedly agreed to send his cow to graze in pastures of faceless anonymity. There would be no fountains of milk, as Vijaykar would discover later in the day.

Shoot started sharply at noon at Powai lake. It was decided then that the script would be developed as we went along and improvised at will. Two heroes, Shinde and Pa came

306

from H7, while Radhika and Priti came from H10. This was a coup scored by Jetu, Sood, Khosla and gang. Rather than getting guys dressed up as women, they managed to get 'the real thing' as Jetu said. It was quickly decided that Radhika would be the heroine and Priti would be the gangster's moll. Shinde was decidedly more handsome than Pa and also owned and wore a denim jacket and 'non-slippers' and was selected unanimously. Pa had started a week ago with 'I don't mind being the hero' to 'I'd like to be the hero' to finally 'Please make me the hero'. Though ousted, he was sporting enough to break the coconut he had bought from Y Point to mark the token start, and he also did a mock muhurat clap shot. Shinde and Radhika sat in a boat whose ropes were held by Alexander while Shinde pretended to row the boat and Radhika pretended to sing a number from the film *Tere Mere Sapne*. Lyrics were *'Jeevan ki bagiya behekegi, mehekegi'*. During dubbing however, the song was changed to *'Yeh jeevan hai'* and nobody gave a thought to how the lip-synching would look on D-Day. Shinde and Radhika then stepped out of the boat hand in hand while the short cute athlete Bhinge playing the comedian got up from the boat (where by implication, he was hiding) and jumped into the lake. The newfound film makers in us decided to mimic the veterans to the extreme. We now shifted our action to Vihar lake in the same manner that a lead pair starts singing a song at the Eiffel Tower and finishes it at Qutb Minar. We needed Powai for the boats, but Vihar was more photogenic and gave us access to the pipeline where we had the car chase scene.

While the cameraman Shesh and a few others drove in Chintya's black Fiat to Vihar and other trudged their way there, we realized that my bike would carry me and Shinde while Chintya's car would carry the villain and the kidnapped heroine Radhika and Shesh would need another vehicle to film the car chase scene. That's when we hit upon the idea of roping in DOSA Isaac, ostensibly to play a guest role, but in reality, to provide his scooter for the cameraman. Jiten and I rode to Isaac's cute bungalow, A-11 by the lakeside. Isaac was not thrilled to see that 'Bak Bak' was back on campus after promising to stay away. The aftermath of the recent scandal 'Campus Call Girl' was still fresh in everyone's mind and Isaac was already frowning hard and loud on seeing me. I had to go down on my knees twice, I said his non compliance would cost our 'crew', thousands in damages. Jiten laughed his trademark loud Ha Ha every time I made a fresh attempt at melting Isaac, who finally relented when he knew I would not leave without him. He did ask what role he was to play in the movie, I told him truthfully I didn't know (except for the scooter part). 'The director will decide', I said. He was unconvinced, but came to Vihar all the same. At Vihar, after a hurried discussion, we gave him a pair of binoculars and asked him to look toward the lake and snap his fingers to summon an imaginary sidey. In the film, he would look through these field glasses at Vihar and espy Shinde and Radhika alight from a boat in Powai, and his snapping fingers were deleted and rather than a Boss, he was transformed into a sidey who tells his boss, 'Bass! *Panchi aa gaya hai.*' Bass was the tall, mean-looking Meshram from H7 who had shaved his head for the role. Boss was seen sitting on the banks of Vihar with his moll Priti (not our Boss Patil and his real life Priti), telling her how they would escape with the 'sona' after abducting Radhika. The Shinde-Radhika duo who had alighted at Powai was now walking, same hand in same hand, except that it was at Vihar now. They were still singing the *'yeh jeevan hai'* to the lip movements of *'jeevan ki bagiya'* while Meshram quickly moved behind them and grabbed Radhika's hand and ran off with her.

Shesh was on the camera, there was nobody to direct as such and improvisation was the decided order of the day. Radhika brought in a new dimension to the script by running fast along with villain Meshy while screaming a sing song 'bachao.' Shinde was quick to run in the opposite direction looking for his lost Radhika who was still in the frame while Shinde ran away. Shinde ran to a Charsi 'sadhu' sitting under a tree and replied to his question of where Radhika was, 'Gone man! Solid gone.'

The 'charsi sadhu' was an H7 guy from Assam called Topno. He was a very good short distance sprinter, and a smoker who once organized a basketball match of smokers vs. non-smokers. It was one of the few recorded instances where the smokers kicked non-smokers' butts.

—Rohan

Shinde then turned towards the pipeline and saw me sitting on my stationary mobike while singing, *'Musafir hoon yaaron. Na ghar hai na thikana.'* Vijaykar was seen scratching his bald head wondering why Kalidas's cow had acted up. Shinde jumped on my mobike and I started it and raced off towards the direction of Meshy's getaway car. Eventually, I caught up with the car and then saw Shesh sitting backwards on Isaac's pillion, ahead of the car, filming the scene with a heavy wobbly camera resting on his unsteady hands moving up and down due to Isaac's bad shock absorbers. Later, we could see that when he zoomed into the car to catch a shot of Meshy and Radhika, they were seen laughing while Radhika was still shouting 'bachao'. A damsel in lesser distress was never seen before. An excited Shinde decided to catch the car by its window when we got there and almost got us killed by getting my mobike pulled close to the car. I started hitting Shinde's hand to detach it from the car. It was captured on film.

The light was fading and Isaac had to go out and we decided to pack up shooting and continue next day at Kol Dongri sanctuary at the edge of Powai. Kol Dongri was an ideal setting for the villain's den as it had some old crumbling walls which would crumble when a hero threw a villain's sidekick into them. Before shooting the next day, we had an interesting and an animated discussion about how to film a scene where a hero dodges twelve armed villains by jumping backwards from the 'ground level' to a landing or a floor or a wall top that could be classified as 'upstairs'. The motion had to be smooth and fluid and nonchalant as in the real thing seen in not-so-real movies. Again, many intelligent engineering minds stepped in and offered solutions including filming a guy jumping down and then pasting each frame in reverse order. Fortunately, a few idle minds concluded that holding a camera upside down would also do the trick. The scene shot at the villain's den was the best, in my opinion. The villain's lackeys were bare-chested and went down one by one in double slow motion to Shinde's dishum dishum. One degree of motion was due to Shesh filming in slow motion. The other degree was the guys themselves falling down in slow motion, unaware that Shesh's borrowed cam would do it too. When the last sidey was hit, he was made to collide against the wall and sure enough, as expected, it came crumbling down. Finally, Shinde and Meshy decide to fight it out solo. Meshy said, *'Main woh toofan hoon jis se takrakar, ped hil jaate hain.'* Shinde struck a match on Meshy's bald head and said as he lit his cigarette, *'Main woh chattan hoon jis se takrakar toofan ruk jaata hai.'* More fisticuffs. A pendant comes out of Meshy's shirt. And suddenly, there is recognition and a finally heart rending 'Sohan' and 'Mohan' kind of reunion between lost siblings. While the duo gets united, Radhika decides to run away with comedian Bhinge into a scene which shows 'The End'.

During screening the projector began to vibrate and made Isaac vibrate to the tune of *'Yeh jeevan hai.'* Shesh stopped the projector but Kohli did not stop the cassette player. Sound travelled at the speed of sound while light travelled at the speed of a faulty projector and we could hear 'Sohan and Mohan' from the Charsi Sadhu who intended to say, 'gone man! Solid Gone.'

All in all, the audience got a gist of what we attempted and as a concept, we got a lot of points for novelty. Jetu touted it as a multi-dimensional project which involved three hostels, faculty and alumni. Isaac was faculty and I was already an alumnus. While leaving the Convo, Isaac was heard remarking, 'These chaps made me look like a fool. I hope that Bak bak has left for good.'

I left IIT and H4, but certainly not for good.

—*Bakul*

~

Memories of some of our mates who did leave us, too soon.

Devi

Satyendra 'Satish' Devi and I were in the same college before he joined IIT, and to my pleasant surprise I found myself in his wing, NWSF, in 1981. He was a final year UG and I was PG freshy then. I feel compelled to share my memories of him.

1977, Sangli—a small place in the politically active western Maharashtra, the college Willingdon. It was the very first batch of Higher Secondary—12th standard class. All of us knew about two exceptionally bright students of the college, Malu and Devi—a Marwari ghat and a Gujju ghat. One fine day, we heard that Devi was going to join the IIT. Believe it or not, that was the first time I had heard of the IIT, leave alone JEE. 'Oh—Devi's mother is a teacher, she must have known about this great institute in Mumbai'—that's what we said. Remember, this was ages before the quota factories robbed IIT JEE of its innocence.

Fast forward to H4: One fine morning Tushar 'Dadu' Chitre strolled in NWSF to inspect and count the new crop of ghat freshies. His mission was to let Velchya know the number so that he could script a play with the right number of characters for the inter hostel one act play competition. Devi promptly introduced me to Dadu. And the rest is history as they say— I won two acting awards for H4.

I still vividly recall when Devi started complaining about pain in his leg. He started visiting hospi regularly. Eventually he moved to the staff hostel where his parents joined him. His mother was a very courageous lady. By that time, I think, they had started on radiation at Shushrusha Hospital in Dadar. Devi had this ability to watch himself in a detached way. One day, he said to me, with a wry smile on his face, 'I cannot squeeze a lemon anymore. That's how weak I have become.' In the rush of the end sem exams I did not meet him regularly anymore. They had moved him to Shushrusha. And one day the news came— Devi is no more. I could not summon enough courage to meet his parents.

—Abhay

Bhaiyya

One of Bhaiyya's (Satish Gupta) many quirks was travelling on local trains without buying tickets.

He was quite committed to the idea of not buying tickets—not because he couldn't afford to but because he felt it was, in principle, the wrong thing to do. It was something the UP-ite in him just couldn't accept. He reasoned that he not pulling the chain in front of his house—which would have been the proper thing to do if you were travelling by a train in UP—was a good enough deed. He was true to this no-buying tickets on trains thought throughout his life at IIT. Later when he started his own business and became the second largest Bromine and Brominated compounds manufacturer in India, he would buy a first-class railway pass, but only on alternate months. Of course as a man who had honed his ticket-less travel skills to a fine art, he was seldom caught by a TC.

Once, at his absolute and manic insistence and his refusal to allow us to commit the sin of buying a ticket, Chavan, Rod and I once travelled from Kanjurmarg to Dadar on a train with him, without a ticket. At Dadar, he walked confidently past the TC, but us three trainee ticketless travellers were promptly picked out from a sea of humanity, caught, and made to pay a fine. Rs 2 per head, (if I remember correctly), leading to a premature end to our budding careers as sons-in-law of the Railways.

So there was this one time that Bhaiyya finally met his match. Changing trains at Thane to go to Dombivali from Kanjurmarg, the great Bhaiyya was caught by an unsuspecting Maharashtrian TC. Cool as a cucumber, Bhaiyya flashed his IIT id card and asked the TC, '*Hum* IIT *mein padhta hai. Tumko kya lagta hai,* IIT *ka* student *log* without ticket travel *kar sakta hai?*' We learned one more thing about Maharashtrian genes that day— that when faced with such profound questions, the automatic response from a good middle-class Maharashtrian TC is respect for the yet-to-be-earned degree over any empirical data about basic human nature. So the TC, after duly apologising to him, told Bhaiyya to buy a ticket sans any fine. Bhaiyya's response was, 'Purse gum gaya hai, paisa nahi hai'. The TC took him to the ticket office and bought him a ticket with his own money. Bhaiyya's only regret was that he hadn't tried to convince the TC to hand him the money for the ticket.

It's been said before, and I'll say it again: in IIT, you learned 10 per cent from teachers and 90 per cent from your friends. This is certainly true for a barely 6.5-er like me. Ever the resourceful and worldly wise Satish aka Bhaiyya taught us many a thing about a life we never knew or had guts to do. Thirty years after I first met him, and ten years after he passed away, I still remember him often, as I am sure those who knew him do too. May his soul rest in peace.

— *Tarkas*

~

Campus Call Girl

As in most universities across India during the '70s and early '80s, IIT Bombay too had its share of left-aligned students. Young impressionable minds tend to be idealistic, and in that era, Marxism and socialism in any form was considered fashionable and liberal as well. Contrary to popular opinion, IITans were not obsessed with only technology. Metaphysics, existentialism, Advaita, poetry, lateral thinking and various other schools of thought occupied this set of intelligent minds.

Marxism in IIT was not restricted to a boring and an endless discussion on economic imparity or the theory of surplus value. Few practitioners did stretch it to the jargon limits of historical determinism and dialectic materialism. For most Marxists, espousing women's liberation, fighting with the 'establishment' and a 'high handed' institute, championing the cause of mess workers and trying to unionize them was an end in itself, even if it meant being a 'commie'. Commies might have preferred 'radical' or 'progressive' as labels, but the not-so-silent majority was not so charitable.

Commies were easy to identify in their de facto uniform. The mandatory beard, unkempt hair, soiled kurta with equally soiled pyjama or jeans, a jhola (sling bag). The jhola carried reams of cyclostyled anti-establishment pamphlets which these 'lalbhais' and 'red Indians' plastered all over IIT. More than these obvious physical distinguishing marks of Marx and his ism, the commies also carried on their faces contempt for all who were not 'concerned' enough about their deprived fellow humans and who instead wasted their time pursuing academic excellence, and then higher studies abroad, cheating the taxpayer who subsidized their IIT education. In commie eyes, a person who did actually pay taxes was a villain too, because he had money while most could not afford to pay taxes. And their contempt also embraced people who flocked to the universities in the capitalistic, morally bankrupt West while there were perfectly good universities in Moscow and Leningrad.

A joke doing the rounds was that CPIIT, Communist Party of IIT, was founded by Lo Marx. This arose from the fact that many of these gentlemen were in IIT long past the normal five years, and then aligned themselves with low-performing students like themselves.

Authorities at IIT treated them as troublemakers. Fellow students saw them as the butt of unkind jokes and unconcealed sniggers. Any attempt by any of these folks to contest any election at any level ended with a sound trouncing.

CDTs (Champions of the Downtrodden, as they were sarcastically referred to) put up protest banners at every Mood Indigo rock concert denouncing Western culture and values. Through the year, they published reams of cyclostyled newsletters. One of their prized publications was called *'Campus Call'*. This had an unattractive brown logo. The contents were predictable. Denounce IIT, Diro, G Secs, DOSA, Mood Indigo, APEC (Academic Performance Evaluation Committee), rock music, Gandhi and anyone who did not give his life to fight for permanency for the mess workers.

Leading this pack of commies was one MG Rao, often referred to as RG Mao after Zedong, and, like the original Zedong, this one too did not sport a beard or wear kurtas. In fact, he was quite handsome for a commie. Another visible left-leaner was bearded and very hairy Sudheendra Kulkarni who resurfaced after almost a decade in a saffron Rath Yatra, but that is another story.

~

Summer of '82. Like most summerians who did a repeat course, Sid Nag and I were in the cafeteria. The café overlooked the sprawling green gymkhana grounds, a lovely spot to spend countless hours sipping tea. The location and view were free, the tea was bought on credit. Soon enough, a bearded guy with jhola and sense of purpose walked in. He took several sheets of the latest *Campus Call* out of his jhola and placed one at every table, including empty ones, and left. Sid, irked, said 'Who is interested in this shit called *Campus Call*? If it was a *Campus Call Girl*, it would be more fun.'

Within twenty four hours, all talk was about creating a parody to the Campus Call and naming it in accordance to Sid's genius outburst. The organizational structure drawn up for achieving this task was something future management gurus would write about. Members of our informal committee were soon writing material for the *'Campus Call Girl'* or CCG as it came to be known. The original plan was to take pot-shots at the commies. But soon we were creating a document with smutty and ribald jokes and affectionately ribbing well-known faces in IIT, particularly girls. Freshy Rohan Menezes was bullied to add cartoons of *Playboy* bunnies to *Campus Call*'s unimaginative logo to make it appealing. CCG would be produced using now prehistoric cyclostyling technology. For this, four stencils were stolen from the Chem Engineering department. A ream (500 sheets) of foolscap papers was obtained from DOSA Isaac's office by seducing his secretary Shanta. Sanjoy Gupta typed out the matter on the stencil in the Warden's office at H4 on Hall Manager Pillai's typewriter. In those days preceding MS Word, typing was done without a spell checker, without pagination and without alignments, indents and copy/paste functions. Only the exceptionally gifted could type a magazine in one shot without using expensive erasing fluid. Matter had to be altered and added as one typed in order to fit within a page. When it overflowed into the next page, an imaginative line had to be concocted to keep the flow intact.

The final production was done in my room on my portable 'cottage industry' cyclostyling machine which needed strong arms to run a roller dipped in ink on the glass plate above the paper. As expected we ran out of ink and finances. Computer Centre's Ramnath printed 300 copies for us in return for a peek at a pondy.

21st July was distribution day. Waghamare was in charge. He howled 'Aaaaaah-ooooooooooooooh', the freshy-beckoning call. Twenty freshies, in pairs, were dispatched to place copies of CCG at the entrances of ten hostels. The time of 6.30pm was carefully chosen—guys would be either in their rooms or in the sports field.

The rag was a runaway hit. Beyond our expectations. Spy visitors to different hostels saw folks guffawing away in their messes and lounges, marvelling at the audacity of the title and the contents.

I had volunteered to be the face of CCG in the event of any unpleasant fallout since I was a few days away from graduation. The commies were understandably chagrined, but the strength of their anger two days later was beyond our expectations. The commies saw their chance to get back at Fish who had just been elected GSSA (Gen Sec Students' Affairs), defeating their 'nominee' by a thumping margin.

After a week of tension and angry notices, the commies 'gheraoed' Fish and me at the cafeteria. Angry exchanges followed. Coercion tactics were used. Fish was asked to resign for not being able to reign me in. The drama lasted all night. I refused to name anyone involved in this saga.

INTRODUCING IIT'S VERY OWN MAGAZINE OF ROMANCE

Vol.1: No 1: Period of Issue: 28 Days

Note: Any resemblance of the title to any magazine dead or red is
      purely INTENTIONAL.
Added Note: Any resemblance of the title to any short bespectacled,
            portable woman (hopefully dead) is even more INTENTIONAL;

EDITORIAL

Hi there, 'Average IITian'- the most analysed, dissected, pipetted,
titrated and categorized being. From academic reformers to democratic,
investigative, oppressed, suppressed, repressed, depressed, progressive,
journalists, you are the prime object of their concern or so they say,
- or so you think.

Reality, we all know, is otherwise. Let's face it, dear Guinea
Pig- despite the balderdash doled out by the professors, secretaries,
technicians, ~~tentakkey campus callers and partisans~~, the average IITian
remains, an obscure, lacklustre and faceless guinea pig.

~~This then, dear GP , is where we come in, to give colour and~~
sensation to your lives. Remember any exciting episode in your lives
ever since your kindergarten teacher caught you wetting your knickers
in class? No?? Well then, this magazine, devoted to the romance
movement in IIT, promises to appease your passion/ curiosity/desire
etc. Keep tuned for all types of malicious gossip, scandalous scoops,
revealing rumours, lovers'laments, guest columns, articles, PJs, and
lots of fun.

See ya again in 28 days dahlings and until then- Mowwwwaaaaooooow.

                                                        - CUPID.

STATUTORY WARNING:
FLIES SPREAD DISEASE
KEEP YOURS BUTTONED.

OVERHEARD: I don't know why, but I hve this insatiable desire for
            travelling in crowded local trains.
                                                M.S. Kamath

For those who did not hear DOSA's address, we print it overleaf.
Please turn over for the same.

This incident led to a groundswell of popular opinion in our favour. People began to question even the commies' newfound views on morality and their definition of vulgarity, leave alone their behaviour at the cafeteria. The Gymkhana's official publication *Technik* ran a good analysis of the incident supplemented by several reactions from students and faculty which was overwhelmingly in our favour. Signature campaigns were thwarted by counter signature campaigns. There were a few hurried legal consultations from both sides. The *Campus Call* came out criticizing all who didn't condemn CCG.

But my best memory of this episode is the fact that some girls who could not read the original CCG (since many copies were destroyed by the commies) asked us secretly for a copy.

The day I left IIT, I ordered a reprint of fifty, and handed out autographed copies to the girls who wanted them. That was my crowning moment.

—*Bakul*

~

For no good reason and with no particular objective in mind, we would often end up at Bombay airport. Maybe it was to see international (female) passengers, maybe it was a sense of the world out there, or maybe it was the planes themselves, I don't remember now.

One such time three of us from H4 and a fourth, Fatso Gads Gadgil, from H8, found ourselves aimlessly walking around the check-in area and other counters. This sounds odd now, but those days, around 1972, security was just not an issue. At one of these counters, a sleepy guy sat limply at the far end of the stall, and a wooden sign sat temptingly on the counter. It was about 18' long with the words 'Air Insurance' hand-painted on it. There is a tradition for students in hostels and college dorms all over the world to pinch signs and display them in their rooms. I once got myself a 'Central Bank of India' metal sign. It was yellow with black lettering, about 24'x8', and it was nailed to the door of my room, 242.

It was the end of the month, my father dispatched sorely needed funds with a colleague who was visiting Bombay. My father instructed him, if I was unavailable, to slip it under the door of Room 242. I was unavailable. He stood outside Room 242 and looked at the sign on the door. My wing-mates patiently told him that it really was my room, the sign was put there by me just for fun. He refused to believe it, saying there was some 'tomfoolery' going on. He refused to wait for me or to slip the envelope under the door and went away, carrying the money with him. I had to scrounge from my always ready-to-help wing-mates to pay mess dues, I had to smoke Charminars (33 paise for a pack of 10) and beedis as my WILLS Navys were beyond my means. It was payback for my sign thievery. Or in this case, no payback.

This experience unfortunately did not spring to mind at the airport when one of us suggested we filch the 'Air Insurance' sign. Before a plan could be hatched, one of the guys eased up to the counter, picked up the sign, tucked it under his wind-cheater, and walked toward the door to the drive-way outside. We followed. We were barely out of the building when we heard a hue and cry behind us. The sleepy Air Insurance guy was now fully awake and running after us along with three havaldars from the Bombay police force.

As guys do when they are being chased by cops, the guys took off running. Some instinct caused me to pretend I was not one of them. The guys were running away, I walked deliberately slowly and even stopped to look busily for some papers in my shirt pocket. One of the chasing cops stopped and stared at me. I gave him my most surprised and innocent look. It worked. He took off after my three buddies. All three were caught and dragged off to the airport police station. I followed them discreetly. To this day, I cannot make up my mind whether I let my buddies down by not getting arrested with them, or made a smart move so I could somehow get them out.

I spent the next half hour running to the police station and peering in, and running to the airport to make phone-calls to H4 to figure out someone with connections who could do something to have my guys released.

The guys in the meanwhile were shoved into a room and made to strip to their underwear. They were given a tongue-lashing by the havaldars with choice words in Hindi and Marathi. They were clueless in their underwear, pondering their fate. A hefty fine? A few days in jail? Worse? They were told the Inspector-sahib would decide. An agonizing and nerve-wracking interval later, Inspector-sahib arrived. The guys in their underwear plaintively told him they were not crooks but students from IIT, Powai. This information incensed him further. He screamed at them for being from a 'good college' and acting like common thieves.

He then turned to a cop and asked for full details of what all things these boys had stolen. The cop proudly produced the 'Air Insurance' sign. The inspector was silent for a second, and then burst out laughing. He had assumed that there had been a regular, proper, actual robbery involving actual money or goods of value. He gave the guys a stern lecture, told them to put on their clothes and get lost.

My fretting came to an end when they walked out from the building fully clothed but sans the 'Air Insurance' sign. They were angry about what they had experienced in there, but were also embarrassed.

Of them all, Fatso Gads was the most relieved. His intense relief came from his father not having found out about the incident. He feared his father intensely, and he was willing to go through anything—a fine, a beating, a week in jail, even all three, as long has his father did not find out.

If Fatso Gads had mentioned that his father was the Airport Manager of Bombay Airport, the cops would have let them all go in a second.

—*Vicky*

~

Planes and trains. The famous Railway strike of 1974 called by union leader and later day Union Minister George Fernandes was one of the biggest strikes in recorded history with almost 1.5 million workers abstaining from work for over twenty days. With over 900 million metric tonnes of cargo being ferried by the Indian Railways over tracks measuring 39,000 miles and a passenger traffic of over 18 million every day, this strike virtually crippled India's economy and is believed to have been one of the considerations for imposing the dreaded Emergency.

And it was during this major crisis in India's history that volunteer motormen from H4 drove Mumbai locals, much to the relief of agonized passengers, and in spite of dire threats and goondaism.

Bombay Suburban

I was one of the handful of guys who ran local trains in Mumbai during the All India Railway strike in 1974 organized by George Fernandes. This opportunity came thanks to Aditya 'Punk' Srinivasan, whose father was in the Central Railways.

On the morning of the third day of this adventure, I was alone with one driver in the gloomy and desolate staff room at VT station. He was extremely nervous. He was one of those defying the strike, for reasons probably related to his job and economic future, but, crossing the picket line is a dangerous act, and he knew it. The strikers and general hooligans were hanging around all over the station, and were not in a good mood. We stepped out to take our train out. By now the man was sweating and really scared. In hindsight, I should have been too, but I was too naïve then.

We had two policemen escorting us, and the four of us walked toward the platforms on VT Station. We got to the train without incident. The motor man stepped in the motor cabin and I was just up the steps when we saw the station

324

master hurrying towards us, a few policemen around him. He was a large beefy Anglo-Indian guy (a remnant of the several Anglo-Indians who often took jobs in the Indian Railways back in the day).

He was eight or ten feet away from me when an unkempt man rushed forward from the crowd with a dirty looking knife in his right hand, yelling. He stabbed the station master in his back, below his shoulder-blade. All hell broke loose then, with the police surrounding the stabber, the station master shouting and trying to wrestle him, and people reacting with panic. Fortunately, it was not a fatal wound. The station master was still yelling and screaming as the cops dragged him away from the platform, presumably taking him to a safer place. We did the safest thing possible. We shut the motor cabin door and slowly took the train out of the station.

That evening back in the hostel, we were told that union gangs were issuing threats against students who were interfering in their strike. They actually came to the campus to carry out their threat, and Mudgal, Head of IIT Security, informed them it was illegal for them to enter the campus. He told them they could wait for us outside the main gate if they wanted. Mudgal then told us to sneak in through the Y-Point gate and stay put in the hostel. We never saw them, and they, fortunately for our health, never saw us.

Several months later, I graduated, and was in Pune about to start my new job. I got a phone call from a policeman in Mumbai, telling me that since I was witness to the stabbing of the station master, I would have to attend the court proceedings in Mumbai, voluntarily, or they could issue a summons.

I had to stay in Mumbai and be available at the court for twelve full days. The accused sat close to me and occasionally gave me blank looks. His family members were there too. They were poor folk who seemed to have no clue what was going on. The prosecutor, a Parsi gentleman, asked me to describe what happened, which I did. He asked me how I could see the incident so clearly, I said I was between eight and ten feet away. He asked me how I could say it was eight to ten feet. I looked at him confidently and told him I was an engineer, a graduate from IIT, Bombay, so I could estimate such distances very well. That answer was good enough for him.

Then the station master was called to the stand. As he was asked the first question, this large, brooding guy suddenly turned into a hyperactive mix of Amitabh Bachchan, Rajesh Khanna, and Mehmood, all rolled into one. He was in his element. He began enacting the scene with 'this bugger came from my back', pointing at the accused, and acted out violent stabbing motions in the air. Then he said, 'This fucker stabbed me. I turned round quickly and caught his right hand. Bastard tried to run away. I twisted and put my other hand on his shoulder. I said 'Motherfucker, where do you think you are going? What did the bastard think? He could just stab me and run off?' He was unstoppable, in spite of the prosecutor trying to interrupt.

At end of that day, I begged the prosecutor to let me go home as I had finished my work as a witness. I promised I would come back immediately anytime he wanted to question me again. Luckily he relented, and I went back to Pune.

I have no idea what the final verdict was.

—*Vicky*

~

Yes, that was an eventful summer vacation. It was not yet time to return (escape?) to Powai for summer courses—I had convinced my parents that these courses were reserved for the very best students to hone their skills. My father and I were eating our breakfast—idly sambar—when the phone rang. The General Manager of the Railways had called an emergency meeting to review the strike which had virtually halted suburban trains the last three days, and wanted all his department heads to attend the 10.30 meeting.

'The city's coming to a standstill,' my father grumbled, returning to his breakfast, 'BEST can't handle this, and now people are walking from Andheri to Churchgate. Damned strike might go on another week.'

'It's what—the suburban train drivers?' I asked him. I hadn't paid it much attention, and it hadn't affected my movement through the city—I either walked or took buses, and didn't need to travel far.

'Yes,' he said, 'it's the motormen's association. Also the guards.'

'Well—I can get my friends to help, and we'll run the trains,' I mused aloud.

My father seemed preoccupied, barely listening, and soon left for the office. An hour later my father's secretary called. 'Sir, please come to the office at VT. Your father is in a meeting still, but asked me to send the car for you.'

I was alarmed. Had my results been sent to his office address?

'The General Manager wants to meet you, so please hurry up, Sir,' the secretary said. That puzzled me, but was less threatening, and I went to the Railway HQ office at VT.

Later that afternoon, a valiant group of H4 students assembled at the Driver's Rest Room at VT. We were addressed by a railway officer who thanked us for volunteering our help to run the trains during the strike, and gave us instructions. We would serve as guards, working the back of the train, and we would have a training run that afternoon. The pay was twenty five rupees per day.

The next morning, the gang again assembled at VT. Karl, Gautam, KR Dog, Homi, Glandu, Vaanya, Camel, Pakshi and I, and then several others joined us as the strike dragged on through the week. Though we were not allowed to drive the trains by ourselves, we learned how to, and the few drivers on duty were happy enough to allow us to try. These were men who had serious violations—mainly to do with alcohol—and were breaking their union rules to curry favour with the railway administration and retain their jobs.

Vicky was walking to the train through a dense crowd at VT Station with a burly engine driver one morning when there was a scuffle and a shout. He gasped to see the blood flowing from the thick forearms of the station master, who stood his ground, shouting at the retreating figure who had stabbed him. The union had struck back.

After this incident a police escort surrounded us when we walked to the train at VT, and switched ends at the terminus. The atmosphere in the motormen's room was tense.

One Sunday evening at the end of the eventful week, the gang met at the Grand Oriental for drinks and dinner. We were flush with unexpected funds from the Central Railway.

ger in Sri Lanka

ESTABLISHED 1838

IMES OF

BOMBAY: SUNDAY, MAY 12, 1974

'I'm in trouble,' Homi said, 'all my aunts and uncles insist I stop doing this. That picture on the front page of TOI really did it.'

'But because of the publicity even guys like Sant are joining in. Your Gear4 T-Shirt looked nice. Stood out.' I told him, 'and now there will be twenty-five guys in that stinky driver's waiting room.'

'What about you—family not telling you to stop after your picture got into *Loksatta*?' Homi asked me, sipping his London Pilsner.

'No,' I told him. 'For one thing, I don't have old Bawajis for aunts. But mainly we're a Railway family. We all know this strike is unfair to Bombayites and want it to stop. So? Will you stay home?'

Homi laughed. 'No way, I'm having too much fun. I just stopped answering the phone.'

—*Punk*

~

The day that picture came out, our home phone started ringing non-stop from 6 in the morning with all my Mom's friends and my Dad's friends telling them that since I was now identified my life would be in danger and that they should not let me go drive the trains again, and that if I insisted, I should shave off my beard so that they would not

recognize me. Much to my mother's consternation, I refused to either stay home or shave. From that day on the railways gave us an armed police escort. The picture in the paper embarrassed my parents. I was on the front page of *The Times of India* in chappals. The next day I wore sneakers in case I needed to run fast.

—*Homi*

~

End of final semester. BTPs just done. A big group of H4ites all waited for the bus to arrive. Someone said, 'Hey, god alone knows when we all will be together again.' And that was it. Guys who had spent the best part of their lives together with each other through thick and thin and sick and sin and tests and quizzes and matches and competitions, through mugging and cogging and ragging, pondies, beer and mosambi and narangi, were last together at the 396 Bus Stop.

That moment defined for me my stepping out into the world.

—*Sanjay Chavan*

~

We owe thanks to the following:

~ Prof. Chetan Solanki for lending us some rare photos from his *Punctuations*, a book of photographs published by IIT Bombay.

~ Sushma Gawande for her help in compiling the photographs from *Punctuations*.

~ PRO Jaya Joshi for permissions and access to her archives.

~ Damayanti Bhattacharya, COO IIT Bombay Alumni Association.

~ Members of the Board of Directors of IIT Bombay Alumni Association for their patronage.

~ Ram Kelkar and the IIT Bombay Heritage Fund for their patronage and web support.

~ Shridhar Shukla for the use of his K Talk facility for international conference calls.

~ Shirish Waghulde for his legal advice.

~ Pratulbhai from DSK & Associates for advice on royalties and copyrights.

~ Ajit Ranade for his network of contacts.

~ Devdas Kamath for his advice, guidance and support.

~ The graduating class of 1985 for gifting this book to their batchmates on the occasion of their Silver Jubilee Reunion.

~ Hemant Patel for gifting this book to all HATS donors.

~ The student volunteers of SARC (Student Alumni Relation Cell) for publicizing this book on campus.

~ Rajinder Ganju for his care in the production of the book.

~ Saaz Aggarwal for her advice and guidance.

~ The members of the H4Madhouse group—Abhay Dandekar, Abhay Patil, Abhiram Ranade, Aditya Srinivasan, Ajay Marathe, Ajit Limaye, Late Ajit Shelat, Akbar Khan, Amol Mahajani, Anil Bansal, Anil Kamath, Arun Gupta, Arun Jethmalani, Arun Kaul, Arun Wankhede, Arvind Kher, Ashanka Sen, Ashish Khosla, Ashvin Iyengar, Bakul Desai, Balaji Raghavan, Benoy Desouza, Birjoo Mehta, Chetan Chitnis, Christopher Fernandes, Clarence Pinto, CR Seetharam, Darsh Maheshwari, Deb Mallick, Deepak Avasare, Deepak Patil, Deepak Shah, Deepak Tiwary, Deven Waghani, Dinar Bhatkar, Edgar Dias, Gaurav Jain, Girish Shrotri, Hari Narayanan, Harishankar Ramachandran, Hasmukh Tavadia, Hemant Shah, Hemendra Godbole, Hiren Malankar, Homi Byramji, Huzefa Mehta, Jamal Kothia, Jayant Kulkarni, Jayesh Shah, Jiten Apte, Keith Rebello, Kenneth Robertson, Ketan Kapasi, Kishorebabu Kamatham, KY Philip, Madan Mohan Rao, Mahavir Meghawat, Mahesh Khandeparkar, Mahesh Navani, Mahiuddin Laskar, Makarand Gokhale, Manjunath Pai, Manohar Parrikar, Milind Kurve, Mukund Karwe, Nandakumar Saravade, Nandkishore Gotarkar, Narendra Chaudhari, Neville Nagarwalla, Nikhil Tikekar, Nilesh Mehta, Nilesh Shah, Nishad Kelkar, Nitin Apte, Parag Joshi, Paresh Vora, Pinakin Patel, Pradeep Fulay, Pradeep Mittal, Pradip Chavan, Pramod C, Prashant Khambekar, Prashant Shah, Praween Napate, Raghunath Iyer, Rahul Shukla, Raj Laad, Rajan Rao, Rajat Bansal, Rajeev Jorapur, Rajeev Potnis, Rajendra Adhye, Rajesh Devi, Rajesh Valia, Rajiv Deodhar, Rajiv Samant, Rakesh Kapoor, Ramanik Satra, Ramesh Chauhan, Ranjit Patwardhan, Ravi

Krishnaswamy, Ravi Prakash, Ravi Shenoy, Rohan Menezes, Rustom Sethna, S Ketharaman, Sachin Chavan, Sampath Kannan, Sandeep Shah, Sandeep Tarkas, Sandeep Vichare, Sandeep Vijayakar, Sanjay Chavan, Sanjay Jagdale, Sanjay Kohli, Sanjay Kshetramade, Sanjay Pol, Sanjay Tamta, Sanjiv Samant, Sanjiv Sood, Santosh Madbhavi, Satish Baliga, Satish Joshi, Satyen Harve, Shailesh Sabnis, Sharad Prabhu, Sharookh Lashkari, Shashank Shah, Shekhar Bhide, Shekhar Jain, Shirish Dharmadhikari, Shirish Karmarkar, Shobhan Mondal, Shrikant Sathe, Shyam Arora, Shyam Bhat, Shyam Thosar, Sid Nag, Sohag Desai, Somnath Sinha, Soumitra Banerjee, Srinivas Kethavarapu, Subodh Mhaisalkar, Subodhan Gadgil, Sudhanshoo Maroo, Sudhir Bapat, Sudhir Mohan, Suketu Pandya, Sunil Majgaokar, Sunil Nikhar, Sunil Patil, Sunil V M, Sunil Waghamare, Surendra Sharma, Sutanu Sarkar, Tarang Thakkar, Tushar Chitre, Vasant Joshi, Vasant Limaye, Vasant Prabhu, Vasudev Gharpure, Vasudevan Ramanujam, Vibhash Patel, Vijay Desai, Vijay Nagasamy, Vijay Shah, Vijay Sukhadeve, Vijay Topkar, Vikram Gupta, Vikram Modak, Vinay Deodhar, Vinay Sane, Vinayak Godbole, Viraj Anavkar, Virendra Patel and Vivek Kura.